HAUNTED
LAND

HAUNTED LAND

Investigations into Ancient Mysteries
and Modern Day Phenomena

PAUL DEVEREUX

PIATKUS

Copyright © 2001 Paul Devereux

First published in 2001 by
Judy Piatkus (Publishers) Limited
5 Windmill Street
London W1T 2JA
e-mail: info@piatkus.co.uk

The moral right of the author has been asserted

A catalogue record for this book is available from the British Library

ISBN 0 7499 2207 9

Text design Paul Saunders
Edited by Barbara Archer
Figures 13, 14, 15 and 17 by Rodney Paull
This book has been printed on paper manufactured with respect for the environment using wood from managed sustainable resources

Typeset by Wyvern 21, Bristol
Printed and bound in Great Britain by
The Bath Press, Bath

CONTENTS

ACKNOWLEDGEMENTS

I am indebted to the following people who made their own or collected first-hand accounts of apparent supernatural encounters available to me: Dewi Bowen; Paula, Claudia, and Philip Copestake; Nigel Jones; Andrew Lucas; Sandra Maddox; Guy Routh; Mark Spurlock; G.M. Stocker, and Cheryl Straffon. These accounts have been used in this book, but I also gratefully received fascinating material that in the event was not used from Soma Faye; Vicky and Andy Heaps; Duncan Lunan (who was particularly kind), and Col Veacock.

For their generous help with specific research matters I thank David Clarke; Charla Devereux; Kevin Groves; Eddie Lenihan; S. Longhi; Laurence Main; John Smith; Erling Strand; Damian Walter. I must make special mention of Jeremy Harte, who has spent much time and effort in responding to my queries and providing me with valuable insights and information. I also wish to thank the heroic editors of *Fortean Times*, Bob Rickard and Paul Sieveking, for their kindness in allowing me to make use of the columns of their magazine to elicit research information.

I salute the army of brilliant and dedicated researchers whose work is cited in this book, and I am grateful to Charla and Sol Devereux for individually or jointly sharing various fieldwork expeditions with me.

Naturally, no one mentioned in these acknowledgements, or cited in the main body of the book, is to be associated with any errors I may have made. And I deeply apologise to anyone whose name I may have inadvertently omitted here due to my rather porous memory and chaotic files.

Illustration credits:
Photographs are by the author. Known sources of figures not originated by the author are given in the captions. Figure 22 is reproduced by kind permission of Routledge publishers, London; it appeared in *The Lost Beliefs of Northern Europe* by H. Ellis Davidson.

INTRODUCTION

A T 6.45 A.M. on 7 January 2000, 53-year-old Keith Scales was driving to work. Rounding a bend in White Hill, Wye, Kent, he ran
into a woman standing in the middle of the road. 'I felt the
thump on the front of my motor,' said Scales. 'She didn't try to get out of
my way but just looked at me and smiled as I hit her. She bounced over
my bonnet and disappeared.' Scales admitted to shaking like a leaf as he
got out of his slightly damaged car and looked all around for the woman,
but he couldn't find her. When he got to his workplace in Wye he phoned
the police who searched the entire area around the accident spot but could
find no trace of the woman nor any spillage of blood on the road. It
emerged, however, that local people in the area had previously reported
seeing a ghostly white female figure in the area.

What is going on here? Incidents of this kind, typical of so many hauntings,
ghost sightings and the like, were among the reasons I felt compelled to
write this book. I wanted to explore why we continue to see ghosts and
spirits in the landscape, what they might mean, and what answers I could
find in the past.

This is no ordinary ghost book, in that it is not simply a list of spooky
stories or a ghost-buster's manual. While there are many chilling and eerie
accounts of strange encounters in the following pages, they are but a part of
what is a thoroughgoing investigation into the issue of the haunted land –
of spirits in the landscape. This book traces the subject from far back in

time right up to today's reported experiences of road ghosts or other apparitions in the 'great outdoors', and ends by briefly considering the implications they may hold for our culture's view of reality. It is a journey that
takes us from ancient tradition and still poorly understood magical and spiritual practices, through superstitions and actual experiences, and ultimately
brings us to profound questions that are usually associated with books dealing with consciousness studies. *Haunted Land*, then, tells a ghost story on a
grand scale, without becoming enmeshed in the theoretical aspects of spiri-
tualism or psychic research. What I reveal in these pages is that landscape
hauntings and spirits are not the outpourings of madmen or ignorant
minds, but rather are a phenomenon that is objective and deserving of serious study. I show that shamans of old had a message to share that is still
profoundly relevant.

The story that unravels in these pages did not start out as anything to do
with ghosts or spirits. Let me explain. I had been editor of *The Ley Hunter*
journal for 20 years, a specialist publication dealing with 'leys' (alignments of
ancient sites), or 'leylines' as they are more generally referred to nowadays. I
began enthusiastically in the early days, drawing lines on maps and believing
all the modern popular notions about how leylines were supposedly lines of
dowsable energy or flightpaths of UFOs, and other colourful ideas. As my
knowledge and experience deepened over the years, however, I became gradually disillusioned with the general unwillingness within the circles of leyhunting and geomancy to move on to deeper understandings. I felt it had
become a kind of self-serving club. There were nevertheless certain lines of
enquiry touched on by some leyhunters (or geomantic researchers) that were
of genuine value, and though there was never such an archaeological entity as
a 'leyline', there were nevertheless some ancient alignments of sites and mysterious linear features in the archaeological record – features such as the
famed Nazca lines in Peru, for example. In an effort to find out more about
the legacy of the human past rather than the fantasies of the human present,
I decided to focus directly on the archaeological linear features themselves,
which were to be found in various lands, and to further some of the embryonic strands of enquiry that had developed within leyhunting.

Eventually, I came to realise that the common thread that linked otherwise different archaeological linear features was the ancient practice of
shamanism – one of humanity's earliest organised spiritual expressions that
took the form of specialised practitioners making trance-based ventures into
supernatural otherworlds. Further research revealed that this ancient source
had at different times and places subtly transformed into associations with
the dead and with spirits of various kinds. This led me to the subject of spir-

its and ghosts, which eventually brought me back to the modern world and people's reported experiences of encountering landscape-based apparitions. It was only then that I realised I had taken a circuitous route through the haunted land; that I had been on a ghost hunt of sorts.

This book is an invitation to you, the reader, to accompany me on this curious but mind-opening excursion. It will reveal to you a forgotten but powerful part of our human heritage, and provide fresh insights into some of the mysteries that still surround us all.

The story of this investigation is partly autobiographical and is presented in a personalised narrative form in order to give a little of the flavour of some of the extraordinary places that research has taken me, and of some of the people involved. I wanted to convey how understandings came about – to include the personal, human dimension to the quest. When research is presented as an essay, it comes as a ready-made package like something arriving in the mail; here I wanted to indicate to some extent how the package was put together – research is never as neat and tidy as hindsight accounts so often imply. Also, a narrative style allows certain observations and asides to be made that are not always possible in other forms. Despite this, the text has been referenced copiously for those who want to follow up specific items or lines of enquiry. Otherwise, the following chapters can be read like a detective story – one that deals with mysteries of both the human mind and the soul. Although you can simply let the story unfold, it covers some areas that may be unfamiliar, and so I sketch here how the book is laid out, to give a basic framework of reference.

Mapping the journey

Part One describes recent expeditions to remote desert locations where shamans of old had left signs carved on rocks that had resulted from their journeys into otherworld realms and their visions of spirits. I then look at some of the fundamental differences between the worldviews of the modern age and preceding eras. I describe my earlier visits to rather weird ancient ground markings and linear features throughout the Americas. Such features, which represent one of the earliest examples of archaeologically detectable human recognition of the haunted land, were my intended primary focus of interest, but, as becomes clear, I decide to extend and deepen my investigation.

Part Two traces my attempts to find similar archaeological features in the Old World of Europe. Instead of shamanism I keep encountering associations with the dead, for the 'spirit roads' and other European linear features I discover all seem to occur in funerary landscapes of varying eras. I discover a body of scholarship that identifies a central Asian source of shamanism that could lie behind both the relatively pristine American shamanic landscapes and the more complex developments in Europe. In the process, this research opens up a Pandora's box containing witchcraft, werewolves, vampires, and very strange beliefs and practices of the past in Europe. I realise that in order to continue the investigation I have to go beyond archaeology and explore the ancient mind itself.

Part Three looks at the 'invisible spectral country' of ancient peoples. I explore the spiritual significance of archaeological features and sites throughout western Europe, and journey into folklore and anthropology.

Part Four explores contemporary reports of spirits in the landscape. Studying representative accounts of ghostly encounters taken for convenience primarily from my own land, Britain (though it could be from anywhere), I set about learning what it is exactly that people claim to be seeing, and discover some interesting patterns and characteristics that are to lead to yet deeper questions which challenge the very way our modern culture views reality.

Part Five brings us full circle to the recent rock art expeditions in the Americas described in Chapter One. I find that the traditional explanations for ghosts as offered by both believers and sceptics to be inadequate and follow lines of thought that lead to the frontiers of recent research and thinking about the mind and its relationship to physical reality.

Each of the long main chapters is subdivided into mini-chapters, and those in turn contain subheadings to assist the reader in processing the information *Haunted Land* contains.

This, then, is the basic structure of the book, but the map of a journey is not the journey itself. That experience awaits you in the following pages, where there is chronicled an extraordinary adventure of the mind.

Paul Devereux
Cotswolds, England

PART ONE

SHAMANISM AND ANCIENT MYSTERIES
OF THE
NEW WORLD

CHAPTER ONE

SIGNS OF THE SPIRITS

THE CHEVY BLAZER bucked and bounced along the miles of dirt road leading out into the desert wilderness of New Mexico some miles north of the United States' border with Mexico. I gripped the steering wheel as the vehicle's four-wheel drive engaged with the ruts and dips of the track, realising that yet again my specialised kind of 'ghost hunt' had landed me in an unexpected situation. I was investigating the archaic and deeply-rooted idea of there being spirits in the landscape by studying archaeological evidence and folklore material worldwide, along with its continuation in modern reports of actual encounters. On this occasion, I was on the trail of ancient American Indian spirits.

We were heading for Cooke's Range, rising ahead of us like a rugged island in the flat, arid scrub country all around. Cooke's Peak itself gleamed with a light dusting of snow: the beginning of November 2000 had ushered in an unusually early taste of winter. The dramatic landmark, over 8,000 feet (2.4 km) high, had attracted people long before my son and I had set out on our modest expedition – notably the Mimbres people whose culture emerged around 250 BC and became extinct about 1,000 years ago. The Mimbres were a branch of the larger population of Mogollen people who had inhabited the whole vast region of what is now southern New Mexico and Arizona, and northern Mexico. They disappeared mysteriously about AD 1400, and the Apaches later occupied some of their territory. The heartland of the Mimbres culture had lain immediately to the west of Cooke's Range.

Our route led along the forbiddingly named Starvation Draw in the foothills of Cooke's Range. I was looking for signs of the mysterious markings the Mimbres had carved into the rocks. New Mexican archaeologists had given us directions to an area called Pony Hills where such markings – 'petroglyphs' – could be found. It was a remote spot and the rock art there had not yet been properly catalogued. What had seemed to be clear-cut directions in the comfort of the office of the Bureau of Land Management 60 miles away in Las Cruces, became a more challenging proposition out here in the wild. We wasted a couple of hours mistakenly exploring a Martian-like landscape of red-brown rocks forming a barren ridge. It was bereft of any human signs, and the scurrying lizards kept their own secrets. Travelling on, we at last identified a line of low hills that proved to be our intended destination.

The rock art we were seeking is generally termed 'Jornada Style' and is identified by scholars' various subdivisions, but in general terms Jornada Style rock carvings or petroglyphs depict a wide range of animals, human figures, horned serpents, animal and human tracks, and geometric designs with recurring motifs. There are also some examples of face – or rather mask – images known to researchers as 'Tlaloc masks', in reference to the Mexican rain god, because many archaeologists now think the great prehistoric civilisations of Mexico extended their religious practices and mythic beliefs northwards to these regions. The American Indian artists made the markings by scratching away the darkened patina or oxidised surface of the rocks (an effect that occurs commonly in desert regions) revealing a lighter surface beneath. Some of these petroglyphs are not much more than scratched doodles, but others are well-crafted designs etched deep into the rock surfaces.

Signatures of Shamanism

We left the vehicle and scrambled up the hill slopes. At first we saw no markings, but within a few of the rocky outcrops along the summit ridges we found the reason why this apparently undistinguished line of hills had been so important to past peoples: it harboured spring-fed rock pools. As in so many cultures around the world, whether Celtic springs in Europe or Mayan subterranean lagoons in the Yucatan, water-sources had been perceived as sacred. It was indeed easy to feel such sanctity here, standing next to these small pools of crystal-clear water surrounded by an otherwise unremittingly arid landscape. The rocks around each pool were decorated with petroglyphs depicting turtles or horned snakes, complex geometric designs, a recurring motif of a human figure holding a ceremonial staff, and carvings of bear paw-prints. The turtles or horned serpents were mythical images, and the other motifs revealed that the rocky outcrops around these remote, crystal pools had been the haunts of ancient shamans.

The Nature of Shamans

Shamans occupied an elevated position in tribal societies in many cultures around the world. They were the healers and knowledge holders, the keepers of the tribal myths, the storytellers. Above all, they ventured into the dangerous spirit world to divine information, to obtain supernatural power, to guide the souls of the dying to the realm of the ancestors, to placate the gods, and to struggle with hostile spirits or rival shamans in magical battles. In order to allow their spirits to travel in the supernatural otherworld, shamans had to enter into a trance state, and it is this state of out-of-body trance ecstasy – often depicted as an aerial journey, a spirit flight, expressed by bird symbolism – that distinguishes the role of the shaman from that of the simple healer or witch-doctor. The shaman was a religious functionary, and it was from shamanic origins that many of the more structured religions developed. Primitive shamanism survives today in a few tribal societies in some parts of the world, though sadly it is becoming ever more marginalised. Once, however, it was a major form of human spiritual expression. Men and women who became shamans often had a natural ability to enter trance states because they possessed specific mental and physical characteristics or peculiarities. Otherwise, entry into the requisite visionary state of altered consciousness was achieved by employing trance-inducing techniques such as chanting, dancing, drumming, fasting, going without sleep, and the taking of mind-altering plants. Usually, a combination of such methods was used.

While all the specific details of the religious practices of the Mimbres, or Mogollen peoples in general, cannot now be directly understood such a long time after their passing, much is known about the religious practices of recent and surviving Indian societies of the American Southwest and Mexico which certainly enshrine traits that originated long ago in pre-Columbian Indian cultures. American anthropologists of the nineteenth and twentieth centuries were able to record considerable traditional tribal information, and it is possible to apply this material to interpretations of some of the pre-Columbian societies.

For example, all known Indian groups of the American Southwest are thought to have practised shamanism, and most if not all took mind-altering drugs derived from plants. These included jimson weed (Datura) preparations, peyote (a cactus containing the hallucinogen mescaline), and a range of beans and mushrooms that could promote visionary, trance states. These drugs were considered to be sacramental, and were sometimes used in conjunction with sleep deprivation and fasting during 'vision quests'. This practice was traditionally performed by many American Indian cultures (and Siberian tribes), in which the shaman or initiate would seek a special vision or 'dream of power' by resorting alone to a remote spot for a number of days and nights. In some societies, most men would undergo at least one vision quest in their lives as a rite of passage, but shamans would perform vision quests frequently in the service of the tribe, perhaps to conjure rain or seek otherworld assistance in dealing with some crisis or enemy confronting the tribe. Vision questing sites were often unembellished wild places known to individual shamans, but sometimes they were slightly more structured, and could take the form of subtle enclosures of rocks or arranged platforms of stone.

The Relics on Pony Hills

Here on Pony Hills it was not difficult to imagine that some locations near the pools had been used as vision questing sites centuries ago. I could almost feel the presence of the old shamans, a sense created, at least in part, by the recurring petroglyphic motifs of the bear paws and a figure holding a staff. One sloping slab of bedrock on the approach to a rock pool had particularly dramatic examples of both motifs. There was an image over two feet (60 cm) in length of a human being in an apparently ritual posture holding a tall upright stick with an umbrella-shaped top (Figure 1). Images of these ceremonial staffs, 'prayer sticks' or *pahos* also appear on Mimbres pottery, and examples have been unearthed by archaeologists. Some researchers have suggested that their shape derives from that of hallucinogenic mushrooms. Looking at the carved figure in the bedrock at my feet it seemed to me that this was a reasonable if not downright obvious interpretation. The carved bear tracks on the same rock surface were also probably emblematic of shamanism, because in the Pueblo Indian world of New Mexico even today 'the bear track stands for the curing power of the bear'.[1] It is known that certain Pueblo Indian shamans would put on what were effectively bear-paw gloves and boots so as to 'become bears' during healing rituals.

Close to some of the bear tracks at Pony Hills were carved life-sized

FIGURE I: The rock carving at
Pony Hills depicting what seems
to be a shaman engaged in a
ritual involving a mushroom.
The carved footprint alongside is
lifesize.

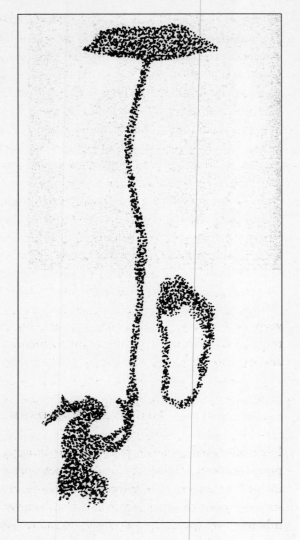

human footprints. I interpreted this association to mean that the footprints
were more than likely of shamanic origin. This association was repeated along
the top of the Pony Hills – in one case a tall upright outcrop of rock had
human-sized footprints on one of its vertical surfaces and three bear paw
prints on the opposite side. Footprint petroglyphs are sometimes interpreted
by experts as relating to mythical figures or legendary migrations of the 'first
people'. This might be the case in some instances, but I was confident that I
was 'reading' this rock art accurately. In fact, I had the disturbing sensation
that the ancient imagery emblazoned on the rock surfaces around us was
somehow being 'translated' for me: my rational self told me this was due to

FIGURE 2: One of numerous rock-carved bear paw-prints at Pony Hills.

years of literature research on my part, but it *felt* as if elusive agencies a respectable scholar would not want to mention were guiding both my eyes and my thoughts.

In the Footsteps of Spirits

I was delighted to encounter footprint imagery, as that had been one of my prime motives in coming to this remote place. My long and many-faceted interest in ancient worldviews, particularly in the various ways most of the societies prior to our modern one had believed the physical landscape to be inhabited by spirits, had recently led me to the work of a British archaeologist, Richard Bradley, based at Reading University.

The aspect of his work that currently intrigued me concerned prehistoric rock art in southern Sweden, where horizontal or slightly sloping sheets of exposed bedrock can be found carved with a range of recurring motifs, footprints being one of them. It had been the typical approach in archaeology to see a panel of rock art, whether painted or carved, almost as if it were a framed picture, an isolated artefact, but Bradley was one of the pioneers in viewing rock art in its landscape setting.

He noted, for instance, that the images of ships, one of the most common and striking motifs in Scandinavian rock art, occurred near what had been the prehistoric coastline (the sea has receded along the west coast of

FIGURE 3: The typical style of prehistoric 'ship' petroglyph to be found in Scandinavia. (After Coles, 2000)

Scandinavia, due to the land rising after the last Ice Age). Rather than being concerned with sea transportation, these images were more likely to be symbolic of death, for the sea was the way to the realm of the dead in Old Norse belief. We know from archaeological findings and surviving written accounts of Viking funerals that the bodies of chieftains were placed in boats and buried or pushed out to sea and burned, and some prehistoric and Viking graves are marked by standing stones arranged in boat shapes. Bradley suggests that the 'fleets' of ship carvings that were 'sailing' across the rock surfaces may have been intended to convey the idea of the sea on areas of dry land that had once been under the waves, and which lay at the foot of hills that had formerly been islands on which were placed stone burial mounds (cairns), just as actual islands off the coast also contained Bronze Age burial cairns. Isles of the dead, both real and symbolic.

What was of particular relevance to my investigation was that by viewing the footprint motif as a landscape phenomenon rather than as isolated marks on individual rocks, Bradley had seen that a *route* across the landscape was in effect being depicted in some areas. So at Bohuslän, on the west coast of Sweden near the border with Norway, for instance, Bradley saw that petroglyphic footprints appeared to cut paths at right angles through the generally horizontal zone of ship carvings, the symbolic sea, between the higher land containing the burial cairns and the areas of settlement and agriculture on the fertile, reclaimed coastal strip below, and, ultimately, the actual sea beyond.

Bradley wondered if these footprints represented the dead.[2] According to ancient Norse lore, the dead existed beneath the ground and were upside-down relative to us, walking on the underside of the ground's surface, so sometimes the soles (and indeed the souls) of the living and the dead might briefly touch. Is that what was being portrayed here? Was the rock art showing the spirits of the dead in the Bronze Age cemeteries walking down to the sea on their journey to the realm of the afterlife? This idea was supported by

FIGURE 4: Prehistoric
Swedish rock carvings
of a pair of soled feet.
(After Coles, 2000)

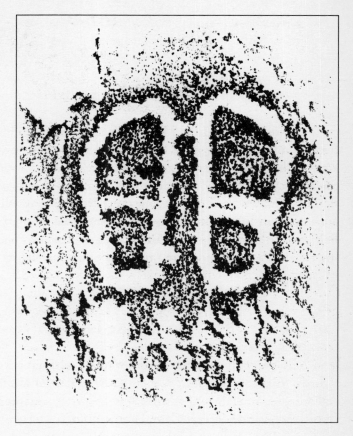

the fact that many or most of the footprints were shown as being shod. This
is pretty much the case throughout Sweden where the footprint motif occurs
in the rock art. Another British archaeologist, John Coles, notes that the petroglyphic footprints in Uppland, Sweden, are sometimes shown as simple
outlines or carved-out foot shapes with narrow insteps, but that other footprint carvings 'are furnished with a cross-strap, either a single strap or a double strap'.[3] Drawing again on what is known of Old Norse lore, Bradley
wondered if the shod footprints at Bohuslän were referring to the *hel-shoes*
that the Norse newly-dead were said to be given to help them on the long
journey to the realm of the dead.[4]

Bradley went on from Bohuslän to study another Swedish site, Järrestad,
in Scania at the southern tip of Sweden, and saw the same phenomenon
repeated, but on a more compressed scale. Järrestad is basically a rock outcrop topped by a prehistoric cemetery containing the remains of two or
three burial mounds. The sloping rock surfaces are carved with various
motifs, including ships and, most strikingly, depictions of shod footsoles

and bare footprints. Bradley could clearly see that the footsoles originated in the cemetery and proceeded down the rock slope, some of them apparently lingering at a pool, on a route that if extended would have led down to the sea. 'If the footsoles do represent the *hel-shoes* of the recently deceased,' Bradley concludes, 'they may record the path from the grave to the world beyond.'

Interestingly, the unshod footprints at Järrestad do not follow such a distinct route across the rock surface as do the shod footsoles: most cluster around the edges of exposed rock surface, and a few actually point uphill towards the cemetery. Could these bare footprints represent the Norse shaman's presence accompanying the newly-dead on the first part of their journey from life, which is the traditional role of the shaman everywhere? Fortunately, more is being learned about the existence of Scandinavian shamanism, and an increasing number of archaeologists are researching the subject.

In the Desert

The Scandinavian countries seemed a long distance in every way from ancient, native New Mexico, but the new, more holistic way of seeing the rock-carved footprints of Sweden as effectively mapping routes of spirits through the land was very much in my mind as we clambered over the rocks of Pony Hills. I was in no way presuming a cultural link between the ancient Norsemen and the Indians of the American Southwest, but I was keen to study the latter's footprint petroglyphs to see if there had been an attempt to use the medium of rock art for a similar purpose – namely, to convey the idea of spirits moving invisibly through the physical landscape. With the bear paws and life-sized footprints (which were unshod) I felt there was some similarity, for the bear tracks represented the transformed shaman – it was a widely held belief the world over that when in trance, shamans changed into the form of a wild animal or bird. While this seemed to me a reasonable interpretation of the petroglyphs, it wasn't quite what I was looking for. But the old Mimbres shamans had more to reveal.

As our exploration progressed along the ridge of Pony Hills, we came upon a particularly large rock pool. The unusually high number of images etched into the rocks in its vicinity marked it out as a special place. Then we saw them – a whole trail of footprints leading up and over rocky ledges and across flat rock surfaces towards the pool. It was immediately obvious that these were different to the human and bear-paw prints we had seen so far:

these footprints were tiny – human in shape but barely a third of the size of an adult human footprint (Plate 1). With a thrill of realisation, it dawned on me that these were specifically the depictions of spirit tracks.

Tracking the Water Baby Spirit

As we traced the trail of tiny footprints, I remembered reading about rock art research that had been carried out in the Great Basin – the huge area that straddles western Nevada and eastern California. One of North America's leading rock art experts, David Whitley, had been making a detailed survey of ancient rock art left by peoples like the Shoshone who had inhabited the Great Basin, and had also trawled through largely forgotten ethnographic material compiled by earlier researchers and which had subsequently been overlooked by rock art scholars. Whitley has been able to demonstrate that the ancient (and not-so-ancient) Indian peoples of the Great Basin region had been shamanic, and that the rock art related specifically to the activities of shamans, often shamans who specialised in rain-making. Because of his investigation of the old ethnographic material, he was able to link shamanism with lines of small engraved footprints in rock art areas he was studying. 'In the Great Basin, small human footprints were attributed to the Water Baby, a diminutive human spirit who lived in springs and pools and served as a particularly potent spirit helper for shamans . . . The sight of Water Baby's tracks was thought to signify a supernatural experience.'[5]

The Water Baby was envisaged by Great Basin Indians as being a short, male humanoid entity wearing traditional American Indian clothing. The sighting of a Water Baby was believed to result in death, but Whitley discovered that 'death' in this context was a metaphor for an altered state of consciousness, the shamanic trance. The Water Baby was one of the most important of the shaman's spirit or dream helpers, and the designs and imagery engraved on the rocks were said to have been executed by Water Baby spirits, or at least had been 'dictated' to the shaman by a Water Baby. In the Great Basin region the word for shaman was *poagunt*, meaning both 'medicine man' and 'a man who writes'. The earlier ethnographers had also noted that their Indian informants referred to the rock art imagery as 'writing'.

From the photographs I had seen of the Great Basin petroglyphs, the miniature footprints now confronting us at Pony Hills were identical to those recorded by Whitley. I could not have asked for a clearer archaeological expression of spirits in the landscape, complete with a link to shamanism,

FIGURE 5. The probable depiction of a Water-Baby spirit carved on the rocks at Pony Hills.

than these spirit tracks. What was remarkable, though, was finding these Water Baby footprints in their traditional rock pool setting some 600 miles away from where Whitley had been working. The Mogollen were a different people to those who had lived in the Great Basin, but it was possible that ideas and influences had travelled such distances. (Either that, or the old shamans everywhere were seeing the same spirits.) It seemed that the Mimbres shamans had allowed me a modest discovery.

As we began to work our way around the rock pool, which now looked particularly deep, dark and mysterious in the shadows being cast by slanting rays of the late afternoon sun, I suddenly found myself looking down at a large and startling image on the flat rock surface that edged the rock pool (Figure 5). I called my son's attention to it: we didn't know whether to gasp or giggle, for it looked like a modern cartoon drawing of a ghost, and wouldn't have looked out of place wisping around in a *Ghostbusters* movie. We went on to find similar motifs near other rock springs. At least one rock art writer has referred to these wraith-like images as depictions of tadpoles,[6] but this is simply a modern guess bereft of the rich spiritual context within which these rock images were created. My own guess was that here were the depictions of the Mimbres' conception of Water Baby spirits – ancient American Indian shamans used only natural forms to depict spirit realities.

We had tracked the spirits of this wilderness to their lair.

Time pressed, and we returned to the Chevy Blazer and headed out of Cooke's Range. As we drove across the desert flats the setting sun cast the earth's deep violet shadow onto the pinkish dust haze in the eastern sky. Our next journey would take us 100 miles or so in that direction, to where shamans of old had left their visions on the rocks – the Three Rivers petroglyph site, 30 miles north of Alamogordo.

Cultures in Collision

Although Three Rivers is a better-known rock art site than Pony Hills, it is still remote. The site, a low and seemingly unremarkable ridge, is dramatically positioned, being set amid the foothills of the Sacramento Mountains rising to the east, and the vast emptiness of the Tularosa Basin stretching out to the west. Why should the ridge have been deemed so special? We can never know for certain, but what has been gleaned from past and present indigenous peoples of the Southwest allows some informed guesses. Rock art scholar Polly Schaafsma, for instance, suggests that concentrations of petroglyphs on landscape features away from habitation sites 'may have marked places where mythic events took place and/or supernaturals were said to reside'.[7]

For whatever reasons, the Three Rivers ridge was clearly of importance to the Jornada Mogollon of a millennium ago, for tens of thousands of petroglyphs survive there. As we combed the dark, basalt rocks we came to fully appreciate this, with images springing into view at every turn. There were crosses within circles, birds, animals, abstract designs, sunbursts, terrace designs representing clouds, masks, and many more motifs. In one place, small footprints traced a path over a boulder, and there were a few isolated life-sized carved footprints, but the footprint motif was generally less in evidence here than at Pony Hills. However, there were quite a large number of depictions of animal and bird tracks. These were

probably representations of spirit animals, a key feature of shamanism –
shamans had their 'power animals' just as European witches had their animal
familiars.

Images of Transformation

A recurring image, particularly at Three Rivers, is that of a winged human
being, sometimes displayed in association with bird imagery. This is the classic symbolic representation of the shamanic trance or ecstasy – the aerial journey, or what we would more commonly refer to today as the out-of-body
experience. It represents the human being sprouting wings, and often tail-
feathers, symbolic of spirit flight. A few of these depictions show a halo
around the human figure's head (Plate 2). Harvard anthropologist, Joan
Halifax, has written with insight on this depiction in ancient American
Indian rock art:

> The nimbus or halo emanating from the head of these shamans . . . is a
> visual expression of intellectual energy in its mystical aspect, or of super-
> natural power. The sun itself is symbolic of the heroic principle of all-
> seeing and all-knowing . . . [8]

Magnetic Rocks

The ridge at Three Rivers was patently a haunt of the old shamans; here they
undertook their vision quests. On impulse, I took out my compass and held
it near some of the rocks we were exploring. The needle began to spin, sometimes settling up to 90 degrees or more off north. The rocks were magnetic. I
had come across this phenomenon before, not only at other American Indian
'places of power', but also at Celtic and prehistoric holy places in my native
British Isles.[9] There was nothing supernatural or unexplained about this – the
rocks contained iron magnetised in ancient geological upheavals, but such
strong anomaly spots were noteworthy, and often seemed to coincide with
ancient sacred places. There is experimental evidence to show that the human
brain is susceptible to quite small changes in the ambient magnetic field, and
that this can trigger sensations that are commonly considered as being visionary or paranormal.[10]

I can only guess at what an ancient Jornada shaman might have experienced out here at Three Rivers, after ritual activity, perhaps primed with

drinks containing jimson weed, sitting down to have a dream of power along-side a magnetic rock, or with his head resting against one. Such rocks would have been seen as 'spirit rocks' that could enhance visionary experience; a doorway to the other world. Such speculations about geophysical anomalies at sacred places tend to be frowned upon by mainstream scholarly research, so its study goes begging. Yet it has always seemed logical to me that ancient and traditional peoples who we increasingly appreciate had developed detailed and sophisticated knowledge about the plant life surrounding them, would have had an equally sensitive and exact knowledge concerning what we would call the geological and geophysical aspects of their environment. Anything that enhanced visionary experience was prized in the ancient world.

Patterns in the Mind

There is a plethora of geometric, abstract imagery at Three Rivers, similar to what we had found at Pony Hills. Many leading rock art scholars now believe such imagery frequently derives from mental patterns, universal in all places and times, that are generated in the human brain during the onset stages of trance. In an anthropological context this effectively means during shamanic practice.[11] Technically known as 'entoptic phenomena', such internal visual patterns fall into specific classes of imagery – zigzags, nets and lattices, dots, nested curved lines, concentric circles and tunnel-like effects, and other basic categories of geometric mental patterns known as 'form constants'.[12] These mind-patterns, while having the same basic appearance to all people everywhere at all times were nevertheless given different symbolic meanings specific to the cultures that used them. This kind of abstract imagery often graces rock art sites worldwide, strongly hinting at the trance-related origins of rock art.

A Flash of Light

As we continued to explore the Three Rivers site, I discovered places I concluded had been the vision-questing sites along the ridge. Typically, these were small areas of smooth ground set amidst enclosing clusters of rocks, which were invariably inscribed with petroglyphs. At any one of them, I could picture an old shaman sitting upright and experiencing his strange dreams, leaving the record of his visions on the surrounding rocks. While my son climbed up to explore and photograph some of the more inaccessible

places, I wearily and thankfully settled down in one of the presumed vision-
questing places. It overlooked the Tularosa Basin, and I found such a vast
expanse of space to be in itself mind-altering, a sensation enhanced by the
extraordinarily deep silence – a quality I have noticed occasionally elsewhere
in wild mountain and desert locations.

I sat and pondered the core underlying issue being raised by my investigation of the spirits-in-the-landscape theme – namely, the gulf of worldviews
that existed between our modern, globalising culture and the ancient world.
The contrast could not be starker than at Three Rivers, because 50 miles
away to the northwest is the Trinity site, the place where the first atomic
bomb was detonated. The device, code-named Trinity, was exploded shortly
before dawn on 16 July 1945, and for a split second it released four times the
heat of the sun in a blinding white flash that was seen 250 miles away and lit
up the surrounding terrain more brilliantly than the noonday sun. Even ten
miles away the heat could be felt on the face like that of a furnace, and the
sound of the explosion was so powerful it broke windows at a distance of 120
miles. The initial fireball turned to red then purple, and a column filled with
fire and dust rose into the air, its top spreading in the atmosphere to look like
a giant mushroom, a mushroom that grew seven miles tall like something in
a grotesque fairy tale. Scientists observed the awesome event in bunkers several miles from Ground Zero, and their leader, Robert J. Oppenheimer, was
moved to mutter a phrase from the sacred Vedic texts of ancient India: 'I am
become death, the shatterer of worlds.' Shortly after the false sunrise of the
explosion, the true sun rose: there were two dawns in close succession on that
day and at that place which saw the start of the nuclear age, a legacy our culture has bequeathed to the rest of time.

I found myself on the verge of tears. What would my imaginary shaman
sitting here centuries ago have made of such a happening? The giant nuclear
mushroom of our time could not have been more different from the magical, visionary, mind-altering mushrooms he may have known. While we
explosively split the substance of nature with devastating violence, he lived
with the natural world – the wind, the clouds, the animals. He followed the
slow cycles of sun and moon, and prayed for rain and participation in the
natural order, not for dominion over nature. His calculations resulted in
ceremony and ritual related to the natural rounds of the seasons and the
inner sun of the visionary otherworld, not the glare of an atomic fireball.
My shaman's legacy was his visions marked upon the rocks, while my culture's bequest was a horror that can never leave us. I couldn't help but wonder if, during his visions, my shaman had not glimpsed precognitively the
flash of baleful light marking out this awe-full event on the vast landscape

lying before him. And if so, was he confused by what his inner eye saw, or did he understand its significance? Did he keep it from his people, harbouring a dreadful memory of the future as part and parcel of the shaman's burden?

It is easy to be romantic, and there is no doubt that warfare and a measure of human cruelty was familiar to the culture my imaginary shaman inhabited, but, crucially, it was the type of conflict that did not challenge the order of nature. Our culture's violence does, however sanitised we try to make it with high-tech methods. My shaman took his mind and spirit into the heart of things; we use our brainpower to tear atoms apart.

I had experienced being outside my own cultural frame of seeing and thinking numerous times when in the Australian Outback with Aborigines, or in the rainforest with American Indian tribal peoples. At such moments, the attitude common to modern culture that ancient and indigenous people are superstitious becomes distinctly reversed: it becomes mildly laughable to think that the land around us is empty of spirits. I now had the same experience sitting here, staring out across the Tularosa Basin from Three Rivers, where the spirits still signalled from the rocks. I had the sensation of the old shamans still somehow being present, and giving me mental gifts. A gift of remembrance, reminding me that it had not always been like it is now in the world; that for untold ages prior to the few fragile centuries of the modern world the land had been understood by all humanity to be inhabited by spirits as much as by human beings, and that there was a fully conscious interaction with them. Only three or four generations ago, my own forebears believed in spirits and today there are still societies that live in a world inhabited by spirits, but these societies are suffering cultural erosion and will soon fall silent.

West Mesa

I went alone to Boca Negro Canyon, the final petroglyph site I was to visit in New Mexico on this expedition. It presented another graphic symbol of the marginalisation of the old worldviews. Now known as Petroglyph National Monument, the canyon runs through the dark rocks of the West Mesa escarpment near Albuquerque, and contains tens of thousands of petroglyphs, forming one of the greatest concentrations of such markings along the entire Rio Grande. Most of these markings are referred to by archaeologists as the 'Rio Grande Style', dating to between AD 1350 and 1680, and belong to a Pueblo Indian heritage. These petroglyphs include depictions of 'star-beings'

– star-like geometric forms with headdresses and features.

But there are other images there that are much older. These include abstract markings belonging to the 'Desert Abstract Style' of around 1000 BC, and there are animal and stick figure images, handprints and sandal prints, belonging to the early Anasazi of around AD 800. (The Anasazi, 'the Ancient Ones', are thought to have merged with or originated from the Pueblo peoples when their great culture finally collapsed around AD 1400.) Along the escarpment there are also dozens of archaeological sites testifying to human presence there for at least 12,000 years. And to the east, across the Rio Grande from West Mesa, the huge bulk of Sandia Crest rises against the sky. This is one of the sacred peaks of the Pueblo nations, and has yielded (controversial) evidence of the earliest human activity in the Southwest.

West Mesa incorporates a line of five extinct volcanoes that have been sacred for countless ages, and are still used for ritual practices by Pueblo people. The greater the outrage, then, that its status as a protected area has come under pressure. Albuquerque, typical of most American desert cities, expands remorselessly in a horizontal grid fashion, and its urban sprawl threatens the integrity of Petroglyph National Monument: there are powerful political and economic pressures to build highways and extend housing developments through the area. Our culture threatens to swallow the visions of the past in its everyday expansion. Because of this threat, the governors of five local pueblos were moved to publish articles in a local paper. One read:

> The petrolgyph area is where messages to the spirit world are communicated. It is here that our Pueblo ancestors 'wrote' down the visions and experiences they felt. This special place . . . is the center of great spiritual powers! . . . We consider each of these petroglyphs to be a record of visions written here of some spiritual being, event or expressions. The Petroglyph National Monument should be a place of reverence and prayer and used in this manner.[13]

Another of the writers stressed that the monument's area encompassed 'spirit trails travelled by the dead',[14] bringing me directly to my theme – spirits in the landscape.

Monoculture

Such ancient worldviews are in danger of being rendered extinct by the modern world, which is turning into a monoculture at every level. Ecologically we are remorselessly reducing biodiversity on the planet and creating a monolithic agribusiness based on ever more controlled species of crops. Commercially massive corporations are already merging with one another to form inter-continental conglomerates with combined resources greater than that of many nations. Socially and intellectually our radio and TV stations are beaming out around the world the same ideas and concerns. Despite its undoubted usefulness to us, the Internet is also functioning as a kind of *coup de grâce*, reducing all thinking to the same shared levels. The World Wide Web could too easily become like the spider's web that indiscriminately traps anything flying in its vicinity. And in the physical, geographical sense we are not only destroying the habitats of plants and animals, but also of traditional peoples. The ancient forest and desert societies of the world are being relentlessly edged towards extinction, leaving their members as lost souls stranded on the fringes of our encroaching global culture. When they go, their knowledge and different perspectives of being in the world go with them. Soon, within a generation or two, this modern culture of ours will be its own sole referent – it will know only of itself. It will become, literally, self-consuming.

As I GAZED out over the urban sprawl of Albuquerque I saw it as symbolic of the way in which our culture is eclipsing all former knowledge, for it looked like an encroaching tide eating hungrily away at the foot of West Mesa, and it made me understand why I felt a sense of urgency in trying to make a coherent picture – a snapshot at least – of this ancient and virtually universal idea of a haunted land.

I had already conducted enough field and library research to be aware that in addition to rock art, there was other archaeological and anthropological evidence in both the Old and New Worlds testifying to a belief in the haunted land that could be traced back to remotest antiquity, and enough modern encounters to make me question the foundations of our current views of reality.

I sought somewhere to sit where I could contemplate the long but fascinating and instructive journey I had been making over previous years through the ancient Americas and parts of the Old World of Europe . . .

CHAPTER TWO

PATTERNS OF POWER

I WAS BEING TAKEN to where God sits. I was experiencing mild trepidation, as one would, but I was also slightly nervous for other reasons. Here in this Manitoba forest we were in bear country, and I'd already had a brief brush with a black bear a few days earlier while roaming around on my own elsewhere in this Canadian wilderness. Tom, the guide for our small party, had stopped up ahead on the narrow forest track and was pointing to the ground. 'There's a big one a short ways in front of us,' he said, indicating a large bear track still oozing in the black mud. Then he added for good measure: 'And there's a timber wolf around as well.' I was beginning to feel that I'd had enough of the 'call of the wild' experience, and was ready to go back the 100 miles or so to my hotel, but Tom reassured us that such wild creatures wouldn't bother us, it was our species that was the dangerous one, and in any case we only had a few miles further to go . . .

The Archaeology of Shamanism

We arrived at locked gates in a chain link fence – a most incongruous sight in the depths of the forest. 'Welcome to Tie Creek,' Tom beamed. He unlocked the gates and removed his boots. He explained that as an initiated member of a local branch of the Midewewin, an Indian 'medicine' society that has shamanic roots,[1] he was obliged to show respect for the holy ground on which we were about to tread, but as respectful visitors with genuine interest we would be forgiven if we kept our footwear on.

We walked through the gateway onto a dramatic sweep of bare, grey table-rock. Bushes and small groups of trees jutted up here and there from the smooth rock surface, but it took me a moment or two to discern in the distance small rocks and boulders running off in various configurations in all directions. There were bewildering curves and triangular shapes, grids, straight lines, complex patterns, and wandering lines leading out from some of the huge designs to link with others, or to eventually peter out on the tablerock. These great landscape designs, known to scholars as 'boulder mosaics' or 'petroforms', were what I had come to see.

They had been laid out many centuries ago, and their antiquity was evident by the thick encrustation of lichen on the rocks themselves and around their bases. Precise dates are not known, but an ancient native campsite amid the boulders had yielded pottery and stone tools dating to around AD 500. No one knew for sure who had built the designs, though it was thought likely that their makers had been early Ojibway people, or their immediate predecessors in the region, and today's Ojibway or Anishinabe Indians claimed the spiritual legacy of the designs, which are to be found on various glacier-exposed areas of tablerock in what is now known as Whiteshell Provincial Park. The Anishinabe refer to the area as *Manito Ahbee* (Where God Sits), a term that apparently gave rise to the name of the province of Manitoba itself. Tie Creek is the largest and best preserved of the known boulder mosaic sites.

As well as the who, there was the why. The sheer scale of the patterns at Tie Creek precludes any idea that they may have been idle doodles or mere decoration. The Midewewin believe that they were built by spirits, or laid out by people under instruction from the spirits, and that they were teaching places and doorways to other worlds. Tom led us around the huge tablerock area, stopping at one design, then another.

At a great grid-like feature (Figure 6), he quietly pointed out details to a young woman accompanying him who was seeking to join the local branch of the medicine society, then informed the rest of us that the feature was understood by the Anishinabe to have been associated with the 'shaking tent' ritual. This was a key act in recorded Ojibway shamanism: at the time of a tribal member's death, a ghost lodge (a specially-designed conical tent) was constructed using a frame of tree poles. At sunset, after purification, the shaman-diviner, the *tcisaki*, entered the lodge which magically began to move as he did so. This was said to be due to the 'winds' of the *manitous* or spirit presences. Inside, the shaman drummed and chanted himself into a trance

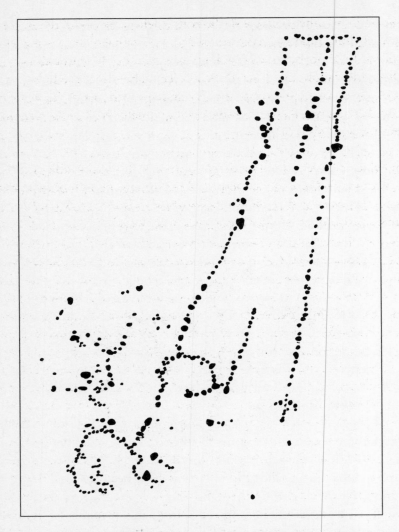

FIGURE 6: Grid pattern of boulders at Tie Creek, Manitoba, about 45 yards/metres long. Thought to represent a ghost lodge arrangement. (Manitoba Dept. of Natural Resources, 1990)

eventually making contact with the spirits. When the tent shook violently, the audience outside knew the spirits had arrived within. The shaman's voice would be heard interpreting the messages of the spirits, often using archaic forms of the Ojibway language, and the voices of spirits were sometimes also heard directly. Spark-like lights were said to appear within the tent itself. Some anthropologists have dismissed all this as trickery on the part of the shaman, but one *tcisaki* avowed near his death:

'I can do no other than speak the truth. Believe me, I did not deceive you at that time. I did not move the lodge. It was shaken by the power of the spirits. I did not speak with a double tongue. I only repeated to you what the spirits said to me. I heard their voices. The top of the lodge was filled with them, and before me the sky and the wide lands lay expanded. I could see a great distance around me, and believed I could recognize the most distant objects.'[2]

Tom led us to another boulder design near one edge of the tablerock area. He said that today's Anishinabe interpreted this strange pattern of rocks as representing the sweat lodge of Waynaboozhoo – the First Man, the Oldest Brother. Yet another boulder mosaic was interpreted for us as representing in

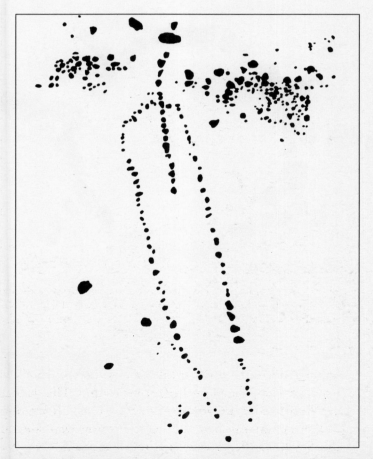

FIGURE 7: Pattern of boulders at Tie Creek believed to represent a birch bark scroll. About 28 yards/metres in length. (Manitoba Dept. of Natural Resources, 1990.)

rocks a birch bark scroll (Figure 7); these scrolls had been used by the
Ojibway to record their ceremonies, history and beliefs. Some scrolls still
survive.

It was apparent that the Tie Creek features were generally larger and more
abstract than the petroforms I had inspected earlier at the much more accessible Bannock Point tablerock site several miles distant. There, the boulders
were smaller, forming recognisable creatures like snakes and turtles, and bear
and wolf tracks made from rocks forming giant versions of the actual bear
and wolf tracks I saw on my way to Tie Creek. It was as if these metre-wide
displays had been formed by gargantuan mythical creatures padding out onto
the exposed rock area from the surrounding forest. But Bannock Point has
been subject to much recent human interference, and stones have been
moved in some of the designs. There were nevertheless some features that had

FIGURE 8. A stone circle in the form of a turtle at Bannock Point, Manitoba.
(Manitoba Dept. of Natural Resources, 1990.)

remained undisturbed for many centuries judging by the display of lichen
cover. This was particularly true of some of the turtle-shaped stone rings
(Figure 8).

As we continued our tour of the great ceremonial ground of Tie Creek, I
was concerned by how much today's Indians thought the boulder mosaics
reflected the true meanings lying behind the features. To be fair, the
Anishinabe stress that they offer only their own readings of the boulder patterns, with interpretations varying even among themselves, and do not insist

that these were necessarily the original meanings.[3] This is refreshingly honest, because on other occasions I had encountered questionable claims of surviving traditions by some representatives of indigenous peoples.

Leylines

This 'reverse anthropology' is a consequence of an insatiable New Age appetite for ancient traditional wisdom, and some people both from within and outside of traditional cultures are prepared to manufacture it or fudge authentic examples of it to feed that market. This has led some American Indian elders, for example, to write to a popular journal on shamanism complaining that weekend courses on the use of the sweat lodge were demeaning tribal spiritual legacy.

At a British New Age centre, I had once heard an Australian Aborigine talk about alignments of sacred sites. 'We Aborigines call them leylines,' he said. As editor of *The Ley Hunter* journal for 20 years I knew that to be untrue – alignments of ancient sites had been called 'leys' by English businessman, photographer and amateur archaeologist Alfred Watkins in the 1920s, an idea that had been in the New Age efflorescence of the 1960s, when something called 'leylines' first began to make its appearance in the literature associated with UFOs and dowsing.

Why should some indigenous persons make up such tales? Well, why not assume the mantle of a wise elder if people are prepared to fly you around the world to conferences, put you up in fancy hotels, and laud you as if you carried the word of God? The Aborigine in my example said it himself: 'I used to go walkabout; now I go flyabout.' Western audiences believe they are hearing tribal wisdom, but they are only hearing their own fantasies being echoed back at them, or at best simple common-sense ideas they could pick up in any village pub.

It was against the background of these concerns that I turned to Peter Walker, the archaeologist who, along with a colleague from his Winnipeg office, was accompanying me. I asked how much weight could be put on these interpretations and whether the Indians in this region today descend directly from those who laid down these ground patterns.

Peter explained that we simply cannot be sure who built the boulder mosaics or whether today's Anishinabe can trace a continuous line back to them. It could be that today's Indians were simply making up their own folklore about features that mystified them as much as they did us. But, it could also be that they were tapping into some native memory that had partially survived the ages. He added that in any case it was the policy of the province's authorities to engage with the local Indians so they could jointly look after these remarkable sites, even though that meant allowing the Indians to use some of them for ceremonial purposes from time to time – ceremonies that may not necessarily have anything to do with the original purpose of the ground patterns.

As we all fanned out to find our own, solitary places to sit and meditate amidst the ground patterns, I thought more deeply about how to interpret them. The Ojibway had been a shamanic people, even using Fly Agaric (Amanita muscaria), the red-capped, white-spotted hallucinogenic mushroom of Siberian shamanism, and which also figured in their mythology. It is likely that even if their predecessors had made the boulder mosaics they, too, would have been shamanic. So it was pretty certain that the ground patterns were associated with shamanic ritual and religious beliefs, as, indeed, the Anishinabe interpretations implied. I figured that the relatively small, ancient turtle-shaped circles I had seen at Bannock Point were probably vision-questing spots, as were some of the stone rings and smaller enclosures here at Tie Creek, and that the giant stone paw tracks related to conceptions of power animals – and none were more shamanic than the bear and the wolf. But what about the apparently abstract lines, enclosures and complex patterns?

Death Valley Patterns

Comparisons are often useful when trying to untangle knotty interpretative problems in archaeology, and as I sat by a boulder at the end of an alignment at Tie Creek I recalled that there were similar ground patterns far away to the south in the deserts of the southern United States. In the Panamint and Death valleys and areas around southern California, for example, there were lines of small rocks, enclosures, alignments, meandering lines, and a range of stone rings (Figure 9). Unlike the Manitoba examples, where the rocks were laid out on the hard tablerock, the Californian patterns consisted of rocks pressed into the desert surface. Museum curator Jay von Werlhof, a leading archaeological investigator of such features, associates them with the shamanism of people who lived in the valleys when they were in a stage of climatic transition from a moister, more hospitable condition to the harsh arid environments they became.[4] From an analysis of their relationships with physical features in the valleys, such as dried up stream beds, Werlhof suggests that the rock designs represented patterns of magical power with which the shamans

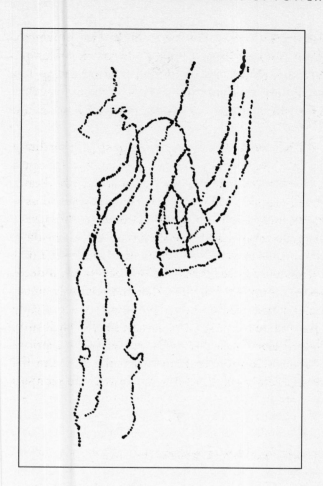

Figure 9: Part of a complex of rock patterns in the Panamint Valley, California. (From Werlhof, 1987)

attempted to 'induce a rejuvenation of a dying ecosystem'. The compacted nature of the ground around certain of the rock patterns indicates that some of them were used for ceremonial dancing or processions. The smaller stone rings Werlhof identifies as 'shaman's hearths', which were ritualistic and non-functional, while the larger rings, as defined with stones or simply as cleared areas of ground, were for vision questing.

Another intriguing type of feature Werlhof found among the patterns are 'spirit breaks'. These are formed by short arrangements of rocks, usually quartz cobbles, lying across some of the ancient trails in the region, or in association with the rock patterns. These were to block evil spiritual forces moving along the trackways or trying to enter the boulder design complexes.[5] Quartz was considered a power stone, and among the ground designs there were places where quartz had been broken up, presumably to release its supernatural power. This may have been expressed in the Indian mind by what we know as the piezoelectrical property of quartz: it produces electric charge when subjected to pressure, and heavy friction or breakage can cause discharges of light, an effect known as 'triboluminescence'. Pieces of quartz were found in American Indian shamans' 'medicine bundles' even into historic times.

Dream Paths

I looked around the expanse of tablerock at Tie Creek. Tom was conducting some solitary observance at one boulder mosaic site in the distance. Were these features, then, like the Californian ground designs, giant shamanic patterns of power? The idea of ground markings being the mapping of various forms of supernatural geography was supported by other research too.

In the Gila River valley of southern Arizona, researcher Tom Hoskinson has made a remarkable study of ground markings at a place called Sears Point.[6] On arid mesa tops at this remote spot there are about 50 ground designs, some made by clearance of the thin veneer of volcanic pebbles and small rocks covering the hard clay subsurface, and others made by the placing of small rocks and boulders as at Tie Creek or southern California. The markings had been made in ancient times by Yuman and Piman Indians, and are comprised of straight and wandering lines, geometric designs, and giant markings depicting human figures and ritual objects. Hoskinson's research concerning one of the straight lines revealed that it pointed to the distant peak of Granary Basket Mountain. Further, Hoskinson found that the alignment of the line on the ground is astronomically significant, in that it indicates the midwinter sunset, when the sun's disk appears to sink into the peak. Looking the other way down the 75-foot (23 m) line, the summer solstice sun would have been seen rising from another distant mountain. At one end of the line there was a boulder with a notch in it like a gunsight, and marked with a solitary rock carving in the style of the Hohokam Indians, ancestors of the Piman, Yuman and Papago peoples. From the various astronomical features, Hoskinson was able to calculate that the ground line was likely to have been made 1,500 or more years ago.

The ethnographical literature available on the Yuman and Piman Indians was able to greatly expand the interpretation of the ground marking: it reveals that Granary Basket Mountain was sacred to the Yuman people, and that their shamans went into a trance or 'dream' by means of a hallucinogenic infusion made from jimson weed, known in its Aztec context as *toloache*. The

Indians said that after taking the potion the ground 'shone with dazzling colours', and the shaman felt filled with supernatural power.[7] Hoskinson picks up the story:

> During a shamanic dream, the dreamer invariably was transported to the summit of his or her tribal power mountain. The tribal power mountain was always the first stop in a shamanic dream; while there, the individual contacted sources of power ... Powerful shamans frequently would solicit the aid (or non-interference) of power mountains belonging to other tribal groups.[8]

Key dates of the year, like the solstices and equinoxes, were considered times of special power. So the winter solstice sun setting into Granary Basket Mountain would have been a major alignment of power, monumentalised by the line on the ground at Sears Point. Putting all the evidence together, it is possible to picture the line being used by *toloache*-inspired Hohokam or Yuman shamans long ago as a kind of spiritual runway, a take-off point for their shamanic dreams – indeed, a semi-circle of stones exists at the other end of the line, reminiscent of a vision-questing site. The ground markings in effect set the trajectory for the shamanic out-of-body dream flight to the power mountain.

The Power of War

The ethnographical literature also revealed other aspects of ancient Indian ground markings, very much in line with Werlhof's general idea of patterns of power. Granary Basket Mountain marked the boundary between Yuman and Piman territories. 'It was believed that this mountain, if addressed with the proper shamanistic ceremonies, would ally itself with another power mountain and magically intervene during a war on behalf of the shamans's tribe,' Hoskinson discovered. The Yuman and Piman Indians were fierce fighters to whom war was a source of spiritual power, and they took pleasure in planning battles and conducting them. Their shamanism was closely bound up with this process. Yuman Indians would magically raise power mountains as a barrier to enemies or harmful forces by drawing a line on the ground. In the same vein, a shaman might draw a circle on the ground around himself so as to set up a protective circle of power, or around a sick tribal member during a healing ceremony so the healing power of a special song or chant could be contained and concentrated.[9] With the same logic, a

Piman shaman might draw a line across a pathway to magically become a deep canyon to prevent an enemy's or rival's progress. As strange as these ideas are to us, they were part of the ancient American Indian's view of reality.

Monuments of Shamanism

My thoughts were interrupted as Tom signalled for us to get up from our respective places around the Tie Creek sacred ground in order to gather together once more. As I picked my way through the lines and circles of rocks forming the feature that supposedly represented a ghost lodge, I recalled an Indian sketch I had seen in an old book depicting the layout of a ghost lodge and the path taken towards it by the spirit of a deceased person (Figure 10). If

FIGURE 10: Ghost Lodge arrangement. The circle on the right represents the wigwam of the mourner; the rectangle on the left represents the ghost lodge itself. The horizontal line joining them represents the path taken by the ghost. The other depictions relate to other features of the ritual arrangement. (After an Indian's sketch in W.J. Hoffman, *The Midewewin or Grand Medicine Society of the Ojibwa*, 1891)

the Anishinabe interpretation of this boulder mosaic design as representing the ghost lodge ceremony was correct, then the long line of boulders leading from the circular enclosures probably represented such spirit paths. I was beginning to see that the ground markings of the ancient North American Indians were the physical mapping of a curiously interrelated set of concepts – the trance journeys of shamans, the patterns of supernatural powers and the paths of the dead. Because shamanism was considered a subject for anthropology, the idea of there also being an *archaeology of shamanism* had tended to be overlooked, and I had not encountered it in the academic literature. Yet here it was: a monument to shamanism constructed with rocks laid out on a vast scale for all to see.

Before we had gone off to our chosen locations among the boulder mosaics of Tie Creek, Tom had asked us to see if we could become aware of a special rock he did not identify. He now queried us about our findings. The group looked mildly perplexed, and no one answered, but I had in fact noticed an unusual boulder: the *whole* stone was pink and free of lichen, yet growth around its base showed it to have been standing in situ for ages. I hesitated before suggesting it might be the rock in question. Tom nodded. He told us that one day he had brought an elder from a distant Ojibway group south of the Canadian–United States border to Tie Creek, at the old man's request. The fellow had never been to Whiteshell before, but he wanted to make contact with a 'grandfather rock' he knew was at Tie Creek. Tom said that as soon as he had let the elder into the site, the old man had made his way directly to the small boulder, which is located out of sight and at quite a distance from the entrance gate. 'So there is a living esoteric tradition among the modern Anishinabe, then?' I suggested to Tom. He beamed once more. A twinkle was in his eye, but he said nothing. It was time to leave Tie Creek.

A Search in Secret America

The Manitoba petroform sites had certainly acted as teaching places for me, and helped to inform my ongoing research into other ground patterns and shamanic monuments, elsewhere in the Americas. My research was largely literature based, but as and when possible within my means, I conducted fieldwork on sites widely scattered over the Americas.

Effigy Mounds

One of the most extraordinary experiences on this quest occurred when I was picking my way through a Wisconsin wood one humid summer's day. The sunlight streaming through the foliage cast a vividly contrasting dappled pattern on the ground, and it was with straining eyes that I suddenly picked out the giant earthen form of an eagle lying amidst the trees. The earthwork was about three feet in height and dozens of feet long. It had its head to one side, and I could walk along its beak and down its back. I also came across the earthen effigy of a cat-like animal elsewhere among the trees, and then another: I wandered for an hour finding one huge effigy after another in what is now called Lizard Mound County Park, but was formerly a sacred landscape belonging to an unknown people the archaeologists call the 'Mississippian Indians' for convenience.

Lizard Mound is just one example of a cluster of effigy mounds to be

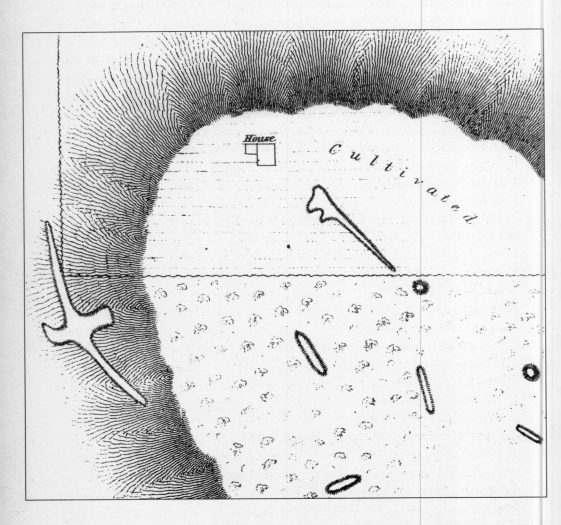

FIGURE 11: Detail of a nineteenth-century plan of Wisconsin effigy mounds, showing bird, quadruped and geometric forms. (I.A. Lapham, 1850)

found in Iowa and Wisconsin and a few other states depicting birds, serpents, lizards, bears, creatures usually referred to as 'panthers', and other
quadrupeds that might be wolves. Most effigy mounds, though, are geometric – circles, ovals, conical forms, rectangles and other shapes (Figure 11).
Thousands of these curious mounds still survive – usually near lakes and
rivers – but many more had been ploughed out or otherwise destroyed by
white settlers. They had been made between c.AD 350 to c.AD 1300. I visited
many more of these curious earthen features, some of them relatively small,
others gargantuan. Archaeologists found that some had burials within them,
often where the heart would have been found in the actual creature, or
where a wing or limb joined the main body, but others contained no burials
at all.

The most famous effigy earthwork in North America is probably
Serpent Mound, situated on a bluff overlooking the Miami River in Ohio,
and this quarter-mile-long (400 m) sinuous effigy is thought by most
authorities to date back 1,500 years or more to the shamanic Hopewell people, and possibly to the Adena, who preceded them. It contains no burials.
The Hopewell people also built vast geometric earthwork enclosures of
hexagonal and other regular forms (Figure 12), as well as a 60-mile-long (97
km) dead straight ceremonial road linking two such sites. The existence of
this remarkable road has only recently been uncovered by dedicated
investigation using old documentation, field study and aerial infrared
photography.[10]

No one truly knows what the purpose was of either the Hopewell or
Mississippian earthworks. A burial mound would not be shaped as an animal
or bird unless there was a reason, and in any case not all the effigy earthworks
were burial mounds. The Hopewell culture is known to have been a consor-
tium of tribes united in their practice of a shamanic religion, and the
Mississippian Indians were probably similar, for archaeological remains of the
Mississippian Indians such as stone tablets and incised shells show winged
figures, or people wearing winged costumes, referred to in the scholarly
literature as 'flying shamans'.[11]

What could the connection be between shamanism and the effigy
mounds? It seemed likely to me that the animal shapes referred to shamanic
'familiars' or power animals, and perhaps some of the Mississippian burials
were of shamans or shaman chieftains. And I could not help but wonder if
the geometric earthworks were a reflection of those mind patterns seen in
trance. I was in little doubt that I was yet again encountering the monuments
of shamanism.

But what of the straight ceremonial road stretching across Ohio: should it

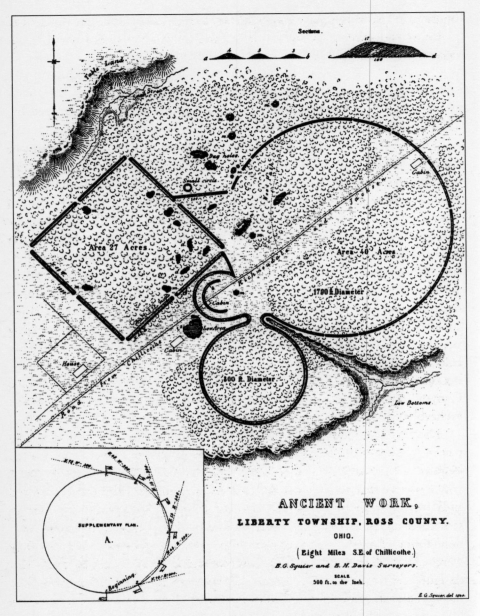

Figure 12. Nineteenth-century plan of a group of Hopewell geometric earthworks, Ohio. The large circle encloses 40 acres. (E.G. Squier and E.H. Davis, 1848)

and the numerous shorter ones running between Hopewell sites also be included in what I was interpreting as a shamanic geography? As I travelled further southwards I was to discover that mysterious ancient roads were to figure large and it would become apparent to me that roads and pathways had a deeper significance in the world of ancient American Indians than we accord such features today.

Roads of the Ancient Ones

I was brought face-to-face with this fact in the San Juan Basin where the modern states of Colorado, Utah, New Mexico and Arizona meet. This is the ancestral territory of the lost Anasazi Indians, the 'Ancient Ones' as their name means in the language of the Navajo Indians who much later occupied their lands. One of the chief holy places and ceremonial centres of the Anasazi was Chaco Canyon, a shallow rift a few miles long in high desert country in northwest New Mexico. I visited this remote and arid site a number of times, as well as many other Anasazi sites across the San Juan Basin.

The Anasazi, who lasted as a definable culture for about 1,000 years before disappearing somewhat mysteriously around AD 1400, were accomplished builders and astronomers. Much has now been written on these fascinating people,[12] but the focus of my interest with this lost civilisation was its carefully engineered roads. These are often referred to as 'Chacoan roads', because most of the longest lengths have been discovered around Chaco Canyon. It is only in the last few decades that there has been any extensive archaeological work on them.[13]

The Chacoan roads are in the main distinctly straight, reaching to over 30 feet in width (10 m), and aerial infrared photography has revealed that some lengths of the roads had up to three parallel sections. No one understands why a society that had neither wheeled vehicles nor beasts of burden needed such freeway-scale highways. The roads seem to have connected up pueblo structures archaeologists call 'Great Houses', which, judging from the midden (rubbish) heaps, were occupied only intermittently, indicating that they were ceremonial buildings. The architecture of the Great Houses was designed to accommodate the roads, in that gates in walls allowed the roads passage, and in some cases rooms in the Great Houses had no internal access but opened only onto the roads. The roads reach right to the rimrock of Chaco Canyon, and rock-hewn stairways lead down the canyon walls from them, though these stone steps are now eroded to virtual invisibility in many cases. The Great Houses scattered along the canyon floor were connected by similar roads.

Although some lengths of road have now been mapped around the canyon, as a consequence of aerial photography and selective field archaeology, the full extent of Anasazi road networks in the San Juan Basin is still unknown. The roads certainly extend tens if not hundreds of miles from Chaco, and segments have been found as far afield as Colorado, Utah, and southern New Mexico.

Shadow Lines

Trying to see the roads from ground level is a frustrating business for the investigator, because the depredations of time, weather and people have almost erased them. I found that though armed with maps and aerial photographs I still couldn't see a Chacoan road even when I knew I was looking at one. Then late one afternoon I climbed up to the rimrock of the canyon, and reached the ruins of a Great House called Pueblo Alto, where I stood looking northwards along the line of what archaeologists had dubbed the Great North Road, as a nod towards the great Roman road that runs north from London. I could see mountain peaks almost 100 miles away, and I knew the desert in between contained the course of this great straight Anasazi road. It was initially invisible, but as the sun sank towards the horizon I very gradually realised I was beginning to see the road. On the ground, its course is marked by a shallow and normally barely detectable depression, but as the sunlight became nearly horizontal this showed up as a faint, soft-edged shadow running though the desert. As the sun sank even lower, the shadow became stronger, and other roads began to appear. For a few fleeting moments at sunset I was looking at a desert landscape criss-crossed with soft, shadowy lines. It was as if the desert spirits were casting spells for me.

The Anasazi roads seem to have linked ritual centres across the entire 400-mile-wide expanse of the San Juan Basin, but we are as yet only detecting fragments of the system. The roads had clearly been ceremonial, or, at least, had had ceremonial attributes even if they also served practical purposes as well, as it was obvious that they had been deliberately engineered to be more than simple trackways. One Navajo elder told an archaeologist in the 1920s that the Chacoan features may look like roads, but they were not roads. I was to return to this conundrum as my research continued.

La Quemada: Citadel of Mysteries

Another expedition brought me to the remote and little-known citadel and ceremonial centre of La Quemada, also known as Chicomostoc, near

Zacetecas in northern Mexico. Here, the remnants of stone structures clad a rocky, twin-peaked hilltop overlooking the broad floor of the Malpaso Valley. An enormous stone stairway leads up the lower slopes from a precinct containing a truncated pyramid. Higher up the hilltop, ancient paths wind around the rocks, leading past the ruins of temples, shrines and ceremonial platforms and plazas built onto terraces which had been cut into the hillside. No one is quite sure about the origins of the site, but it is thought to have been a product of a little-known culture archaeologists refer to as the Chalchihuites. La Quemada seems to have reached its heyday between c.AD 600 and c.AD 800. What took place there is by no means clear, but religious concerns were certainly important, as revealed by the large percentage of ceremonial and ritual structures making up the ruins.

A quiet mystery still hangs over the site today. The Huichol Indians of northern Mexico studiously avoid La Quemada when crossing Zacetecas state during their long, annual pilgrimage to the Wirikuta plateau in San Luis Potosi. There they 'hunt' the hallucinogenic cactus, peyote, basketloads of which they bring back home for their religious ceremonies over the following year.[14] Anthropologists suspect that the rituals enacted by the Huichol at Wirikuta hark back to extremely ancient times, possibly even as far as the supposed Eurasian origins of the American Indian.[15]

Having climbed to one of the high terraces on the rocky hilltop, I could see the large, now roofless building called the Hall of Columns, situated on a lower terrace. As its name implies, it contains a series of columns – massive cylinders comprised of small rocks. This reminded me that there was one exception to the Huichol avoidance of the citadel – they hold a secret peyote ceremony here every year a few days prior to the spring equinox. No outsider seems to have yet plumbed the Indians' curiously ambivalent attitude to La Quemada.

As I raised my gaze from the Hall of Columns to the great expanse of countryside stretching out below my vantage point, I was able to pick out remnants of long, straight causeways running through open land, their courses revealed by the tell-tale growth of cactus bushes and stunted trees along the jumbled remains of their masonry, now largely buried in the ground. When my eyes became trained to the task, I was also able to make out light brown lines marking the course of major causeways amidst the plantations of nopal cactus near the foot of the citadel.

These straight causeways crossing the landscape at various angles are mysterious features. The first written study of them was by the British engineer, G.F. Lyon in 1826. He described slightly raised and paved causeways ranging 12–45 feet (3.6–13.7 m) in width that were 'perfectly straight', traversing rivers and mountainsides as well as flat open land. They ran to caves in cliffs, towards distant mountains, and to ceremonial structures like temples, pyramids and plazas. Some of them were mapped by various investigators a little later in the nineteenth century.

Modern surveys conducted by Charles Trombold of Washington University, St Louis, have confirmed the existence of over 100 miles (170 km) of causeways in the region. Some of them converge onto the citadel, and others relate to smaller outlying sites or natural features. Trombold notes that the ends of causeways are often marked by platforms with ceremonial stairways and sunken courts, and that altars are also sometimes found placed on the causeways. Trombold goes on to remark that there are few natural impediments to foot traffic in the valley, and he warns academic colleagues that 'the causeways cannot be used as the basis of economic or social models'. He also finds it difficult to identify any military purpose, concluding that 'almost certainly they . . . were associated with ritual activities'. He suggests that there were several other centres in northern Mexico in addition to La Quemada that had similar networks of straight roads, and makes the further important observation that the causeways:

. . . are not casual occurrences . . . Rather they represent the tip of a cultural iceberg in that behind their presence lies extensive planning, engineering, mobilisation of labour and monumental-scale construction. Most important, there was a well-defined and socially sanctioned purpose to justify all this.[16]

As I sat high up on the citadel of La Quemada, reading Trombold's words, I could not help but wonder just what that ancient purpose had been.

The Strange Causeways of the Maya

The furthest south in the Americas my personal field research has taken me to date is the rainforest covering the flat expanse of the Yucatan Peninsula in southern Mexico, which had been the heartland of the ancient northern Maya. The focus of my interest there was yet more ancient straight stone causeways known as *sacbeob* in the Mayan language, a term meaning 'white ways'. They run through the forest between ancient Mayan ceremonial cities, with shorter versions within the cities connecting plazas and ceremonial buildings. With the demise of the high Mayan culture around c.AD 900 (a

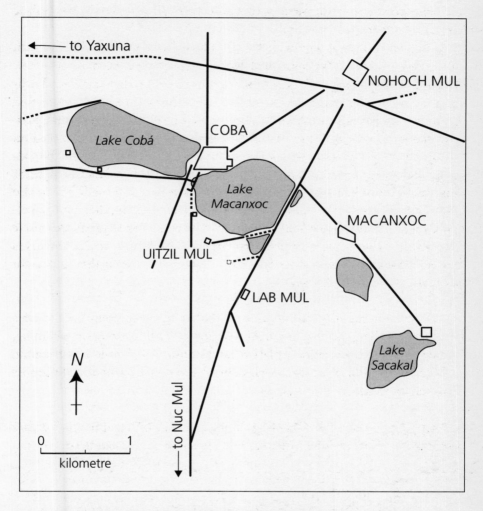

FIGURE 13. Causeways or *sacbeob* within and radiating from the ancient Mayan centre of Coba, Mexico. (Compiled from various sources.)

little later in the Yucatan), the Maya eventually abandoned the sacred cities and returned to the forest. The cities gradually became engulfed by the rain-forest, as did the causeways, most of which consequently became lost.

The longest section so far mapped by archaeologists is the 62-mile

(100 km) causeway in the northern part of the peninsula connecting the great
Mayan centre of Coba in Quintana Roo, from which many *sacbeob* radiated,
and the ceremonial centre of Yaxuna, Yucatan. It was first discovered by the
explorer Thomas Gann early in the twentieth century. He considered it to be
one of the 'most remarkable roads ever constructed', noting that it was 32 feet
(10 m) wide, built of massive stone blocks, and 'straight as an arrow, and
almost flat as a rule'.

I traced short sections of this road through dense jungle but found those
parts of it, at least, to be now sadly ruinous, with great white limestone rocks
tumbled hither and thither among the undergrowth. The only obvious
record of its existence on the ground is a battered sign saying 'Camino Maya'
where the course of the causeway crosses a modern road. Shorter lengths of
causeway have been mapped elsewhere in the Yucatan peninsula, especially
around Coba, and *sacbe* sections within the cleared ceremonial cities had
been restored to some approximation of their former glory (Plate 3). Like the
causeways of La Quemada, some of the Mayan features had altars, ramps and
other architectural features associated with them.

Laying such structures with such straightness through the rainforest was
not a minor achievement. Why was the straightness, the precision deemed
necessary? Walkable routes through rainforest didn't need to have been constructed with such exactitude. What purpose had the causeways served? I
went to see Professor William Folan at Campeche University for some eluci-
dation. I found him in a room stacked high with books and unruly paperwork. I knew he had been conducting fieldwork and mapping *sacbeob* for
decades and that he had developed some far-reaching ideas about the meanings of the causeways not only because of that outstanding fieldwork, but also
from his contacts with today's Maya.[17]

First I wanted to know *how* the ancient Maya had managed to survey
straight ways through the dense forest. Folan agreed that achieving such precision had to have been a formidable effort. He remarked on the innate direc-
tional abilities possessed by the Mayans with whom he worked on his
fieldtrips: in apparently featureless forest, they knew just where they were,
and in what direction to go. Further, he suspected that the ancient Maya had
used astronomy to help them set out the trajectory of the causeways. The
great Mayan pyramids that rose above the forest canopy would doubtless
have been instrumental in this – for instance, a number of causeways radiated
out from various pyramid locations within the great complex of Coba, which
covers some 40 square miles, most of it still covered by trees. Folan felt that
some causeway networks were aligned to celestial features of special significance to the Maya, such as the bright stars Sirius, Canopus, Regulus and

Cygnus, the Pleiades constellation, key sun and moon settings and risings, and those of the planet Venus, all important players in Mesoamerican cosmology. Some causeway networks may in themselves have mirrored star maps.

I asked Folan what he thought the purpose of the *sacbeob* could have been. He pointed out that the long, inter-city causeways and in-city road systems were all multi-functional, facilitating the movement of the ancient Mayan population 'for sacred, secular and military purposes'. This idea of multi-functionalism for a road is alien to modern understanding, but is crucial to an appreciation of the thinking of the ancient American Indians. Folan pointed out that there were not only these larger causeways, but also neighbourhood and even individual, personal *sacbeob*. It was a nested system of intricate social and spiritual significance.

Invisible Roads

As if this wasn't complicated enough, Folan then insisted that all this was only part of the story. He had retrieved ethnological evidence that the physical, 'land-level' causeways were complemented by *invisible* ones. There were the *kusam sum*, aerial routes that were believed to take the form of blood-filled tubes. One of these was said to connect the city of Tulum on the Caribbean coast with Coba, and then onwards to the site now occupied by the modern town of Merida on the Gulf coast of the peninsula; another was said to connect the ancient Mayan ceremonial centres of Dzibilchaltun and Izamul. Then there were mythological underground *sacbeob* – these may relate to the underground passageway mentioned in the ancient Mayan sacred text, the *Popol Vuh*. One was said to run under the Castillo, the stepped pyramid that was the Temple of Kukulcan, the Feathered Serpent, at Chichen Itza. Some mythical *sacbeob* were said to invisibly extend the courses of some actual stone causeway systems.

I left Folan knowing that I had got more than I had bargained for, and deciding that the ancient American Indian way of thinking offered real challenges to the modern mind.

The Nazca Lines

No investigation of ground effigies and straight lines, roads or paths can ignore the profusion of markings on the Andean desert tablelands known as pampas, the most famous example being the Nazca Lines of Peru. General understanding of the markings on the Nazca pampa are unfortunately over-shadowed by populist beliefs that they were landing strips for ancient extra-terrestrial spaceships, a notion generated by the 'ancient astronaut' fad of the 1960s, and which sadly has been revived more recently. This idea simply isn't true, for a variety of reasons, as will become evident.

The Nazca pampa markings cover the whole range of ground features – effigy figures of animals, birds, and plants, geometric patterns, rectangular and triangular or wedge-shaped areas, enclosures and curvilinear lines. And there are almost 1,000 dead straight lines of varying widths crossing the pampa, amidst which are nodes or 'line centres' with several lines converging on them or interlinking them. These line centres or nodes are often piles of rocks or natural spurs. The ground drawings, 'geoglyphs', are on a grand scale, extending from a few hundred to a few thousand feet in length, and the lines can run for several miles in some cases. The patterns and figures are uni-cursal, meaning that the line defining them never crosses over itself, so a per-son can walk, run or dance around them in an orderly, uninterrupted sequence. The oldest markings are perhaps over 2,000 years old, but some are several centuries more recent.

The actual making of the markings was quite an easy task to accomplish. The darkened, oxidised desert surface is removed to reveal a lighter surface underneath – but the laying out of these huge geoglyphs with the fine pro-portions and symmetry most of them display could only have been achieved by use of scale plans (or else, it has been suggested, by guidance from an over-seer in a hot-air balloon). Once made, markings on the pampa last virtually forever, for there is effectively no rain to wash them away, and the wind has long ago removed what was light enough to blow away. The desert surface is so sensitive that footprints and tyre tracks also last interminably, and at the present time it is such careless markings that pose the greatest threat to the survival of the geoglyphs. Indeed, the fact that it is so easy to make long-lasting marks on the pampa, intentionally or otherwise, provides one of the practical reasons why the idea of alien craft landing and taking off here centuries ago is wrong, even if we were to take the notion seriously: there would be marks left by such events, and there are none. The ancient astronaut explanation is a crude modern one; it is with the subtler workings of the ancient human mind and soul that the answer to the mystery on the desert has to lie.

Although my fieldwork did not extend into South America, I digested much of the considerable literature on the Nazca Lines, and I further inter-viewed some of their key researchers. For one such meeting I drove through the stunningly vivid reds, russets and yellows of autumnal foliage in New

York State to speak with Andean experts Anthony Aveni and Gary Urton, both at Colgate University at Hamilton. Aveni is an extremely lively and hospitable man who specialises in the study of ancient astronomy in the Americas, and Urton, a quiet and courteous fellow, is an anthropologist. He has lived with Andean Indians studying their religious and social practices,[18] and Aveni co-ordinated a multi-disciplinary research effort on the Nazca lines over various seasons in the 1980s.[19]

Earlier work[20] indicated that few if any of the Nazca markings have significant astronomical orientations, but Aveni warned that this may only be so with regard to celestial features that modern researchers were familiar with. For instance, Urton's work revealed that dark patches caused by interstellar dust in the Milky Way were viewed as 'dark constellations' by Andean Indians today, and this had probably always been the case. Moreover, the Milky Way itself was a major feature of native Andean skylore. It could be that there were alignments in the lines of native astronomical significance that have not yet been recognised by non-Indian investigators.

Aveni and Urton both pointed out to me that certain mountains, in certain directions, had significance relating to the ancestors and other concepts in the Andean mind, and they reminded me of anthropologist Johanne Reinhard's studies of straight paths in the Bolivian Andes – which are even longer than the Nazca lines – and his conclusion that these and at least some of the Nazca lines pointed to mountains associated with water-giving gods. He had seen Bolivian Indians walking the straight ways up the mountains to petition rain-bearing deities. At Sears Point, in Arizona, I recalled, the Indian shamans 'flew' in their hallucinogenic trance or 'dream' to the mountain peaks to engage with the gods and extract supernatural power. I suspected that the people went to the mountaintop in processions, but the shaman went there in spirit, the weird straightness being related to that otherworldly aspect.

Aveni's own work on *ceques*, Inca alignments of sacred places (wakas) radiating from Cuzco, Peru, showed them to have symbolic association with the ancestors and kinship groups, with astronomical orientations, and perhaps above all, with ritualised linear pilgrimage routes, and he felt that all these three purposes could similarly have applied to the Nazca lines. In addition, the lines may themselves have been sacred features.

Urton had observed the current practice among superficially Christianised Andean Indians of family groups taking it in turns to sweep narrow strips of ground across the square in front of a village church to ritually transform it from everyday, profane space to sacred space prior to the parading of the image of a saint or the Virgin.[21] The team members of Aveni's expedition detected evidence in the way the rocks were disposed at edges of the Nazca lines hinting at a similar kind of ritual sweeping. Persis Clarkson, a Canadian member of the Aveni interdisciplinary team, also discovered that many of the straight lines had been deeply furrowed by people walking along them, yet the lines start or end nowhere that we can understand as being significant. Another of Aveni's team, anthropologist Helaine Silverman, researched a ruined ritual complex called Cahuachi, just off the Nazca pampa, which she felt had been a major pilgrimage centre – possibly an oracle temple and shamanic ceremonial site – and noted that some of the Nazca lines seemed oriented towards it.

Sacred mountains, skylore, the dead, kinship groups, ritual dancing and walking, pilgrimage, water sources – there was such a jumble of potential associations with the Nazca Lines and features like them that my head was spinning. All of them could be right, as I knew it was important to remember the multi-functional nature of many ancient American Indian structures, and also that there were many different kinds of markings on the pampa, probably made at different times. Before I had spoken with Urton and Aveni I had interviewed David Browne, a British archaeologist who had also conducted research on Andean ground markings. He had also cautioned against going for one single explanation – the desert markings in the Andes were, he averred, 'a palimpsest' – a manuscript on which successive texts had been written.

Other Mystery Roads

My enquiries revealed just how many more ground features there were in the ancient Americas than those I had visited or studied the literature on. There were numerous locations in the Andes with straight line markings, Nazca being just one example; in California there were geoglyphs in the Mojave desert and straight Indian paths cutting through the sierras; there were petroform figures scattered across states in the north-central United States, faint remnants of Anasazi-like straight roads in Colorado, ritual paths in Central America, paved sacred ways in Columbia, straight causeways at various locations in the Amazon Basin, and straight paths running down from the eastern Andes into the Amazon that had been spotted by NASA aerial surveys. There were doubtless many such features that I had not heard about, and probably others that have not yet even been discovered. (Such a profusion of the straight line features in spacecraft-unfriendly mountains and forests was another factor that gave the lie to notions about landing strips of ancient spacemen.) These strange landscape features defined the territories of the secret Americas, so secret that they were largely unknown to the mass of the public, and only a handful of scholars were researching them.

Seeking Answers

What was I to make of it all? Regarding the different kind of ground features, it was pretty certain from the ethnology that the *abstract designs*, however constructed, and whether geometrically exact or irregular and meandering in nature, were essentially patterns mapping the contours of supernatural power. From the trance-visionary viewpoint of the shaman, these patterns could be used in various ways: to protect the shaman from hostile spirits or forces sent against him by enemy shamans, to create magical landscapes for protective purposes when conducting sorcery or physical battles, and to combat and re-channel the forces of nature itself. Some abstract designs were ritual dance grounds, and some smaller features were for vision questing. The *figurative imagery* – the effigy mounds and geoglyphs, again however constructed – bore the hallmarks of shamanic spirit animals or familiars when they were not depicting mythological figures or clan totems. Ethnology that I had studied in fact suggested these three functions could be combined in the same features. Then there were the straight lines.

The Straight Line Mystery

Whether in the form of a simple line scratched on a desert, an alignment of small rocks or boulders, a slightly more structured ritual footpath, or a fully developed stone-built causeway in more complex societies like the highly organised and hierarchical cultures of ancient Mexico, there seemed to be a deep and stubbornly undeciphered meaning behind the straightness.

It was this enigma that both fascinated and perplexed me the most. It was a riddle that particularly engaged me as the editor of a magazine dealing with leys or 'leylines', the topic on which I also did some of my writing. It had become apparent that the straightness of the ancient American Indian ground features could not be dismissed by simple pragmatic explanations to do with them being merely roads to get from one place to another through open country: the features were specifically engineered to be straight, and in all kinds of terrain – even forests and mountains, where maintaining such precision had to have been a notable challenge. As Trombold observed: 'If there is one attribute that characterizes New World road systems, it is their straightness.'

This was echoed in a telephone conversation I'd had with Tom Sever, the archaeologist at the United States' National Aeronautical and Space Administration (NASA), an organisation more commonly associated with futuristic technology like rockets and spacecraft, but whose airborne and Earth-orbiting electronic eyes in fact quite often uncover archaeological sites hidden deep within jungles and elsewhere. 'What was the obsessively deliberate straightness all about?' he had openly asked me. He had made a special study of the Chacoan roads, and he mentioned that only when the data were analysed by computer did this factor become so unavoidably evident. In an unpublished report on the Anasazi features he kindly let me see, he emphasised that they were purposeful constructions, not trails that had resulted from repeated use of convenient routes. To the contrary, he remarked that the 'Chaco roads . . . were not efficient routes; they made inefficient use of human resources and the natural landscape in order to maintain a straight route'. Sever stated unequivocally that the Chacoan roads 'appear to be associated with ritual activity', pointing out that shrines are found along their courses, and that they connect to ritual and ceremonial structures, as well as to natural features that were presumably viewed as having sacred qualities.

My own travels and investigations have shown these factors to be also true of most other ancient straight road, path and 'line' features throughout the Americas. To these observations have to be added the views of Indian elders that such straight linear ground features may look like roads but are not roads, and informed opinions like that from the late John Hyslop, who was based at New York's Museum of Natural History and had intensively studied American Indian road features in the field and anthropologically: 'Roads constructed in extraordinary ways may reflect ritual or symbolic concerns . . . Attempts to interpret all aspects of prehistoric roads in purely materialist terms are bound to fail.'[22]

The Entrancing Line

If the straight line ground features – roads, paths, lines or however one chose to refer to them – were part of a shamanic archaeology, to what aspect of shamanism did they relate? The connections I had made at Tie Creek suggested that some of the rock alignments could be marking out the paths taken by the recent dead, but what else might be involved, especially with regard to major features like the Andean lines?

I made an intuitive connection between the straightness and *flight* – 'as the crow flies', 'as straight as an arrow'. Did not the shaman go on an aerial journey during trance? Did he not take plant drugs that specifically promoted the sense of spirit flight? Was not the core of shamanism the experience we refer to today as the out-of-body experience? The answer to all these points was, of course, resoundingly in the affirmative. I suspected that somehow the lines related to the supposed flight of the shaman's spirit.

I had had hints of this from fragmentary sources long before, a notable one being a college friend back in the 1960s who had told of his adventures with old shamans or *curanderos* in remote Mexican villages. He said he had taken their hallucinogenic mushrooms during night-time ritual gatherings and had subsequently 'flown' to distant locations he hadn't previously seen where he met other shamans from other villages. Later, he was physically taken to those locations to meet those people. However, I had not read anything in the scholarly literature about a possible connection between the straight lines and such spirit flights, and I was not confident enough to go into print with the idea.

Fortunately, I happened to mention my thoughts on the topic to Christian Rätsch, a friend and cultural anthropologist who had spent long periods of time living with the Lacandon Maya deep within the rainforests of southern Mexico. I knew he had been initiated into the religious life of the tribe, so he seemed a good person to quiz about the matter. He admitted that there had been little formal study about the subject, though it was instinctively understood among the tribal peoples concerned. However, he informed me that a paper had been written on the topic in 1977 by American anthropologist Marlene Dobkin de Rios.[23] This scholar is well known in the academic world for her work with shamans throughout the Americas. As I read her paper, I was startled to find that here was someone who had taken precisely the same track towards solving the mystery as I was now doing.

Dobkin de Rios states openly in her paper that the ground markings and effigies were built 'due to shamanistic, out-of-body experiences, the so-called aerial voyage'. They were built, she suggests, to express cosmological knowledge, and to make that known to 'supernatural forces . . . to members of the community, as well as other shamans in conflict with the social group'. She emphasises that she had found in her fieldwork that shamans and witches or *brujos* spent much time battling with one another – a feature that would figure prominently in my explorations of European shamanism (see Chapter

Four). She also suggests that the building of these ground features would have enhanced the social power of the shaman, or shaman-chieftain, while helping to cement 'social solidarity'.

Dobkin de Rios confirmed my own feeling that the effigy mounds of the northern United States express recognisable shamanic imagery. She dwells for a considerable part in her paper on the wide use of plant hallucinogens by ancient American Indian societies, and their role in promoting trance 'journeys', specifically flying or out-of-body sensations. She notes evidence showing that the Adena, Hopewell, Olmec and Nazca peoples are all known to have taken such drugs. Not only did shamans engage in such magical flight, they also believed that they sometimes transformed into birds and animals as they did so (see Chapter One). She ends by associating the effigy ground images with such experiences, used in the main as warnings to rival shamans, and the geometric imagery with mind patterns or entoptic imagery produced in trance, just as it is now recognised to influence rock art.

In a later work, Dobkin de Rios reports that ancient Peruvian pottery and textile motifs do show figures flying, with hair streaming backwards, some of them seemingly holding mushrooms.[24] To this could be added the fact that it is now certain that the great cult that centred on the northern Peruvian temple of Chavin de Huantar in the first millennium BC was based on the use of plant hallucinogens, notably the mind-altering San Pedro cactus, and this cult influenced people for many hundreds of miles through the Andes: a highly relevant precursor to the peoples who produced the effigy and line markings on the pampas there.

Webs of the Spirit

I was delighted to learn of Dobkin de Rios's work, and felt more confident in proposing the shamanic solution for the markings, including the straight line features. I felt these were a symbolic representation of the shaman's soul journey, especially in the form of a flight in addition to whatever specific religious and secular attributes and uses were placed on them by the society at large. At heart I suspect they represented what we today refer to as the 'tunnel' experience in near-death and out-of-body experiences. The tunnel is in fact a key entoptic pattern – that is, it resulted from structures within the mind itself – and I felt that the straight line was the ancient American Indian way of expressing this same idea, the same inner sensation. This was supported by ethnological snippets such as that relating to the Sears Point features (above).

There were also other ethnological indications of traditional American

Indian beliefs in straight 'dream' or visionary soul flights that involved lines in one form or another. For instance, one Arizona Indian, Papago Foot, reported to early ethnographers that he went into a sacred cave in a butte near Tempe and smoked a special reed. He fell asleep and he dreamed of a stranger approaching him who told him he would help him to become a shaman. The spirit visitor then tied a cobweb from that butte to other buttes and holy peaks like those of the San Francisco Mountains, and Papago Foot travelled on the cobweb, receiving supernatural gifts of power at each of the mountain destinations.

Another, clearly associated, Yuman belief was that in a dream an eagle or other bird might move the dreamer through the air on a string to the sacred summits: 'They think of the buttes as connected by strings' wrote one ethnographer.[25] Cobwebs and strings linking natural sacred places seems likely to have been the mythic corollary of the ritual ground lines, directing the spirit of the dreamer or visionary to sacred mountaintops. In a similar vein, way down in South America, the former Selk'nam Indians of Patagonia believed that the 'eye' left the body during sleep or trance, flying in a straight line over the land trailing a thread behind it.[26]

In addition to such enthological items, I duly became aware that a living ancient culture, that of the Kogi Indians of northern Colombia, had stone-paved paths that the ordinary people were obliged to walk almost constantly as a sacred act, but which were viewed by the ruling Kogi shamans as physical 'traces' of the paths they followed in the spirit world – that is, when they were in trance.[27] The Kogi paths were holy in themselves, and at least some of them were straight even though they crossed mountainous country.

Getting on Line

Proposing a shamanic interpretation of material remains to the academic, scholarly world is not easy, of course. As Stephen Lekson, a leading anthropological and archaeological investigator of the Chacoan phenomenon has remarked: 'Landscapes are difficult to communicate. Historically, we [archaeologists] don't do it very well.'[28] Lekson has argued recently from the archaeological evidence that the Anasazi migrated from Chaco to a centre now called Aztec, in New Mexico, and then finally to Casas Grandes in northern Mexico. By taking the broader, landscape view, he has been able to determine that these three former Anasazi ceremonial centres fall on a dead straight line hundreds of miles long – a line, moreover, that is a meridian, a true north-south alignment, a feature that occurs both in Anasazi architecture and also in the orientation of the 'Great North Road' out of Chaco Canyon. It seems the ancient American Indians really could express abstract ideas in precise and large-scale landscape terms.

I tried bouncing the shamanic interpretation of the ground markings and features off some of those scholars I was meeting in the course of my investigations. Gary Urton had no problem with it. He told me of a television documentary that showed Amazonian Indians who took the mind-altering hallucinogen *ayahuasca* could recognise the geoglyphs on the Nazca pampa. For the documentary's producers he had found anthropological film footage showing the Amazon Indians taking the hallucinogen in the form of snuff. Urton agreed that the straightness was 'probably physiologically based', or neurophysiologically based, as I would have phrased it.

Folan at first resisted my idea with regard to the Mayan *sacbeob*. I argued that while there is no doubt that the more structured, elaborate straight causeways had ceremonial and social functions, their obsessively straight form went back to an old source – shamanism. I reminded him that the Maya were certainly shamanic people, and as their tribal ways turned into a high culture the shamans developed into a theocracy, a ruling elite of shamanistically inspired priest-kings. After the collapse of their high culture, the Maya returned to the forest, where they continue to this day with more basic, tribal shamanism, using plant hallucinogens as well as other techniques.[29] After a few moments thought, Folan agreed that by taking a more general overview, rather than being immersed in the archaeological details of one culture, it was possible to see a connecting straight-line pattern relating to ground features throughout the Americas.

Browne stated that he had 'no problem' with the shamanic interpretation of the Andean lines, but, like Folan, he resisted the same interpretation of the Mayan causeways. It was really a question, I felt, of realising that by the time the straight line motif had developed a more sophisticated and multi-purpose structure in the complex American Indian societies, like that of the Maya, it was moving beyond its shamanic roots. One had to look behind the superficial structure. As the great anthropologist Weston La Barre put it, 'Even the hieratic architecture and sculpture . . . of the theocratic cultures of Mexico and Peru both derive ultimately from religious ritual'.[30]

IT WAS TIME to turn my attention across the Atlantic to the Old World of Europe and Asia – Eurasia. Could the shamanic archaeology of the Americas, the New World, have any relevance there? The question really revolved around the origin of the American Indians. Most scholarly authorities accept that they originally came from central Asia between 12,000 and 20,000 years ago across a land bridge linking Siberia with Alaska. This opinion is based on certain physiological characteristics, cultural elements, and the fact that very few archaeological sites have been found in the Americas much over 10,000 years old, and the few that have tend to be controversial for one reason or another. Furthermore, no Neanderthal skeletons have been uncovered in the Americas: the Neanderthals were a species of human being that preceded modern humans in Eurasia. It therefore seemed to me that if shamanism was in the Americas, which it clearly was, then it is likely to have come over with the people from central Asia who became what scholars refer to as the 'paleo-Indians'.

My quest was about to take me from ancient ground markings of super-natural forces and the routes taken by shamans' entranced spirits in the New World to what I was to find was a geography of the dead in the Old World. It was a journey that would bring me into contact with some eerie creatures of the night . . .

PART TWO

SHADES OF SHAMANISM IN THE OLD WORLD

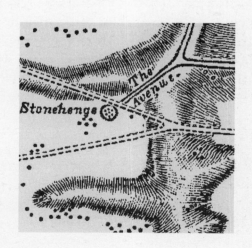

CHAPTER THREE

DEATH ROADS AND FUNERAL PATHS

T HE DAY WAS overcast, and the darkly forested mountain slopes loomed gloomily around the cable car as it slowly ascended. The funereal atmosphere was appropriate, I felt, considering that we were on our way to see a strange ancient burial site. My wife, son, and I were in the Harz Mountains, Germany's most northerly range of peaks, and our guide was Ulrich Magin, a young German folklore scholar and writer who had initially whetted my interest in the site.

The Mystery on Dragon Mountain

We were ascending the Wurmberg, 'Dragon Mountain', the second highest peak in the Harz after the Brocken. On its summit was a curiosity connected to a mystery. The curiosity had already been described to us by Magin.[1] It was a prehistoric site comprised of a circular area about 80 feet (25 m) across enclosed by stone walls with four openings, each facing one of the four compass directions. At its centre, there was a stone burial kist (a kind of stone box) set in the ground within a rectangle of stones. And then the mystery: leading from – or to – the kist feature via the eastern gap in the encircling stone wall was a dead straight road, paved with cobbles. This path, known appropriately enough as the *Steinweg*, 'stone road', extended across the summit plateau and down the side of the mountain.

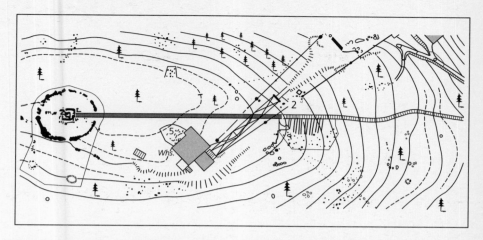

FIGURE 14: Plan showing the *Steinweg* rising up the slopes of the Wurmberg (at right) and crossing the summit plateau to the Ringwall or stone circle.

The cable car shunted to a halt at its summit destination. As soon as we disembarked, Magin led us off around the cable car wheelhouse, muttering that he would first take us to something called the *Hexentreppe* (Witch Stairs). On our way, we passed the display window of a small souvenir shop; it was scattered with numerous articles from key fobs to small dolls all depicting witches with their pointed hats and broomsticks. 'What's all this about, Ulrich?' I asked Magin, indicating the witch-festooned window. He paused in his step only briefly. 'Well, traditionally the Harz was thought to be the location of a major witches' gathering or Sabbath every year on Walpurgis Night, which is May Eve.'

As my later enquiries were to reveal, the Harz was indeed associated with witchcraft – the Harz Sabbath is even the subject of an episode in Goethe's *Faust*. One local legend tells of a tradesman who found himself out on the mountains on the fateful night. He saw flying witches like swarms of flies, but overcame his unease when the witches allowed him to join in the orgy. The Harz region was the last stronghold of paganism in Germany, and so it was no surprise that it generated such stories. It became the natural hunting ground for the brothers Grimm, the famous collectors and tellers of folktales: *Little Red Riding Hood*, forest witches who fattened children for eating, giants and goose girls – they all emerged from this general region that harboured the fading, inchoate memories of what I was soon to discover was the deep, dark secret life of Old Europe.

Simplified Timeline Guide

Palaeolithic	*c.*250000-8500 BC
Mesolithic	*c.*8500-4000 BC
Neolithic	*c.*4000-2000 BC
Bronze Age	*c.*2000-800 BC
Iron Age	*c.*800 BC-historic era
Romano-British	*c.* AD 71-410
Anglo-Saxon/Viking era	*c.* AD 400-1000
Mediaeval	*c.* AD 1000-1550
Early Modern	*c.* AD 1550-1800
Modern	*c.* AD 1800-present day

After a short distance we came to a set of broad, uneven stone stairs or ter-races on the steep shoulder where the level summit plateau gave way to the mountain slope below. I asked whether these were the *Hexentreppe*. 'They are the top of them,' Magin replied. 'The rest are lower down.' We all followed what we now discerned was the *Steinweg* down the slope from the terrace steps. Sure enough, we saw that its straight and narrow course was comprised of stone steps leading down and then merging into a stony pathway. 'They are also known as the *Heidentreppe*, the "Pagan Stairs",' Magin informed as we explored them. After a while, we climbed back up to the terrace steps. Gaining the summit plateau once more, we slowly walked the several hun-dred paces along the *Steinweg* towards the *Ringwall*. Magin mentioned that there was some suspicion that the mountaintop had, in fact, been artificially levelled in the remote past. The path's course across it was decidedly straight, with exact edges (Plate 4). The *Ringwall* itself was a circle of low stones, with uneven gaps. I asked Ulrich how old the site was. He explained that there had been apparently several features occupying this site over the course of time, so archaeologists dated the site as a whole to between the Neolithic and Iron Ages – a span of 2,000-3,000 years. However, it was the stone path that was the real mystery. Archaeologists had conducted pollen analysis, and the dates they came up with ranged between the eleventh and thirteenth centuries AD! Basically, it was a mediaeval path connecting to a prehistoric site.

Nor was that the only riddle on Dragon Mountain. There were remains of another stone path leading on to a further circular-walled site a few hundred yards away. I asked Magin what the archaeologists made of it all. He said they could find no evidence to suggest any military use of the site, which had been one initial (but rather curious) idea. In short, they simply did not have a theory to explain the purpose of the stone road on Dragon Mountain.

Connections and Missing Links

Taking my cue from the American Indian features, I was trying to find out about linear features like paths and 'lines' in Europe that provided the equivalence of the shamanic archaeology I was learning about in the Americas, but my enquiries were constantly encountering ritual roads and linear features that seemed to be associated with what archaeologists refer to as 'funerary landscapes' rather than a shamanic geography. I felt perplexed as I strolled back along the *Steinweg*.

My working hypothesis was that the still visible archaeology of shamanism in the Americas must have had its roots in the Old World, if, as most scholars agree, the American Indians – or most of them at the very least – had originated there, specifically in central Asia. If there is one thing that the hunter-gatherers who followed the big game over the ancient, temporary Beringia land bridge between Siberia and Alaska would have brought with them it would have been their religion, which in those far off days was almost inevitably shamanism. The American mythographer, the late Joseph Campbell, was very clear about this transference to the Americas of earlier Eurasian traditions:

Passing eastward across Siberia into America . . . shamanism traveled as but one element of a living compound that included . . . an elaborate complex of social regulations, ceremonials, and associated mythological ideas . . .[2]

Scholar Frank Linton identified an Arctic culture that left its mark on the Americas as well as on China and Europe.[3] La Barre similarly refers to 'a Siberian-Asiatic origin for the American Indians':

Shamanism of a specifically Eurasiatic type is distributed from ancient Scandinavia to eastern Siberia, and continues from Alaska eastward to Greenland and southward to Patagonia in the New World.[4]

In the Americas the time-depth is relatively shallow and it is therefore easier to see the remains of this archaic shamanism and all its works there, than in the Old World of Europe and Asia (Eurasia), which has been the stage for much greater human flux over much longer spans of time and so has been affected by infinitely more numerous and complex cultural layers.

Landscapes of the Dead

I was puzzled by the association of the *Steinweg* with an ancient burial site, yet I should have been more prepared for the death connection, for I had already encountered the first hint in the Americas. NASA aerial sensing technology had detected prehistoric footpaths running through mountainous rainforest in Costa Rica, Central America. Follow-up field research showed that the paths dated to between AD 500–1200, and that they were distinct from contemporary roads, cattle paths or other recent and historic or linear features.[5] In contrast to these other features, the newly-discovered pathways 'follow relatively straight lines as they travel across topographic changes rather than around them' the investigating archaeologists noted.

Clearly that curious 'shamanic hallmark' of straightness associated with ancient ceremonial roads and landscape lines in the Americas was evident, but the field investigators found that the paths were linked specifically with funerary activities. At one village, they found an ancient path running over the top of a hill to a cemetery some distance away. The villagers still used it to carry corpses for burial, to convey large quantities of laja, a volcanic stone used for building tombs and cemetery walls, and to visit the cemetery for ritual purposes. The investigators found other similar paths radiating out from the cemetery to other villages, and to sacred places like springs. They found evidence for 'long-duration ceremonies in the cemetery, perhaps directed towards the ancestors and other spirits'.[6] To this clear-cut case, I could have added clues like the 'spirit trails travelled by the dead' reported in the traditions of present-day Pueblo Indians (see Chapter One), or the ghost paths seemingly monumentalised by some of the boulder mosaic markings in Manitoba (see Chapter Two).

As I walked the *Steinweg* deep in thought, I realised that I had also already foreseen a death link with Old World linear features and traditions back in the late 1980s, when I had written a chapter called 'A Passage of Spirits – The Sanctity of the Straight' in a book I co-authored.[7] There I noted that many ancient straight paths and other straight linear features seemed associated with the idea of the passage of spirits in one form or another – in the *feng shui*

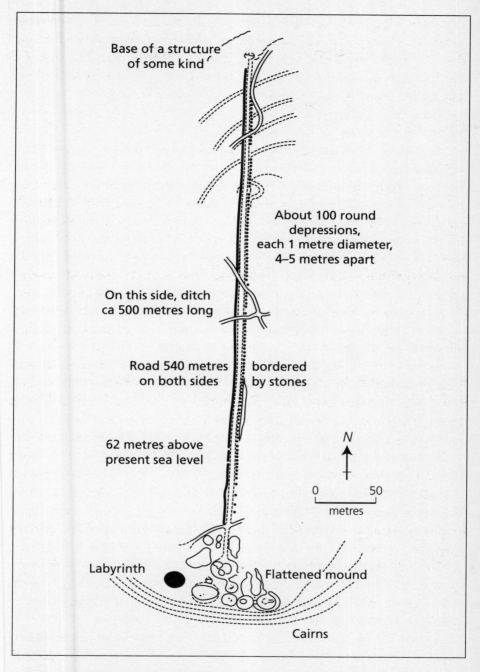

Base of a structure
of some kind

About 100 round
depressions,
each 1 metre diameter,
4–5 metres apart

On this side, ditch
ca 500 metres long

Road 540 metres
on both sides

bordered
by stones

62 metres above
present sea level

N

0   50
metres

Labyrinth

Flattened mound

Cairns

FIGURE 15: The straight ritual road at Rösaring, Sweden. (After Upplands-Bro
Kulturhistoriska Forskninginstitut)

system of Chinese land divination, for instance, in linear ceremonies in the Sudan, and in linear features associated with sacral kingship (divine kings) in Indo-European territories.

In particular, I had noted the existence of a curious Viking processional road at the archaeological complex of Rösaring in Uppland, Sweden.[8] Situated on one of the largest glacial ridges in Scandinavia, the site as a whole had been noticed by antiquarians since the 1670s. On the ridge, which once had been an island, are Bronze Age burial cairns and a large stone labyrinth (see Chapter Six). The mysterious road, which was discovered only as recently as 1981, is about a third of a mile long (540 m) and roughly four feet wide (3.5 m), and is dead straight. It is oriented almost exactly north-south and leads to a flat-topped mound in the Bronze Age cemetery at its southern end. It is not known if this was a grave or a ceremonial platform, and there is evidence that it was constructed after the road. The foundations of a small structure of unknown purpose were found at the other, northern end of the road. Radiocarbon dating of road material yielded a date in the ninth century AD – the prime Viking era. The purpose of the road remains unexplained, but phosphate levels in the roadside ditches indicating horse or ox dung suggest that a ceremonial wagon may have been drawn along it. It may have been a death road for a Viking chieftain, or a processional way for the image of a god. Whatever the case might be, I could see startling similarities between the basic characteristics of the Swedish Viking road and the later mediaeval German one I was now walking slowly along.

My book chapter and subsequent journal articles I had written on the same theme had produced a response from a handful of researchers who had similarly noted an apparent relationship between ancient linear features and funerary sites. Magin was one of these researchers, and that was why I was now scratching my head on Dragon Mountain.

Could there be a connection between death and shamanism? Was there a link I was missing? As I thought about it, I could dimly see that there might be: when the shaman went into trance, he was considered to have temporarily died by most if not all the tribal societies the ecstatic phenomenon occurred in, whether in the Old or New Worlds, and he travelled 'in spirit' into the otherworlds of the gods and ancestors – the realm of the dead. But this conceptual link was not in itself sufficient to bridge the gap between the funerary features of various times and places I was starting to find out about in Europe and an ancient stratum of shamanism. If I had been sufficiently alert, I would have realised that the stone path in the Harz mountains was indicating the connection, but all I could think of at the time was how infuriatingly obscure the feature was, hovering as it did between worlds and

times. I was not yet ready to understand that perhaps it was telling me something by its very contradictions.

Ways of the Dead

John Palmer was another of the researchers who had responded to my sugges-
tions of apparent links between ancient linear features and funerary sites in
my book chapter. He is a talented British artist who lives in the Netherlands.
I met up with him at his apartment in The Hague. With a Dutch-style
peaked cap and an intense brow he reminded me of one of the figures in Van
Gogh's painting, *The Potato Eaters* – he looked more stereotypically Dutch
than most of the native citizens! He had written to me telling me of Dutch
Doodwegen (death roads) he had found out about while conducting other
research in old, obscure Dutch documents, and as its editor I had immediately put an article by him on the subject in *The Ley Hunter*.[9] After a meal at
his apartment, I grew impatient and asked if we could visit examples of these
Doodwegen. Palmer willingly explained that although there were vestiges of
these death roads at locations all around Holland and elsewhere, the easiest
ones for us to see were on the Westerheide between Laren and Hilversum.
'And by the way,' he said, 'It's pronounced "DODEwegen".'

We drove the 50 miles (80 km) to Westerheide, parked the car and strolled
onto the heath. The death roads were immediately apparent – well-kept pathways cutting across the heathland. There were three of them, all scrupulously
straight, now partially maintained as leisure trails. They converged on an
isolated cemetery, St Jankershof, which was mediaeval, though there was
some evidence of it occupying an earlier pagan site. Although prehistoric sites
are dotted across Westerheide, two of the death roads are mediaeval, and the
third early modern (1643). They had been used for the transportation of
corpses from outlying communities to the cemetery. 'Although alternative
shorter and better roads existed in many cases, preference was consistently
given by funeral parties for following the old death roads,' Palmer remarked.
He also noted that the tradition of death roads in general in the Netherlands
goes back to at least the twelfth century, as a mention is made of them in
mediaeval Friesian law codes, though in his fieldwork he consistently found
evidence of earlier pagan features being incorporated into the courses of the
roads.

We explored lengths of all three of the pathways, then sauntered down one
of them in the opposite direction to the cemetery, as I wanted to see what

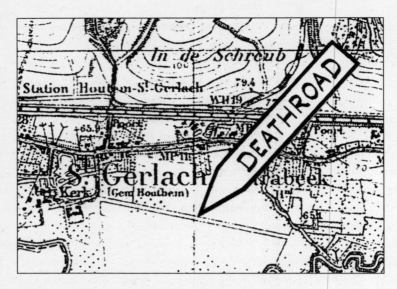

FIGURE 16: Detail of a map prepared by John Palmer showing the location of a section of a death road at Houthem-St.Gerlach, Netherlands.

happened the further back along we went towards the edge of the heath. As we proceeded, it became clear that Palmer had found out a considerable amount about the *Doodwegen*. Roads in many parts of old Holland and Flanders had specific purposes, such as mill roads, bride or marriage roads, church roads, inter-village roads, inter-town main highways – and death roads. In some regions, Palmer noted, the death roads also served as church roads and bride ways. They all had specified widths, and they were inspected annually by official surveyors. The width that had to be maintained for a death road was between six and eight feet (1.8-2.4 m). The death roads went by a variety of names other than *Doodwegen*, including *lijweg* and *lyckwey,* (corpse road).

As we walked along, Palmer nudged my elbow and pointed out an excellent example of Fly Agaric mushroom, the classic 'fairy toadstool' with a white-spotted red cap, growing alongside the death road. The Fly Agaric mushroom is hallucinogenic, and was a staple means of obtaining visionary states for some central Asian shamans, and also for certain American Indian tribes (see Chapter Two). Palmer squatted down beside the mushroom, laughing at the symbolism of it all, for he like me felt elements woven into the death road traditions harked back to distant sources in an earlier Eurasian shamanism, even though the mediaeval features were not themselves directly shamanic features. We walked on, but the clear-cut, restored death road

degenerated into a straight woodland path, then a track, before finally peter-
ing out.

In following years, Palmer went on to report his meticulous explorations
of a number of Dutch death roads,[10] and he also cast his research net further
afield, finding examples of death roads in France, Belgium, Poland and
Germany.[11] As with the Westerheide examples, they were all perfectly
straight, or had long straight sections, and I could not fail to notice the
straightness motif recurring yet again. This was intriguingly emphasised in one
of Palmer's studies concerning a death road running through the Meinweg,
an area on the German-Netherlands border strongly associated with witchcraft in former days but now a national park comprised of forest and heath.[12]
The road runs from the German village of Oberkrüchten across the border
into the Netherlands. It passes in a straight line through the Meinweg, where
it is marked on the map as a *Leichenweg* (corpse road), but after it crosses into
the Netherlands it is marked as the *Hooibaan*, travelling towards Etsberg.

When I remarked on the straightness of the Dutch death roads in subsequent articles it was dismissed as coincidental by some critics, primarily on
the grounds that the roads passed over the flat Dutch landscape. This made me
think how many of the American Indian roads could be so superficially
explained, running across deserts as many do, yet the straightness was also
found in forest and mountainous landscapes in the Americas, revealing it as a
prevailing, deliberate characteristic. Other critics claimed the death roads were
merely re-used Roman roads, or the result of a seventeenth-century Baroque
fad for creating long straight avenues. Palmer answered his critics on all these
grounds. He was able to argue convincingly that the Dutch death roads could
never have been Roman,[13] and in any case the straightness had been a noted
characteristic of the features by those who used them in mediaeval times:
Palmer uncovered a mediaeval law code document that cited an oath Dutch
mourners had to make confirming that they took corpses to burial only along
'*den rechten lyckwegh*', 'the *straight* corpse road' (my emphasis).[14]

While the straightness motif was thus confirmed as being a conscious element in the Netherlands, and ancient roads leading straight to old chapels
were discovered by Palmer in Belgium, France, and Poland, death roads in
Germany and Britain have proved to be a more complex matter.

German Death Roads

Some straight old roads associated with churches or cemeteries in Germany
were noted both by Palmer and Ulrich Magin. For example, Magin

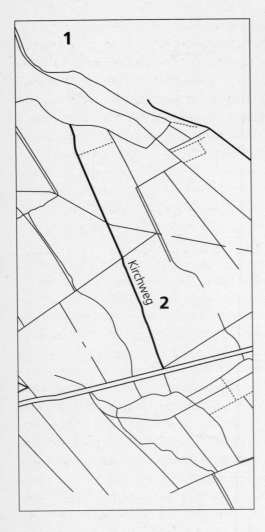

FIGURE 17: Simplified map detail showing the surviving section of the Kirchweg or church road near Mutterstadt, Germany. The Kirchweg is marked by the figure 2; figure 1 marks the former position of Hillensheim church. (After H. Eyselein, *Geschichte Des Dorfes Mutterstadt*, 1938.)

researched an early mediaeval straight path in Mutterstadt, a small town (now a suburb) founded in the sixth century AD.[15] To the north there had formerly been a hamlet, Hillensheim, which had had a church, but eventually became deserted and forgotten as all but a site. To the south there had been a *Hardtkirche* (forest church), which had been the focus of a pilgrimage path from Hillensheim. This has been remembered in folklore as a secret tunnel above which a straight path was once said to have existed. Magin found a stretch of this still surviving north of Mutterstadt. 'It is the Kirchweg, "church road", and is dead straight,' Magin stated (Figure 17). He also noted that near the former forest church there had been a pagan Celtic site. However, it became clear to Magin that many German death or corpse roads – referred to, variously, as *Totenwege, Hellwege, Notwege* and *Leichenweg* – were not straight. He consulted authoritative folklore sources and found out a number of points about them: corpse ways were special cemetery roads that 'must not be blocked or built upon', they were not necessarily the shortest route to the cemetery, a corpse way used for a person's funeral would be the same special route the deceased person would have taken to go to church during life – thus indicating that corpse roads were also church roads, and they could also be used for marriage and baptism processions. The corpse way was 'the road for persons who are taboo'.[16] It was also apparent from the documentation that German corpse ways would often take circuitous routes and detours to cross water and avoid fertile fields. As Magin put it, 'it appears straightness even had to be avoided!'.[17]

British Corpse Ways

In Britain, death roads go by various names that are generally interchangeable – church ways, church paths, coffin paths, burial roads, lyke ways (from Old English *liches*, corpse), and corpse ways, among several other appellations. Here, too, the matter of directness versus detour was confused, because there are three kinds of corpse way: one that follows a direct course,[18] another that seems to wilfully detour and wander like the proverbial English drunkard, and a third where the corpse way even appears to form a circuit embracing various churches.[19] Whether this was an intentional set of distinctions, or simply the result of the vagaries of time or different people defining corpse ways at various times and to different requirements, is not clear.

I knew about the Dutch death roads before I was fully aware of British corpse ways, which was somewhat shameful of me. My British 'awakening' occurred when I was visiting the ancient church of St Levan's in the Land's End district of Cornwall. As I wandered around the small, circular churchyard, almost certainly a pre-Christian sacred place originally, I noticed a stile in the churchyard wall. I saw that a large stone at the foot of the stile was the shape and size of a coffin. I looked beyond the stile, and sure enough, there was a straight path crossing the fields from a distant hamlet. The path was marked by a short Celtic cross perhaps 1,000 years old. A similar cross was placed on the churchyard wall by the stile. I later discovered that local historians date the coffin stone to the eleventh century, though this has been questioned by others because the coffin apparently did not come into use until the seventeenth century, corpses being carried up to that time in stiff canvas bags strapped to wooden frames known as biers.[20]

I went on to explore many parts of the country for further signs of corpse ways, and numerous other people have subsequently been undertaking similar research. This revival of interest is welcomed, because corpse ways are a heritage feature of the landscape that is rapidly disappearing. I traced several corpse paths marked on old tithe maps that in the field had effectively disappeared, with fences and other obstructions obliterating them. In some cases corpse ways have completely disappeared, and can be traced only by studying parish field-name maps because indications of the former presence of a corpse way can be revealed by names such as 'Churchway Field' and similar. Sometimes elderly people retain the memory of corpse ways in their districts – researchers found that in parts of Cornwall they had been known as 'coffin lines'.[21] In a number of cases, though, corpse ways survive and are identifiable as sections of metalled roads, named tracks, or simply as country paths that have continued to be used.

As Palmer, Magin, myself and others increasingly drew attention to death roads in articles for various specialist journals, opposition to viewing them with any significance bubbled up from some quarters. The basis of the criticism was that the death roads were simply mediaeval features providing a functional means of allowing corpses to be transported to cemeteries that had burial rights, and were nothing to do with any archaic tradition.

On the surface, this seemed to be straightforward enough. In England in the tenth century, for instance, when there was a proliferation of village churches being built within the territories of existing mother churches or minsters, burial rights became an issue. There was a demand for autonomy from outlying settlements that minster officials felt could erode their authority, so they decided to ritually bind their parishes together by instituting corpse ways that led from outlying locations to the heart of the parish, the mother church, which held the parish's rights of burial. For some parishioners, this meant corpses had to be transferred quite long distances, sometimes over difficult terrain. Most of the funerals conducted along these corpse ways were walking ones. At points along such routes there would be wayside crosses or rough-hewn, often lozenge-shaped coffin stones where bearers could rest their burden, and where prayers would often be said or hymns sung. Ancient sites, useful as landmarks and perhaps as recognised symbols of sanctity, were also sometimes incorporated into a corpse way's course.[22]

Despite these clear-cut and uncontested historical facts about the origin of mediaeval corpse ways in Britain, and by implication those of other countries, I could not help but feel it was only a surface history. There are two kinds of history. The standard, mainstream one most scholars concern themselves with that deals with rulers and social upheavals like wars, invasions, changes in religious practice, and major technological developments; the other involves the beliefs and practices of rural people that are much less documented and thus out of sight of the more public overall cultural phenomenon of a society. As the Italian scholar Carlo Ginzburg has observed, historians are poor at studying 'invisible mental structures' of this kind.[23] I suspected that the creation of corpse paths may have helped to fossilise beliefs already existing in isolated rural populations. The corpse ways must have attracted such lore to them like magnets, for they ran not only through the physical countryside, but also through the mental terrain of mediaeval countryfolk – the invisible country.

In order to address this problem properly, I had first to delve into that dark secret life of Old Europe, the nightside of history, and for that I had to look to the work of more gifted and resourced scholars than myself.

CHAPTER FOUR

THE SECRET LIFE OF OLD EUROPE

U NTIL THE MODERN era, the peasants, the core agrarian populations, stayed living on the land, no matter what ruler came or went, or which god was fashionable. Crops and livestock had to be tended no matter who was in power. For centuries and even millennia little of essence changed for such populations, and where it did it tended to incorporate previous elements – rural culture is conservative culture. Witchcraft was part of the history of this marginal rural world.

Witchcraft

With only a few exceptions, witchcraft was for a long time not a favoured topic for the attention of modern scholarship. Then, in the last few decades of the twentieth century it suddenly became very popular. The actual nature of mediaeval witchcraft was cause for argument and debate. Most modern scholars dismissed it as delusion and superstition on the part of a peasantry browbeaten by Church demonologists, and focused instead on the social dimensions of the persecution of a section of the mediaeval and early modern populations, a primarily (but by no means an exclusively) female one.

However, some scholars argued that there was an actual witch cult, even if outrageously demonised by the Church. The most notorious of these proponents was Egyptologist Margaret Murray, whose 1921 *The Witch-Cult in Western Europe*[1] caused a stir, and is now discredited by most scholars. She felt that the actions attributed to the witches, shorn of the demonologising prejudices placed on them, to have been actual events, so she had problems with factors such as night-flying and human metamorphosis into animals, two very powerful, recurring motifs in witchcraft. But one aspect of her theory, that witchcraft had deep foundations in a pre-Christian fertility cult, came to be supported in a qualified way by some later scholars, notably the celebrated Italian historian, Carlo Ginzburg. He brought a sharper perception to the problem of witchcraft than most of his contemporaries, and I came to realise that his findings held great significance for my own research dilemma.

Night Battles

The launch pad for Ginzburg's approach was provided by Church documentation dating to the late sixteenth and early seventeenth centuries concerning testimonies given in witch trials of various country individuals known as the *benandanti* who lived in Friuli in the extreme north-east of Italy, a region where German, Italian and Slav customs mix. The *benandanti* were people who were born 'with a caul', that is, covered with the amniotic sac or placenta: it was claimed that this gave them the power to enter trance states and compelled them to go on soul journeys, especially on certain nights in the year. During these nocturnal ventures, the *benandanti* would battle in spirit against malevolent male and female witches for the fertility of the fields, livestock and the vineyards. They were armed with fennel sticks, and the witches fought back with sorghum stalks. These tales astonished the inquisitors who tried to make them fit their invented image of the diabolical Sabbath – a supposed diabolical nocturnal gathering of witches out in the wilderness beyond town limits. Despite pressure on them to conform to this image, the *benandanti* held on almost 50 years before succumbing.[2]

What Ginzberg saw emerging from his investigation of the documents was evidence revealing the existence of an 'agrarian cult of ecstatic character' that pre-dated the Church's demonologising zeal. As Ginzburg pointed out, the image of the Sabbath emerged around the middle of the fourteenth century, first in the western Alpine region, but eventually spreading throughout Europe. When the witch persecutions eventually and mercifully ended, the image of the Sabbath dissolved away, for it had been a mirage created by the Church demonologists. Yet, the Friuli material provided clear evidence that a belief in soul journeys and night flying did truly exist in the region before the paranoid concept of a heretical and dangerous 'witch cult' was introduced by the Church. Whether or not the *benandanti* amounted to an actual, physical organisation (and the documentation did not contain evidence to be conclusive either way on the matter), it was clear that there existed 'a deep stratum of peasant myths lived with an extraordinary intensity' as Ginzburg observed.

Earlier works by other scholars on the Friuli region had omitted any direct study of the *benandanti*, and the term was treated as being synonymous with witches; it was only when Ginzburg managed to overcome the difficulties of access to the original archive in the Curia Arcivescovile in Udine and subject it to a searching examination that the subtler situation came to light.

The Wild Hunt

The Italian scholar detected two principle themes with regard to the *benandanti*, the night battles for fertility, and processions of the dead. Both were entered into in a state of ecstasy, that is, with the *benandante's* body lying in a cataleptic trance at home while his or her spirit seemingly went out into the silent night on its mission.

The idea of a nocturnal procession of the dead was widely disseminated across Old Europe, and was of enormous antiquity. The basic image was of a powerful mythical figure – a god, goddess or legendary personage – leading a hunt through the night skies that swooped to gather up the souls of the dying in its course across the countryside. It went by many names and there were various versions of it, according to which culture described it. In northern Europe it was known as the Wild Hunt or the Furious Host, elsewhere as the Troop of the Dead or the Troop of Souls, and the Good Company, to mention just a few of its names. Depending on when and where the belief appeared, it was variously seen as a beneficent procession, or one peopled with wild, dangerous and resentful spirits – spirits not only of the dead but also the temporarily exteriorised souls of living people, such as witches and sorcerers. In its oldest and most widespread form, the nocturnal procession of spirits was led by a goddess, variously named as Diana (the 'goddess of the pagans'), Bensozia, Oriente, Holda, Herodiana/Herodias, Perchta, among others – again depending on the era and culture in which the basic archetype emerged. The Roman version involving Diana led Ginzburg to the suspicion that it related to an older religion.

The idea of there being special people, particularly women, who could join with this procession in spirit, often astride animals, while lying in a prolonged trance at home beside their sleeping spouses, was an old one. These 'night-riders' were well known to the early mediaeval Church, and were lumped together with witches and sorcerers, though at that time the Church was considerably more tolerant than in later centuries, when factors such as famine and the Plague produced the vicious blame culture that led to the witch persecutions. Ginzburg saw in the Friuli material that it was mainly the female *benandanti* who joined in the processions of the dead, and usually the male ones who took part in the night battles against the malevolent witches. At the time, Ginzburg knew of the nocturnal procession theme, but considered the night battle concept to belong just to the Friuli region. (He was to find out that he was wrong in that regard.) The more he studied the archive in Friuli, the more impressed he became as to how the two themes of battles and processions were unified in the beliefs of the *benandanti*. He made a crucial observation that was daring in the academic circles of the time: he suggested that the activities of the *benandanti* were 'very similar to that performed by the shamans'.[3]

Creatures of the Night

It transpired that the *benandanti* were only the tip of an iceberg: Ginzburg and other scholars have subsequently gone on to show that Old Europe had many rural supernatural specialists of similar type – there were 'many more cases and aspects than research had generally assumed', leading Hungarian folklorist Eva Pocs has admitted.[4] She, too, sees the vestiges of an 'agrarian shamanism' being unintentionally revealed in the mediaeval and early modern witch trial documentation throughout Europe. There were differences and distinctions amongst these village specialists across the continent, but such variations on a theme only reinforced the existence of the theme.[5] There were witches and magicians of every stripe in which the telling element of trance ecstasy was involved. Folklore had it that like the *benandanti* they had been born with the caul, or had some other distinguishing feature at birth, and were the enemies of malevolent sorcerers, witches and supernatural forces. Confusingly, the evil witch and the good witch or ecstatic magician could in some cases be one and the same person! As Oxford scholar Diane Purkiss has commented, the term 'witch' was not a fixed descriptor, nor is it now. Indeed, it is 'highly unstable'.[6] A few examples of these varied supernatural specialists from different parts of Old Europe must suffice here.

Trance Practitioners

In the Balkans there were the *kresniki*. There were slight variants of this figure, such as the *negromanat* and *zduhak*. The *kresniki* were born with the
caul, and while entranced their spirits would emerge from their mouths in the
form of black flies. Once free, their spirits gathered at major crossroads where
they fought sorcerers who often took the shape of animals for the abundance
of the crops, dairy produce and other bounty of the land. These battles took
place at various significant pagan times of the year that had been appropriated
by Christianity, including Christmas night.

In the northern Caucasus region, there were the *burkudzauta*, who went
into caves and inhaled smoke from burning rhododendrons in order to enter
a deep sleep in which they could conduct divination or travel to the land of
the dead. Their souls travelled there on a variety of mounts – scythes,
brooms, bowls, horses, cows, doves, dogs.

In Corsica, there were specific people known as the *mazzeri* (among other
names) who went 'out in spirit' roaming the countryside while they slept.[7]
During these dream journeys they felt compelled to attack animals, and for a
fleeting moment they were able to see a human face superimposed on that of
an animal they had killed. This would be the visage of a person from the
community who was soon to die. At the end of July or the beginning of

FIGURE 18: A weather magician at work. (Olaus Magnus, Rome, 1555)

August (harvest-time – Lammas to Christians, Lughnasa to the pagan Celts) the *mazzeri* from one village would fight those from another, usually one with ethnic differences or on the other side of a mountain. The night battle was conducted in spirit, of course, and the *mazzeri* wielded stalks of asphodel. The communities of the losing sides were destined to suffer more deaths in the course of the year than those of the victors.

In Hungary, there were the *taltos*, who could be male or female, but were usually male. Such persons were marked at birth by some physical anomaly, such as being born with the caul, with teeth, or having an extra finger. The *taltos* usually fought their night battles a few times in the year – or even every seven years – in the shape of bulls, stallions, or lights or flames. They fought one another, or witches, or the souls of those from other lands that were likewise transformed into the shapes of animals or lights. The winner ensured plentiful harvests for the following several years for his or her community. Tasks the *taltos* additionally involved themselves in included uncovering hidden treasure, healing those smitten with evil spells and identifying witches. They also were not above threatening people with bewitchment when it suited their purposes.

Eva Pocs points out that the term *taltos* has been applied somewhat indiscriminately, and she has identified a wide range of what she calls 'mediator specialists' in Hungary and central and southwestern Europe generally. These include weather magicians who in spirit, in trance, fought malevolent witches who tried to blight the fertility of a community's fields by stealing rain, 'picking dew', or causing hail to damage the crops.[8] There were witches who specialised in contact with ghosts and with fairies, and there were a great many more types of 'seers who are capable of trance' throughout Europe and over long periods of time. Even back in the Iron Age there were shamanic aspects to functionaries like the Celtic druids, for example.[9] Norse and Celtic legends are replete with gods and mythic heroes who display the attributes of shamans such as shape-shifting, magical flight and journeys to the realm of the dead. These in turn were almost certainly echoes of even more archaic traditions.

Animal Magic

As the *taltos* tradition testifies, it was a characteristic of some of the ecstatic practitioners of Old Europe to change into animals rather than merely ride them. This is, of course, a profoundly shamanic image. Pocs particularly picks out the figure of the 'mora witch' amongst the rich variety of such magical individuals peopling Old Europe. These were witches whose spirits took on the form of animals when they went 'out' – creatures such as frogs, cats, horses, hares, dogs, oxen, geese, jackdaws and, frequently, bees and wasps. There was a variety of such people throughout Europe going by similar names: in Germany they were known variously as *mara, mahr, mare*; in Slavic countries terms included *mora, zmoras, morava* and *moroi*; in France, such a witch was the *cauchemar*. Pocs traces the core term back to the Indo-European root *moros*, death. Like the other trance practitioners mora witches traditionally owed their abilities to being born with a caul. In their metamorphosed form they could fly through the night (other names for them in Slavic countries was *nocnica*, 'night woman', or *ejjeljaro*, 'night-goer'), walk on or hover above water, and travel in a sieve. Dead mora witches could also return as ghosts.

The Werewolf

The mora witch was closely associated with the werewolf, but while most mora witches were women, most werewolves were men. Ginzburg's own introduction to the fact that the nightside of the Old European mind was of a vastly extended and more complex nature than he had initially supposed, was documentation on a reputed werewolf from Livonia (a formerly Russian Baltic region that is now divided into the states of Estonia and Latvia).

In 1662, a man named Thiess gave an account to inquisitors in which he claimed that he was a werewolf, metamorphosing from man to animal on three nights of the year – St Lucy's night (13 December – the winter solstice in the old Gregorian calendar, thus the longest night of the year), the night of St John (24 June), and of the Pentecost (Whitsun) – when all the werewolves of Livonia 'went to hell' to fight the devil and sorcerers. The werewolves used iron whips, while the sorcerers used broomsticks wrapped in horse tails. The battles were for the fertility of the fields; the sorcerers stole the shoots of the grain which had to be won back in order for the community to avoid famine. Thiess refused to state that he had made a pact with the devil as his interrogators wanted him to, claiming that to the contrary werewolves were the sworn enemies of malevolent sorcerers.

Ginzburg naturally recognised the same basic themes in the man's story as occurred in the accounts of the *benandanti*. The same motifs were appearing in traditions located as far apart from one another as the shores of the Baltic and the shores of the Adriatic. His detailed analysis convinced him even more of the similarities. This included the times of the year mentioned by Thiess, which roughly concur with the times the *benandanti* said they roamed abroad in spirit (and 'on Thursdays' as one *benandante* insisted).

More research revealed further examples of were-animal traditions around the continent and their links with similar motifs revealed in the *benandanti* cases. Some of these traditions were very old – for instance, the fifth-century BC Greek historian Herodotus picked up rumours about a certain race in which there were men who turned into wolves on particular nights of the year, and the first-century AD Roman scholar Pliny mentioned certain families in Greece who transformed into wolves. Throughout the continent, from Ireland, where people in a certain region were said to be prone to turning into wolves, and France, where roamed the feared *loupsgaroux*, to central and south-east Europe, the rumours of werewolves and were-animals in general were rife.

In Norse tradition, there were the Warriors of Odin – the shamanic god of death and warriors – known as the ulfar, wolves. This cult was closely related to that of the *berserkers*, the legendarily fierce warriors said to fight with bear skins over their mail, or, alternatively, bare skins (that is, without a mail shirt). They fought in a rage 'like dogs or wolves . . . as strong as bears or bulls' according to the mediaeval *Ynglinga Saga*, gnashed at their shields with their teeth, and were thought to be impervious to fire and iron. One older man who had once been a *berserker* was frequently observed to become withdrawn and drowsy as darkness fell, and at night was believed to have 'often roamed about in a changed shape (*hamrammr*)'.[10] This *ex-berserker* fellow was referred to as *Kveldulfr*, evening wolf, in his community. These ecstatic warrior cults (*gangs*) seem to have been a specialised development of the militaristic aspects evident in the accounts of the night battles of 'agrarian shamans' such as the *benandanti* and others.

A 1560 treatise by Caspar Peucer stated that Baltic werewolves changed forms from human to wolf during the 12 days of Christmas (Christmas Day to Epiphany) in order to fight witches, and this was also traditionally the period when the restless dead returned to the human world. Olaus Magnus, Bishop of Uppsala, Sweden, similarly stated that werewolves roamed abroad on Christmas night in Prussia and Lithuania. In the seventeenth century, treatises on the subject of werewolves from some German universities recorded that the metamorphosis from human to wolf was preceded by a profoundly deep sleep or trance.

The *liderc*, the werewolf-magician figure of Hungary and surrounding regions, was understood in multiple ways – a human being who transformed, an animal spirit that is the 'shadow' or 'double' of a magician, or a ghost or

demon. Werewolves in central and south-east Europe generally were thought
to have been born with the caul, or with teeth – or even double sets of teeth –
or with two hearts. Werewolves who attack humans seem to have belonged to
a specific tradition confined to eastern Hungary and Transylvania.[11] In
Romania, the *strigoi* were werewolf witches who were born with the caul, had
the power of trance, and took part in 'quasi-shamanistic soul battles'.[12] There
were also traditions of ecstatic practitioners who could transform themselves
into dragons. Dragon magicians were believed to appear as flying fiery light
phenomena (see also Chapter Nine).[13]

With regard to the were-animal phenomenon as a whole, Ginzburg
remarked that the connection between witches and werewolves was close,
often being essentially variants of one another, and that werewolves were
demonised in a similar fashion to the witches – the ferocious image of the
werewolf as the devourer of flocks and children appears to have manifested in
the mid-fifteenth century, prior to which werewolves were portrayed as either
beneficent figures or helpless victims of their weird condition.[14] He also
noted a connection with the dead, observing that the time of year favoured by
Baltic, Germanic and Slavic werewolves for their activities was the 12 Nights
of Christmas period, when traditionally the souls of the dead went roaming.
Further, in Old Europe at least as far back as the Etruscans, the wolf was symbolically associated with the realm of the dead.

The Vampire

As well as the witch magicians or agrarian shamans and werewolves, ecstatic
practitioners also included the vampire figure of Old Europe among their
number. As with the werewolf, literalistic representations of the vampire in
modern books and the cinema tend to disguise the ancient and complex
nature of the figure. In the Balkans there are the *vukodlaki*, vampires, who
behave much like the *kresniki*, assembling at crossroads to do battle and are
distinguished by being born with the caul. The Caucasus region had the
Kara-Kondjolas vampires, who fought with magicians in night battles. They
could fly, and were said to have dishevelled hair, gnash their teeth, and to
flash fiery rays out of eyes, ears, nose and mouth. When engaged in combat,
both the vampires and the sorcerers attempted to suck one another's blood.
The Ukranian vampire, on the other hand, was said to be immune from the
attack of witches. Again, like werewolves and mora witches, vampires were
human beings who transformed.

Tracing the Source

The more I poured through this extraordinary area of scholarship, the more I realised that to the people of Old Europe the dark night must have seethed with spirits, whether of the dead or of magicians or witches temporarily joining the cavalcade of departed souls or fighting battles in the sky, the fields, or at lonely crossroads. Even to have stuck one's head out of the window at night must have taken a measure of courage! It was clear that strikingly similar patterns emerge in the traditions of vampires, werewolves, weather magicians, *benandanti* and all the other ecstatic practitioners alike. There are constant links with the dead, and with ecstasy, the out-of-body trance that is the crux of shamanism. Eva Pocs remarks, for instance, that:

> . . . the most important common feature of the mora, werewolf, and supernatural witch are that all of them can send their doubles to journey in the otherworld and they also have dead, demonic variants.[15]

She finds clear parallels between the abilities of the werewolf and of shamanic magicians in communicating with the supernatural, and also emphasises the links with the dead.

Contacting the Dead

There were specific traditions of seers who made contact with the dead. This was not mediumship, in which a person is possessed by a spirit, but rather the opposite—ecstatic contact in trance, in which the practicant enters the realm of the dead. In Hungary, there was the practice known as 'St Lucy's Stool' in which the seer would sit and enter trance between St Lucy's Day and Christmas specifically to gain knowledge from the dead or to be initiated by them. This was similar to *utiseta*, 'sitting out', practised in Norse tradition, where the seer would be seated on a burial mound or in a cemetery for the same purposes. There were also 'ghost witches' in parts of Europe who would put on white sheets or veils to symbolise their ghostly associations, and who would typically practise divination by interrogating the returning ghost of a recently deceased person. There were, additionally, fairy magicians or witches, and Pocs sees fairies and the dead as being 'practically the same creatures'.[16]

Ginzburg similarly realised that the dead provided the central motif in the varied traditions of ecstatic practices. He focused in particular on the

procession of the dead, already mentioned. His investigations convinced him
that there had been an archaic 'ecstatic cult of the nocturnal female divinities'
that during the historic era had become 'habitually severed' into two – there
were furious or wild spectral armies or hunts, sometimes led by a male god
such as Wotan (Odin), and a female throng led by a goddess – Diana,
Hecate, Richella, Madonna Oriente, or some other female deity, as already
noted (even the Queen of the Elves in Scotland). The Wild Hunt tended to
appear as an *apparition* to men, but the goddess procession was joined by
mainly female ecstastics. Ginzburg traced the core procession theme back to
Celtic roots, identifying the goddess leading the cavalcade as Epona, a Celtic
deity closely associated with horses. The evidence he found convinced
Ginzburg that she was the precursor of the Roman Diana.

Ginzburg's work has strongly indicated that this core theme of the procession of the dead was elaborated, demonologised, and woven into the mediaeval image of the witches' Sabbath: the Church claimed people flew off into
the night to consort with demons and the devil, rather than the ancient and
original practice of trance ecstatics joining with the 'good company' of spirits
led by a beneficent goddess.

On the basis of a rich body of evidence, Ginzburg finally concluded that
'the night flights', the 'ecstatic journey of the living into the realm of the
dead' was a 'very ancient theme'.[17] Eva Pocs similarly traces the trance
witches, seers and magicians of Old Europe to an 'archaic strata' of belief, a
'common ancestor'. Whether Celtic, Germanic, or Slavic 'we are actually
talking about common Indo-European (and similarly Hungarian) beliefs'.[18]

Ginzburg realised that although he had traced the nocturnal procession
motif back to Iron Age Celtic times, this did not explain the presence in the
non-Celtic Mediterranean areas of the similar motifs in the beliefs of ecstatic
practitioners. He suspected the presence of a 'Eurasian substratum' beneath
even the ancient Celtic gloss. The Italian scholar knew that the core motifs of
an ecstatic journey to the realm of the dead, often accomplished by riding
some kind of magical steed, and struggles with malevolent figures and forces,
were at the heart of classic central Asian shamanism. This was the source he felt
was implicated in the rag-bag of ecstatic traditions scattered across the face of
Old Europe. But how had such motifs got there from a central Asian source?

Out of the Steppes

In his book, *Ecstasies*, Ginzburg addressed the practicalities of the question.
He identified the key agents in the matter as being the conglomeration of

nomadic and semi-nomadic peoples who lived in the Black Sea area during the Iron Age, whom the ancient Greeks called the 'Scythians'. Around 1000 BC, these nomads had started migrating out of their central Asian heartland, for whatever reasons – possibly drought – both eastwards and westwards in sporadic waves. Thus by their expansions these people, the Scythians, began to form links involving China, Mongolia, and Iran. In the eighth century BC, they pressed on further westwards from the Iranian highlands to the Caucasus and Black Sea regions – the eastern fringe of Europe. We know from ancient Greek literature that the Scythians had a shamanic religion, utilising the inhalation of cannabis fumes and shamanic paraphernalia such as ritual drums and horses fitted with stags' antlers. They also had transvestite soothsayers – and trans-sexuality (or at least cross-dressing) was a common characteristic of Eurasian shamans. Early in the sixth century BC, some Scythian groups began moving further west, establishing themselves permanently in a region that today spans parts of Romania and Bulgaria – a region that is at the extreme western limit of the immense steppe corridor that joins Asia to Europe. The Scythians co-existed with but dominated the Thracians who already lived there. A century or two later saw Celts moving through the area. Ginzburg noted that the Celtic Epona bore a distinct resemblance to the Thracian goddess, Bendis, who was probably Artemis, the 'Mistress of the Animals', of the ancient Greeks. This archaic image was likened by Ginzburg to the 'Mother of the Animals' of some shamanic Siberian tribes, in whose myths she gave birth to the shaman. In Diana, the Romanised goddess of the nocturnal processions, Ginzburg felt we could see the 'remote heir of the Eurasian divinities, protectors of the hunt and the forest'.[19]

In brief, Ginzburg saw a progression that covered thousands of miles and one or two thousand years: steppe nomads – Scythians – Thracians – Celts. The common pattern of the ecstatic journey into the realm of the dead, usually accomplished in animal form, dimly and accidentally visible throughout Europe in the witchcraft trial material, could be traced back to this melting pot. The Scythians are known to have spread to the Baltic Sea, crossing what are now the modern states of Romania, Hungary, Czechoslovakia and Poland among other places.[20]

Connections

A problem with this view, though, is that shamanic beliefs and motifs were shared not only by peoples belonging to the Indo-European language base, which covers most of Europe, but by those belonging to the northern and central Asiatic Uralic language group as well. Ginzburg remarks on a number of links between both language groups. He pictured intricate cultural exchanges taking place over the centuries within the vast territory of Eurasia that would have led not only to the exchange of words, but also ideas, beliefs, customs – and *objects*. He suggested that the decoration on items such as bowls, jewellery, vases, ritual objects and so forth has left an imprint of such exchanges. He traced the occurrence of certain decorative motifs across Eurasia, especially what could be termed the 'animal style' found on a wide range of objects. He considered that this cross-cultural style, and specific motifs within it which he identified, referred to the animal metamorphosis theme in shamanism, and also to the struggle, the 'night battles' in trance between souls transformed into spirit animals.

A classic example of an object revealing cultural exchanges of this kind is the Gunderstrup Cauldron. In 1891, peat cutters uncovered a silver vessel in a bog near the village of Gundestrup in Jutland, Denmark. The vessel is 27 inches (69 cm) across, and almost 16 inches (40 cm) deep. Its sectional sides contain hammered reliefs showing religious images and ritual scenes. It is customarily dated to the second century BC. It belongs to the pagan Celtic era, and some of its imagery does indeed depict known Celtic objects such as carnyxes (animal-shaped trumpets), as well as figures who seem to relate to those in ancient Irish and Welsh mythology. But other images show Asiatic, specifically Indian-like motifs. The part of Denmark where it was found was not culturally part of the pagan Celtic European scene, being inhabited by Germanic peoples. Moreover, neither the European Celts nor Germanic societies carried out the type of silversmith work displayed by the vessel. Fairly recent analysis of the object suggests skills and influences went into it that range as far eastwards as south-eastern Europe and the Black Sea region, so relating it directly to the Scythians.[21]

Archaeologist Tim Taylor has observed that the pan-Indo-European nature of the vessel's imagery, its craftsmanship, and the place where it was found could be explained by known historical events and archaeological evidence. He draws attention to the famous so-called 'Cernunnos' depiction on the cauldron. This shows a human figure sprouting or wearing antlers, in the company of animals, seated in a yoga-like posture holding a torc and a ram-headed snake (Figure 19). In addition, the figure appears to be levitating! Taylor comments that this imagery along with evidence from other sources suggests 'that druidism, steppe shamanism and tantric yoga may have developed as interlinked systems of ritual specialisation in the Eurasian later Iron Age'.[22]

FIGURE 19: Drawing of a simplified detail of the Gunderstrup Cauldron, showing the antlered human figure in meditation or trance posture.

Of Common Mind

Ginzburg did not make a great issue of it, but he conceded that the diffusion of cultural influence regarding ecstatic, shamanistic practices and the range of beliefs surrounding them would probably not have taken hold in the way it did unless there was what he called a 'prior sedimentation'. He accepted that there were structural factors of the human mind and brain that transcended culture and time, and societies everywhere have always had people who were prone to enter trance. This would have been as true of the populations of Atlantic Europe as it was for the incoming steppe peoples. It was just that the latter had perhaps developed it into a more sophisticated cultural feature.

The Effects of Trance

In seeking these common mental structural characteristics Ginzburg seems to have thought along the lines of archetypes, but in addition we might also add the sort of state-specific mental patterns, entoptic patterns, thought to account for certain imagery in rock art (see Chapter One). Not only is the human mind susceptible to such mental imagery in trance, but two sensations are everywhere associated with it.

The most pervasive one is a sense of spirit or out-of-body *flight*, frequently associated with the mental structure of the tunnel, often disguised as the feeling of moving along or through the visionary image of a steep valley, an alleyway, a straight road, and so forth. One Hungarian witch, for instance, described her entry into a trance state, understood by her as being a literal exteriorisation of her soul, as occurring 'with a speed like the wind's . . . rushing down the road'.[23] In some ancient cultural initiatory groups like the Siberian shamans, the Australian Clever Men, or Kalahari Bushmen trance-dancing healers, the same effect was culturally envisioned as climbing along ropes or cords. (It is this core mental structure of a line, be it road, tunnel, thread or similar, that seems to be the basis for both Old and New World linear features associated with shamanism and funerary or 'spirit' sites, however forgotten or transformed such a basis became.)

The second common sensation in trance that occurs in all cultures, ancient and modern, is a feeling on the part of the entranced person of turning into an animal or other non-human form.

Both sensations can be heightened when the trance is provoked by hallucinogenic, mind-altering drugs, and most shamanic societies used such plant-based drugs as part of their visionary toolkit.[24] These sensations can be very powerful, and should not be thought of simply as dreams. They seem totally convincing and real. 'I thought of a fox, and instantly I was transformed into that animal,' reported one nineteenth-century subject who had taken a large dose of cannabis. He could see his long ears and bushy tail, and 'by a sort of introversion felt that my complete anatomy was that of a fox'. The literature on hallucinogens is full of accounts like this, and it is easy to see why earlier peoples felt they had actually changed into animals, especially when there was a cultural belief that this literally took place.

The same point applies to the sensation of flight. One of the first Europeans to take the Amazonian mind-altering *ayahuasca*, a concoction based on the jungle vine *Banisteropsis caapi*, was the Ecuadoran geographer Manual Villavicencio in 1858. 'I can say for a fact that when I've taken *ayahuasca* I've experienced dizziness, then an aerial journey in which I recall perceiving the most gorgeous views, great cities, lofty towers, beautiful parks,' he wrote.[25] The German scholar Hans Peter Duerr remarks that *ayahuasca* (and by implication traditional plant drugs of similar chemical compositions, of which there are numerous examples around the world) 'seems to be specifically a "drug for flying"'.[26]

There are a great many accounts of spirit flight relating to traditional mind-altering plant drugs everywhere. In the mediaeval era, there were rumours of 'flying ointments' being used by witches, and a few recipes were recorded. One 'witch herb' was henbane, and the German toxicologist Gustav Schenk reported on his experiences of trance visions which followed his inhalation of the fumes from burning henbane seeds. He saw animals with 'staring, terrible eyes' and felt himself to be swept along with them in clouds of mist upwards into a 'black and smoky' sky which was filled with herds of animals. Through it all, Schenk experienced 'an intoxicating sensation of flying'.[27] It is easy to see many images common to night flying witchcraft in his account.

Some other poisonous or toxic witches' herbs had symbolic associations as well, for example, hemlock and aconite were sacred to Hecate, one of the ancient goddesses identified in folklore as leading the nocturnal procession of souls. The flying ointments as described in the mediaeval and early modern literature had similarly symbolic ingredients, like goose fat. The goose/gander was a frequently-used metaphor for night-fliers and, of older vintage, for the soaring soul in Vedic literature. It was also the sacred bird of Frau Holda – the Old Norse goddess Hela – who was another leader of the nocturnal procession and who became the English fairytale character, Old Mother Goose.

Mixed in with such ingredients would be mandrake, henbane and potentially lethal weeds such as deadly nightshade (belladonna), known in Old Danish as *dvalebor*, 'trance berry', and thorn apple. Such plants contain tropane alkaloids, notably hyoscyamine which has been described as 'a powerful hallucinogen which gives the sensation of flying through the air'.[28] In a dangerous experiment, the German folklorist Will-Erich Peuckert made up just such an ointment from a seventeenth-century formula and administered it to himself. He fell into a long, trance-like sleep. 'Faces danced before my eyes which were at first terrible,' he recalled. 'Then I suddenly had the sensation of flying for miles through the air.'

Although there is documentation referring to ointments being used in night flying and human transformation into animal forms going back to at least the second century AD, today's scholars are divided as to the extent of the usage of such concoctions during the late mediaeval Church's witch persecutions. It is a fact that they are referred to infrequently in the witchcraft trial literature. Duerr reasons that this is because the Church wanted to downplay the hallucinogenic nature of the ointments, otherwise the 'Devil would then have been left with only a very modest significance, or none at all'.[29] On the other hand, Eva Pocs, for example, suggests that flying ointment was used in the records as 'a metaphor for creating trance, in the context of flying'.[30] It could be that the ecstatic practitioners of Old Europe were people especially prone to falling into spontaneous trances – it is known that shamans in many cultures are personalities with such a predilection for dissociation. The description of the ex-*berserker* given earlier hints that this might be the case.

As a part of my research into this nightside of European history, I conducted a series of experiments in which I took a variety of concoctions based on mind-altering herbs and spices that would have been available to people for centuries or longer in, variously, both the Old and New Worlds. I wanted to know what these experiences were like on the inside, so to speak. Most of the time, this experimentation involved drinking potions that both smelled and tasted (I imagine) like farmyard swill, to precious little effect. However, on a few occasions, when the dosage of the herb or spice was appropriate, and my physiological state was suitable, I did enter into powerful visionary states. Although I never underwent the sensation of transforming into an animal, I did experience soul flight. I want to emphasise that on occasions this felt effectively like actually flying through space, not some mild dizzy sensation. I felt the air passing over my skin as I arched and somersaulted high in visionary blue skies, I saw detailed landscapes laid out below me. As I flew, perspective changed in an authentic way. When I altered direction in my flight I could seemingly feel the muscles in my body flex and relax appropriately.

I live in a culture that knows something of the workings of the human brain and mind and accepts the idea of altered mind states, but it was easy to understand how people in a different cultural flux, who believed in the literal reality of night flying, could readily accept that their souls really had been out and about with the processions of the wandering dead, or fighting evil forces. I was in no doubt that trance, whether drug induced or natural and spontaneous, was involved with the basic imagery that emerged in the sources explored in this branch of scholarship. Having established this, I ceased my experimentation, for it is not to be recommended. It is not only unpleasant, it can be dangerous: one of my most powerful results was later diagnosed as a near-death experience!

Although the structure of the visions in trance and the bodily sensations accompanying them are common to the human brain and mind in all places and times, the *content* of the visions is to a large extent culturally programmed, because the human mind in a trance condition is highly suggestible. So did the night flyers actually fly? No. Did they assemble in wild places? No. Did they believe such experiences to be literally true? In most cases, almost certainly yes. Are the spirits and ghosts they came in contact with also hallucinations experienced in mind-altered states? As I was later to learn, this is a much more complex matter, and a simple 'yes' or 'no' is, well, too simplistic.

Routes with Deep Roots

This mass of mediaeval and early modern European traditions traceable to an archaic Eurasian shamanism gave me a context for my quest for a shamanic archaeology in Old Europe. It also enabled me to understand why it was not as 'clean' as my findings in the Americas and why it kept resulting in features to do with death. The links between shamanism, ecstatic forms of witchcraft, and the dead (and therefore spirits) were now exposed, even if they were intermeshed. The various kinds of death roads I had been looking at were connected with these traditions and I felt confident that we had to look beyond the bald fact that they were simply ways to take people to burial during a certain period of history. As Californian historian Nancy Caciola has remarked, 'spirits seeking bodies haunted the late mediaeval landscape'.[31]

Corpse Ways Revisited

My guess was that the death roads, the corpse ways, designated by the Church (if it was the Church that determined their actual routes) would inevitably have reflected this haunted land context in the rituals and beliefs that became connected with them. These would disclose beliefs already deeply embedded in the folk mind in much the same way that Ginzburg and others showed that the literature deriving from the witchcraft persecutions accidentally exposed older, lurking folk beliefs.

In the later mediaeval and early modern periods there was a schism between the Church and the rural populations of Europe with regard to supernatural ideas. It was older motifs to do with the 'unruly dead' and the old gods disguised as Christian saints that held the populace in thrall, not theological constructs.[32] But Caciola also points out: 'Even as these two systems of thought competed with one another . . . they overlapped.'

The most crucial aspect of this schism was that the Church taught that the spirit left the body at death and went immediately to another, non-physical plane, while rural communities believed that the dead could return and haunt the physical landscape. The Church was remorselessly abstracting the other-world – heaven and hell were in places other than the physical Earth. Somewhere elsewhere. God was in his heaven, and that was off the Earth. The concept of purgatory, which was heavily embellished by theologians during this era, was also a non-physical location. But such abstractions were slow to be accepted by the hearts and minds of ordinary countryfolk, for, in common with most non-literate or semi-literate ancient societies, they saw the dead as being able to continue inhabiting the land along with the living. To them the physical geography was also a supernatural one, shared and inter-mingled with spirits, just as it was for American Indians and probably every other ancient society on earth. The Church taught an abstract cosmology while country populations stubbornly inhabited a literal one. 'In all tales we find the survival of the mediaeval connection between ghosts and locality,' historian Bruce Gordon has observed. 'Ghosts remain attached to particular places . . . '[33] Countryfolk worried about such things as 'certain apparitions, which, passing through . . . fields were troublesome at night', or 'ghostes and spirites walking by nyght'.

The corpse ways thus passed through a physical landscape for pragmatic purposes, and yet simultaneously traversed a land of the mind that was inhabited by spirits and ghosts. Even a brief glance at just a few clues is sufficient to reveal this ambiguous status of the death roads.

In the Netherlands, the death roads, *Doodwegen*, were also generally referred to as *Spokenwegen*, ghost or spook roads, while a death road in Friesland is marked on the map as *Spookhoekster* (ghost corner). Dutch priest, Ad Welters, has written that it was widely believed that ghostly happenings occurred along the death roads and that it was not safe to take such a road at night.[34] People preferred to take the corpse to burial along the death roads because to take any other route would risk the ghost of the deceased person returning to the community. This suggests that the people who used the death roads felt they were in effect managing spirits as well as burying corpses. This is endorsed by a tradition belonging to funeral processions conducted on a death road at Aalst in Belgium where mourners used to intone: 'Spirit, proceed ahead, I'll follow you.' This suggests that the spirit connection was alive when the roads were being used, and is not some later-developed hindsight tradition or folk memory.

German folklore sources state that the *Leichenweg*, the corpse roads, took on 'magical characteristics of the dead' and that they were haunted.[35] German corpse ways could not be blocked, as we noted earlier. This taboo on the blocking of death roads is reminiscent of the custom of not blocking fairy paths in Ireland (see Chapter Six), or of avoiding placing a building facing a straight landscape line such as a road, avenue of trees, a fence or similar feature in ancient Chinese geomancy, *feng shui*. This was because spirits were thought to travel along straight lines. *Feng shui* originated in Eurasian shamanism, and it is tempting to see these other similar notions widely separated by geography as stemming from the same archaic source.

In Britain and Ireland corpse ways were also sometimes reputed to be haunted. Funeral ritual itself on these death roads similarly spoke of them being perceived as spirit ways. It was traditional custom, for instance, to carry a corpse feet first along a corpse way so as to encourage the dead person's soul to not return along it and haunt the living. 'The intention appears to have been to reinforce the funeral as a one-way journey to disposal, deliberately designed to remain unidirectional,' folklorist Ruth Richardson has written.[36] Many corpse ways included bridges, fords, cross-roads and similar features along their courses, sometimes seemingly deliberately singling out such spots. When a funeral went over a bridge the mourners would start singing a dirge, and there was a myth that if a funeral went over a bridge twice it would collapse. Such spots are what anthropologists refer to as 'liminal' places – betwixt and between, transitional locations. Boundaries and thresholds. Such liminal places as well as detours may have acted as 'spirit traps' to prevent the soul of the deceased wandering back out of the cemetery.

This highlights an interesting point. If there is an underlying cross-cultural motif associating straightness or at least fairly direct linearity with funerary features and the passage of spirits, as there seems to be, a corollary would be that deliberate non-straightness would be a way of preventing the ghost of a dead person returning back along the corpse way to haunt the living. According to one interesting British custom it was thought necessary for the funeral procession 'to return from the graveside by a different way to that by which the corpse was carried, in order to render it more difficult for the departed shade to return'.[37] It must be assumed that in such cases the corpse way had been fairly straight and direct, without any built-in spirit traps for protection against haunting, otherwise this precaution would surely have been unnecessary.

Prophets of the Corpse Ways

I came to suspect that there was a link with death roads in the strange practice known in Britain as the 'Church Porch Watch'. This involved a village seer holding a vigil between 11 p.m. and 1 a.m. at the church door or lych gate, or

at some place in the graveyard, in order to look for the spectres of those who
would die in the course of the following year.[38] Typically, this took place on
St Mark's Eve (24 April), which was the preferred time, New Year's Eve,
Midsummer Eve, Halloween or Christmas Eve. The wraiths of the doomed
living members of the community would usually appear to the eye of the seer
as a procession coming in from beyond the churchyard and passing through
the church door, and then returning back out into the dark night. (What is
interesting here, of course, is that this reveals the belief that the spirits of
living people while asleep could also wander the land.) The seers were widely
thought of as being ecstatic witches, or those with 'second sight', or sorcerers,
so falling within the spectrum of the ecstatic practitioners about whom I had
been learning.

My guess was that the concept of the spectral processions coming into the
churchyard would have been related to the corpse ways or church paths leading there. This is supported by the fact that some seers witnessed spectral
funerals rather than the wraiths of living people, and is further hinted at in a
record relating to an old woman at Fryup, Yorkshire, who was well known
locally for keeping the 'Mark's e'en watch'. She foretold her own death by
this means of divination. 'When I dee, for dee I s'all, mind ye carry me to my
grave by t'church-road . . . if ye de'ant, I'll come again,' she warned her neighbours.[39]

The Church Porch Watch custom in Britain may have been a less-
structured variant of a Dutch tradition concerning a class of diviners called
voorlopers or *veurkieken* (precursors), who were specifically associated with the
death roads.[40] They were seers able to tell who was going to die soon in the
community because they had the ability to see spectral funeral processions
pass along the death road they visited or lived alongside of.

Both the Dutch precursors and the British church seers would seem to fall
into the same general class of practitioner as those already discussed who perceived the dead by means of trance on St Lucy's Stool in Hungary, or by 'sitting out' in cemeteries or on burial mounds as in Norse tradition. Probably
another element of this same class of seership is that described in Icelandic
folklore (a branch of Norse lore). It was practised at crossroads 'where four
roads run, each in a straight unbroken line, to four churches', or from where
four churches were visible. The seer would go to such crossroads on New
Year's Eve, or St John's Day and cover himself with the hide of a bull or a wal-
rus, and fix his attention on the shiny blade of an axe while laying as still as a
corpse throughout the night. He would recite various spells to summon the
spirits of the dead from the church cemeteries and they would glide up the
roads to the crossroads where the seer could divine information from them.[41]

Shakespeare had Puck say it all in his penultimate speech in *A Midsummer Night's Dream*:

Now it is the time of night,
That the graves, all gaping wide,
Every one lets forth his sprite,
In the church-way paths to glide.

Taking all these traditions and clues together, I could no longer doubt that there was a complex of similar practices with common roots which are ultimately traceable back to an archaic Eurasian shamanism, if Ginzburg and others are correct about the distant origins of the sitting out and St Lucy's Stool traditions. And the death roads are implicated in this same chain of vestigial lore. While not being themselves shamanic archaeological features, they had been freighted with the spirit lore that abounded in the countryside, which was a reflex of the existence of the various species of trance ecstatics, who in turn were the distant heirs of an archaic Eurasian shamanism. It was like peeling back the layers of an onion.

Prototypes of the Corpse Ways

I next asked myself if the actual basic form of the roads – linear features associated with funerary sites – could be traced back beyond Christianity? The pagan Viking road at Rösaring fitted that bill without a doubt, and the Harz *Steinweg* was also curiously connected with a prehistoric site, in an area redolent with legends of witchcraft and paganism; it was a corpse way without a church cemetery. There are other, similar, tantalising examples as well. Palmer, for instance, has commented upon the Bronze Age and Iron Age burial complex at the Galgenberg, a large prehistoric mound in the province of Drenthe, Netherlands. The complex lies on a prehistoric trackway 'which is aligned straight upon the Galgenberg'.[42] Similarly, Ulrich Magin has discussed an intriguing Iron Age Celtic site in Hesse, Germany. The complex includes an extensive cemetery area and a large mound containing a rich burial. Parallel ditches were unearthed which marked the borders of a processional road about 35-feet wide (10 m) leading on a dead straight course to the mound.[43] There are numerous other such examples dating back variously through the early historical era, the Iron Age, and the late Bronze Age, but the motif of what I came to think of in my more stodgy moments as the 'mortuary linear motif' goes back even further into prehistory than that.

Probably the two key prehistoric archaeological linear features are cursuses and stone rows. I have written at length about cursuses elsewhere,[44] and to a slightly lesser extent about stone rows, so I will do no more than summarise here. Cursuses are parallel earthen embankments (or lines of pits or post holes) a few hundred feet apart that run anything from several hundred yards/metres to a mile (1.6 km) or more in length. They date to Neolithic times, and what their purposes were remain unknown. They typically align to long barrows (elongated Neolithic mounds sometimes though not always containing burials) or else are closely associated with them. Cursuses are usually fairly straight, sometimes precisely so, or straight in sections, and though there are some examples in which sinuous segments occur it is the regularity of the features that is the key characteristic of the monument type. Cursuses have square or rounded ends, where these survive. Most of these vast monuments have been discovered by means of aerial photography because they are now primarily visible only as crop markings from above; on the ground most are ploughed out, and visible earthworks survive on only a few. Archaeological investigation has revealed some evidence of post-holes, cremations, and inner mounds, but for the main part cursuses appear to have been left empty.

The first cursus to be noticed by antiquarians was the monument just north of Stonehenge, in the eighteenth century (Figure 20). This runs for two miles linking an actual long barrow with a fake one built at the same time as the cursus. About a hundred more cursuses have now been found in many parts of Britain. Some cursus-like features have also been discovered in France, Germany and Ireland, where a particularly interesting set of new finds in the Boyne Valley complex containing the famous Newgrange chambered tomb was announced late in 2000.[45] Using electronic geophysical surveying methods, not only was a cursus discovered amidst the great complex, but also a ritual road. 'The geophysical survey has identified a pathway, which I would call an avenue of the dead, 10 m wide and 80 m long which runs, not to the surviving monument, but to the ruins of a tomb which was once east of Newgrange,' archaeologist Victor Buckley reported. Pits had been found outside the edges of the avenue which may contain cremated remains. This 'avenue of the dead' is reminiscent of one that had been found nine years earlier at Godmanchester near Cambridge in England. There, a ceremonial avenue 330 feet (90 m) wide and almost two miles (3 km) long, and therefore remarkably cursus-like, aligned to what had been a Neolithic timber temple. 'There are a number of graves exactly midway between the sides of the avenue,' archaeological journalist David Keys wrote, 'and similar avenues in other parts of Britain are thought to have been used for funeral rituals.'[46]

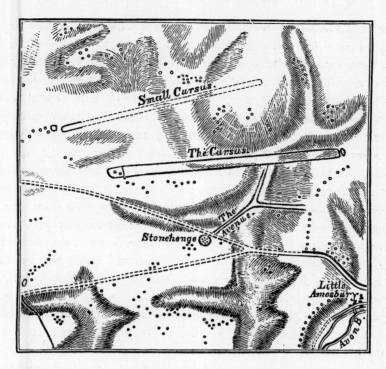

FIGURE 20: A nineteenth-century plan of the Stonehenge Cursus. Note that a smaller cursus is also shown, though little of this now survives. (J. Fergusson, *Rude Stone Monuments*, 1871)

These archaeological remains suggest that the prototype of the corpse ways existed before the Scythians reached western Europe, and long before Church authorities devised burial routes for their parishes. But while these cursus-like features clearly demonstrate the mortuary linear motif, cursus monuments themselves are not roads or avenues, in that they have closed-off ends. They are essentially very long, narrow enclosures in funerary land-scapes. It is probably not without significance that they remain unexplained in the archaeological record – I believe that will continue to be the case until their interpretation is approached from a 'spirit' angle.

Although found in numerous places around the world, stone rows are known of mainly in Britain, Ireland and Brittany. Those on Dartmoor, England, and around Carnac in Brittany are probably the most famous. The monument type is 'an almost unstudied aspect of European prehistory' observes prehistorian Aubrey Burl.[47] Stone rows were built over a 2,000-year period between the late Neolithic and the late Bronze Age. They come in many types, from alignments of a few stones to dozens of them, from a few paces to hundreds of yards/metres in length, involving stones ranging from mere lumps embedded into the ground to tall standing stones, and were laid out in configurations forming single lines of stones to multiple rows, fan-like arrangements, and full-blown avenues. The purposes of the rows, like those of the cursuses, is unknown, but they almost invariably relate to burial sites. A double row on Watern Down, Dartmoor, was known as the 'burying stones'.

Another characteristic feature of these rows is that larger stones than make up the rows themselves are placed at their ends. These are generally referred to as blocking stones, but what are they blocking? I have long suggested that if these rows were seen as marking spirit ways related to the burial sites, the idea of blocking stones as devices to stop the spirits 'escaping' into the open landscape makes sense. Such ideas are fairly basic, and were central to spirit-management systems like that of Chinese *feng shui* and are implied in many other ancient traditions around the world. Furthermore, it was to come to my attention that the concept of the spirits of revered deceased persons like shamans being allowed to roam along specific tracks to act as spectral guardians of certain places can be found in still living shamanic traditions of Asia (see Chapter Six). That the vision of spirits moving around in the land-scape was present in this period of prehistory in Europe is evidenced in the carved stone footprints issuing from Bronze Age cemeteries in Sweden (see Chapter One).

In addition to cursuses, major ceremonial roads or avenues, and stone rows, there is other archaeological evidence of prehistoric associations between linearity and death, whether expressed as simple alignments or as direct roads or 'ways'. Possible evidence for a death association has been found on one of the oldest roads in the world, buried and preserved in the peat bogs of the Somerset Levels near Glastonbury, and known as the Sweet Track. Timber planks were laid end-to-end forming a raised walkway that ran northwards for over a mile (2 km) from high ground to an island within the bogland in 'a remarkably straight line'.[48] The feature has been dated to 3806 BC by tree-ring dating, placing it in the early Neolithic era. Various arte-facts have been uncovered along its length, including a ceremonial jadeite axe, but of particular interest were some yew pins each of which had been whittled and polished to a point at one end. The only comparable objects found at British Neolithic sites were in burials, where it appears they had been fasteners to bags containing cremated remains. In the Sweet Track examples, the peat bog would have eaten away all trace of the leather bags or the burnt bone they had once contained. Investigating archaeologists Bryony and John Coles have speculated that the trackway may have had a relation-ship with funerary and settlement activities on the hills.[49]

Linear earthworks, ceremonial trackways, ancient alignments, all in funerary contexts – these examples of the 'mortuary linear motif' barely scratch the surface of what is in the archaeological record if one sifts it widely and purposefully enough. The motif is detectable from the Stone Age through to the late mediaeval period of the historic era. Although in certain parts of Europe a *prima facie* case could be made for a continued material cultural linkage of the theme or motif through the long periods of time involved, especially from the Iron Age to the mediaeval period, I felt it was not so much a question of a physical cultural linkage as recurring physical versions of a theme that was running like a computer programme in the background, that is, in the ancient folk mind of Old Europe. To keep the analogy, the archaeological features were simply the shifting models of hardware, but it was the software of folklore and belief that provided the true continuity.

That 'software' took the form of a web of ideas and beliefs concerning how spirits could move beyond the body and the grave to wander the land and haunt the living. The kernel of that motif went back to the experiences of ecstasy in the archaic Eurasian practice of shamanism, experiences of soul flight that involved universal and timeless characteristics of the human mind in trance. Physical, archaeological expressions of it manifested here and there in different cultural contexts, but the underlying motif is always recognisable. In Old Europe the long-forgotten shamanic genesis had transmuted into beliefs about the dead and spirits of all kinds on the one hand, and beliefs in night flying witches, werewolves, vampires and the rest on the other, all of it underpinned and constantly revived by the living practice of village ecstatic practitioners of various kinds.

WHAT HAD STARTED out for me as a search for traces of a shamanic archaeology in both the New and Old Worlds had brought me to the matter of spirits and, ultimately, haunting. The concept of spirits wandering the land were, I realised, shades of the shaman, the legacy of beliefs and experiences lodged far back in time. As my enquiries had progressed into the physical remnants of that legacy, I began to get glimpses of an invisible landscape that I was to learn closely complemented the archaeological features.

Now it was time for a ramble along some strange and invisible routes taken by spirits, fairies, gods, mythic heroes, witches and shamans through the landscape. It was time to map the invisible country . . .

PART THREE

THE INVISIBLE
COUNTRY

CHAPTER FIVE

LAST VOYAGE TO AVALON

I T WAS TIME for me to go to Camelot. I had never quite made it there
before, partly because there were doubts as to where it was, which always
presents a problem when visiting anywhere, and partly because it had
never seemed to me to be all that pressing a journey to make. But now,
because of a recent discovery, it had taken on greater significance for me and
fitted in with my newfound desire to explore the invisible – the country criss-
crossed with spectral or mythical routes and populated by spirits; the country
referred to less whimsically by certain anthropologists as a 'cognised landscape'. That country was the haunted land that lay behind the archaeological
features I had been seeking in Europe, the territory belonging to the history
of the night.

I travelled down to Somerset, the summer land. The first stop on my
journey to Camelot was the place where the Wild Hunt came to ground –
Glastonbury.

Glastonbury Tor

It never failed to take my breath away: the sweeping view across to
Glastonbury Tor, dramatically rearing its conical head some 500 feet (150 m)
above the surrounding plain. At the first point in the road that afforded
me a glimpse of the distant, mystic hill I felt the same thrill I had always

experienced on many previous visits. The hill is strange, being visible from afar, yet disappearing from view when in the town of Glastonbury which is at its foot. From some angles it looks like a narrow cone, from others like a whaleback ridge. The vagaries of the scene have always disoriented me; at a given moment's notice I never really know where the compass points are when I am on or around the Tor. 'The irrational scene loosens the grip of the ordinary and gives scope to the fantastic,' the Arthurian scholar, Geoffrey Ashe, has observed. 'Just by a matter of an inch, it jars open the magic casements.'[1] Even as recently as a couple of thousand years ago the Tor and the land immediately at its foot had been one of several islands in a shallow sea of lagoons, swamps and marshes – the remnants of a Roman wharf survive in a nearby village. Only later in the historic era did drainage allow the land to be reclaimed, and even now it is prone to flooding.

Isle of the Dead

The magical allure of Glastonbury and the Tor reaches back deeply into the nightside of history. Was it the symbolic physical location of the fabled though mysterious otherworld City or Isle of Glass of the pagan Welsh Celts? The name it had prior to the Anglo-Saxon 'Glastonbury' was Ynys-witrin which, according to some scholars, means 'Isle of Glass'. Perhaps the later Glastonbury name was a memory of that earlier meaning, or maybe it meant something more prosaic. There has been debate, but no one seems to know for sure. It is more productive, though no less tortuous, to explore the other name for the place – Avalon. This was the Iron Age Celts' Isle of the Dead, the otherworld realm. Many locations have been offered for the symbolic physical location of such a place, from out in the Atlantic to islands off Wales. The actual name Avalon, though, translates as 'apple orchard' in the opinion of most authorities, so how come a connection with the dead? A suggested reason is because in pagan Irish mythology one version of the otherworld was pictured as being in the form of an island, Emhain Abhlach (Emhain of the Apple Trees).[2] Also, apples have been associated with immortality from the remotest times in Europe. Another strand of opinion sees the origin of the name Avalon in that of a Celtic god of the otherworld, Avalloc. Whatever the source of the name and it associations, Avalon was Tir-na-Nog, the Celtic equivalent of the ancient Greeks' Fortunate Isles, a place of sunshine and peace and perpetual youth. They were islands because evil spirits cannot cross water and spoil the blessedness of the otherworld realm.

The association of Avalon with Glastonbury was first mooted in literature at the end of the twelfth century and drawn into the Arthurian romances. Just how it came about remains something of an academic issue, but scholars agree that the mediaeval romances contain some motifs that appear in the Iron Age Celtic myths and tales, motifs such as the idea of a magical cauldron (a proto-grail) snatched from the underworld of Annwn, as survives in the Welsh poem, *Song of Taliesin*, of ancient oral origin but written down in the tenth-century AD. So the mediaeval romances of England and France do incorporate, if at several removes, elements of early British material, but this deep core of pagan British tradition is covered by many layers of mediaeval fashion and fancy coloured by a Christianising bias.

Geoffrey Ashe draws attention to one legend about the Tor that he notes embodies a true folk belief not derived from such literary origins. It is in an account sourced from ancient times of the life of St Collen. The holy hermit lived at the foot of the Tor, the story goes, and one day he was requested to climb up to the top of the hill to meet with Gwyn, son of Nudd (the water god, Nodens), and King of the Fairies.[3] Collen at first resisted, but in the end went to the fateful rendezvous. At the summit he found a beautiful castle in which a glittering company was enjoying a magnificent feast. Gwyn was seated on a golden chair and invited Collen to join in, but the wily old hermit knew better than to eat the literally enchanting fairy food, and instead splashed around holy water from a bottle he had secreted in his garments. The magical scene instantly vanished, and there was only the wind left on the hilltop to keep St Collen company. Not only was Gwyn a fairy monarch, he was also the Lord of the Dead, of the Underworld, Annwn. Moreover, Welsh tradition identifies him as the leader of the Wild Hunt. The ultimate destination of this spectral procession of freshly-abducted souls was always the leader's abode. 'Thus Gwyn's presence goes far to establish a dim but venerable belief in the summoning of the dead to the Tor for passage to Annwn,' Ashe concludes.[4]

Carlo Ginzburg also points to a widespread tradition in Old Europe identifying Arthur as the King of the Dead, and remarks on the twelfth-century floor mosaic in Otranto Cathedral, Italy, showing 'Rex Artú' mounted on a ram leading a wandering band of animals, and later mediaeval references to Arthur leading the Wild Hunt.[5] The theme of the journey to the land of the dead, which I now knew was essentially shamanic, occurs several times in the Arthurian romances, as do mysterious castles, archetypal symbols of the otherworld. Ginzburg also comments on the close similarities between the fairies mentioned in Scottish witch confessions of the sixteenth and seventeenth centuries and the fairies who populate the Arthurian romances.

I could see that a confluence of deeply archaic themes swirled around the Tor like the silvery blue mists of the Somerset Levels that often veil its base, making it appear to float on a diaphanous, otherworldly sea. They all drifted around the same conclusion: that Glastonbury Tor had been an Isle of the Dead. This is the image presented in the later mediaeval versions of the Arthurian myth, in which we last see the mortally wounded Arthur being taken by a fairy barque or barge across the water to Avalon, there to be healed and to stay forever. But this was just mediaeval fancy, wasn't it? In fact, the recent discovery that had prompted my journey not only indicated that the vision of the Tor as the Isle of the Dead might go back much further than even the Iron Age, but also that the journey of the soul to it was envisioned as being accomplished by a ritual boat. I pressed on south and west from Glastonbury through country lanes to Cadbury Castle, the Camelot I had not previously visited.

Camelot

The distinctively isolated hill of Cadbury Castle raises its broad flat summit above its wooded flanks to the same height as Glastonbury Tor. In the Iron Age it was turned into a mighty hillfort with four tiers of bank-and-ditch defences enclosing a summit area of about 18 acres. Only parts of these earthworks are now readily visible. Cadbury Castle has had a documented folklore association with King Arthur for almost five centuries, but there may have been oral traditions for much longer than that. The hill vies with places like Tintagel in Cornwall, Winchester, and sites in Wales as being the true location of King Arthur's Camelot. In addition to the fact that it has the River Cam running beneath it and nearby 'Camel' place-names that are very ancient, archaeological investigation has tended to confirm Cadbury's right to stake its claim.

It is now clear from excavations that the hill was used in one way or another for several thousands of years, with only a few breaks, from the Neolithic era through to the late Saxon period. The impressive defensive earthworks were built and maintained for a long period by British Celts in the Iron Age and the place was intensively occupied. It was probably also a religious centre. In the first century AD, the hill was cleared by the Romans – archaeologists have found jumbled skeletons along with metal spear points, showing that many of the occupants lost their lives in the struggle. In the few centuries following that, little happened on the hill that has left much of an archaeological record, but then activity recommenced with a

vengeance in the fifth and sixth centuries AD – the Arthurian period. At this
time, uniquely among all Iron Age hillforts in Britain, fresh and grandiose
defence earthworks were built onto the old Iron Age banks, and these were
topped with drystone walling 20 feet (6 m) thick with a wooden superstruc-
ture punctuated by watchtowers. In a central position on the high part of
the hill the foundations of what had been a large, well-crafted timber hall
was found – 'Arthur's Palace'. Fragments of imported Mediterranean pottery were also found. This would never have been the romantic Camelot of
mediaeval fancy, but it had nevertheless been an important and impressive
citadel, and many scholars look kindly on the idea that it could well have
been used by the historical Arthur, who appears to have been a great general
if not a king.

Journeys of the Dead

Like Glastonbury Tor, Cadbury Castle is a topographical feature in the invisible country as well as in the visible one. Arthur is said to sleep within the hill
– it was one of the 'hollow hills' of ancient lore. On its northeastern corner
there is King Arthur's Well, and the hill is haunted by Arthur. On
Midsummer Eve, or Midsummer night, or even on Christmas Eve, depending on which version of the legend one opts for, the ghostly hoofbeats of
Arthur and his knights can be heard galloping over the summit and out
through the ancient southwest gateway. On the land below the southwest
entrance to the earthworks are traces of an ancient trackway, whose course is
said to run between the local villages of South and North Cadbury towards
Glastonbury, 12 miles distant. Retained as a bridleway (horse track) until the
late nineteenth century, it was called Arthur's Lane or Hunting Causeway. It
is said that the sound of riders and hounds can be heard passing along it on
winter nights, and a witness in the early decades of the twentieth century
claimed to have actually seen the ghostly horsemen with small flames dancing
around the tips of their upraised lances.

   Did that spectral company ride, then, from Cadbury Castle to
Glastonbury Tor? Does this local legend of the Wild Hunt embody a deep
memory of the journey of the dead to Avalon? The recent discovery that
had drawn me to this place suggests that it does. New archaeological excavations on a spur on the western side of Cadbury Castle have revealed a
host of finds dating over long periods of time, including a remarkable
Bronze Age shield. But the discovery that interested me the most was the
grave of an early Bronze Age man. His skeleton lay in a coffin over eight

feet (2.5 m) in length made from long, narrow slats bound at each end so as to resemble a 'blunt-ended boat'.[6] It was aligned directly on Glastonbury Tor.

Conventional wisdom has it that the Arthurian myth is comprised of archetypal themes, a few drawn from pagan Celtic sources, fashioned in the mediaeval period and then associated with the dim folk memory of a historical figure of the Dark Ages. But the implications of this very early boat burial at Cadbury, at Camelot, are that at least one theme more than 2,000 years older than any historic Arthur, and earlier than the Iron Age Celtic sources, can be found preserved in the mediaeval story of King Arthur. From at least the Bronze Age, and who knows how long before that, souls of the departed here in Somerset were making their last voyages to Avalon, the Isle of the Dead, in a similar way that the Bronze Age Scandinavians and the later Vikings sent their noble dead off to the Isles of the Blessed in their funeral ships, the craft we see pictured in the prehistoric rock art of Norway and Sweden, and in the boat-shaped settings of stones around prehistoric Scandinavian burials. That memory had somehow survived through the Iron Age and lodged itself into the mediaeval Arthurian storyline.

I stood by the excavated grave pit and looked towards the Tor, which formed a distinctive landmark on the northwestern horizon. It did not take much imagination to see before me the blunt-ended fairy barge bearing the dying Arthur across the smooth golden surface of a shallow sea to Avalon, its mystic peak silhouetted against the fiery glow of the setting midsummer sun.

Spirit Routes

The voyage of souls to Avalon, and the ride of the Wild Hunt there, are examples of the kind of spectral routes that traverse the invisible country. I discovered from literature and correspondents that there are many more examples, some of them vague, some quite specific.

Ways of the Wild Hunt

The Wild Hunt followed given routes as it processed through the stormy night skies swooping to collect its retinue of souls and proceeding along the ground before flying off through the air until its next touchdown. While in Somerset it linked two specific topographical features, in Continental Europe its course sometimes linked several locations. In Germany, it was perceived as a roaring noise in the air, usually accompanied by shouts and yells, raucous music and galloping hooves. The sound rose from a distant murmuring to a frightening cacophony. Its most common time of occurrence was in the Twelve Days of Christmas, though Easter and midsummer times have also been mentioned in folklore accounts. If a person was unfortunate enough to be caught in the way of the Hunt, then the thing to do was to lie down on the ground, cross the arms in a specific way and recite certain prayers. With a little luck, the Hunt would just roar by. One man in Mössingen, near Stuttgart, was abducted, though, and carried aloft over the summit of the Farrenberg, but he managed to grab onto the branch of a tree and saved himself.

In any given region, the hunt was believed to always take specific routes. In Swabia, for instance, it was generally understood that the Hunt had 'definite paths' and used certain roads.[7] In the Messkirche district, south of Stuttgart and towards Lake Constance on the Swiss border, the Hunt travelled northwards over 15 miles (25 km) from the Banholz Forest, over the Ablach River, along the town's Herdgasse Street, on through a forest passing close to Rohrdorf, and ending at Veringen. In the country around Stuttgart it could be heard along a Roman road at Mulheim, and on a street at Pfullingen. So specific were the routes of the Hunt that some houses were known to stand in its way – a house at Crailsheim had this misfortune, for instance, and there were many more around Germany. The only thing for the dweller to do in such circumstances was to open the doors and windows at the times the Hunt was due to pass through.

In England in AD 1127, horn-blowing 'black and huge and loathsome' huntsmen riding on black horses 'and black billy-goats' with hounds 'all black and wide-eyed' were seen in the deer-park of Peterborough coursing their way from there through 'all the woods' to Stamford (a distance of about ten miles (16 km). 'Many men of faithful report' saw up to 30 huntsmen in the spectral group.[8]

Despite reference to specific geography and landscape features, it is curiously difficult to plot the whole course of a Hunt on the ground with exactitude, because most routes seem to have been a generalised course, presumably when the Hunt was thundering through the air, with only odd sections where it would follow given roads when galloping along on the ground in order to scoop up the souls of the dying. Overall, the course of a Wild Hunt might change directions from one place to another, but it is unclear whether or not the course between specific locales was pictured as being straight or not – the occasional association with Roman roads and straight streets suggests that it may have been.

Ghost Paths

The Wild Hunt was a large-scale, untidy spectral event, but quieter, individual ghosts had their roads too in parts of Germany and Switzerland, and in what is today Poland and eastern Russia – primarily places with mixed Germanic-Slav populations. Their courses were specific throughout their lengths and were known as *Geisterwege*, literally spirit paths or routes. As befits the invisible country, these paths were invisible too. According to tradition, they are 'always in the same place', that is, they have a definite geography, and on them 'one meets with ghosts quite often'. Without exception, they 'run in a straight line over mountains and valley and through marshes'.[9] As with the Wild Hunt, these invisible spirit paths could sometimes pass through houses, and they ended or originated at cemeteries.

Although folklorists tend to separate these ghost paths from corpse roads (see Chapter Three), they do consider that the concept might have stemmed from the old custom of using corpse ways, on which 'spirits of the deceased thrive'. This of course further underscores the ambiguity with which the corpse ways were regarded, and clearly demonstrates that in the folk mind *straightness* was a key association with the passage of the dead, with ghosts. That formal motif recurs time and again and I interpreted it as being a vestigial hallmark memory of the experience of trance ecstasy as bequeathed by an archaic Eurasian shamanism. Here with the *Geisterwege* it is presented in a particularly pure, conceptual form, but still literalised, for the origins of the motif had long been transformed into ideas about spirits of the dead and their haunting of the physical landscape.

The souls of the dead were also able to fly in straight lines too, if fragmentary folk items are to be considered as the tip of a now-forgotten iceberg of belief. There was one folk notion that the souls of the dead could fly through the air, sometimes making a hissing sound. This made rural folk, especially pregnant women, fearful of possession, in case one of these flitting wraiths decided to seek human form once more. Obviously, the Church resisted such ingrained ideas.[10]

In Nemen, Russia (in a region that was formerly eastern Prussia), there was the tradition of a *Leichenflugbahn*, literally 'corpse flightpath'. The town had two cemeteries, one German, the other Lithuanian. The spirits of the dead in one cemetery would visit those in the other on stormy nights. A straight line connecting the two places was kept clear of trees, shrubs, fences, hedges, houses and walls, because the ghosts were said to fly very close to the ground, and so should not be hindered. On one occasion, a newcomer built a house on this line, despite the warnings from locals. Sure enough, the house was destroyed. Furious, the man built the house again but more strongly so as to withstand the flying ghosts. But it was a futile gesture, for the building was again reduced to ruins. In another incident, a local man wanted to erect a shed between the two cemeteries. However, this fellow had 'second sight' and could see spirits, so he marked the passage of the cemetery ghosts by placing a stick in the ground and erected the shed just to one side of it. Unfortunately, he was careless, for a corner of the roof just protruded onto the course of the flightpath, and the shed was flattened. He had to keep re-erecting it – a hundred times in one year, so the story goes.[11] He was obviously a slow learner.

A less structured legend expressing the same kind of motif comes from Cornwall. In this, a widow who had been deprived of her rights was out walking with a friend when she saw a dog her friend could not see. It transformed into her dead husband who told her to be ready at a certain time when he would come for her. On the appointed hour, the woman put on her bonnet and went outside her front door. The ghost of her husband appeared and he caught her up in his arms and carried her over the tree-tops to Ludgvan Church, where he set her down on the church stile. There she saw 'a good many spirits, some good and some bad'.[12] The bad spirits wanted her to join them, but the good ghosts gave her information that ultimately was to enable her to retrieve her rights. After this stile divination, the spectral husband flew the woman home by the same route. During the flight, one of the widow's shoes caught in the top branches of a tree, but this later reappeared mysteriously on her windowsill. This tale would appear to be a folk-gloss of a corpse way, and the spirit divination associated with it. (Stiles in Cornwall were often associated with spirits, being another example of a type of liminal or threshold spot like crossroads, and stile divination was an old tradition.) A Welsh tradition similarly held that living human beings (or their spirits) could be transported through the air by ghosts – it was said that the person was always given the option of flying 'above wind, amid wind, or below wind'. The latter mode often led to collisions with trees and other objects.[13] It is essentially the same image as that involving the spirit path between the two cemeteries at Nemen.

It is not only ghosts that flit through the air and across the invisible country on their own paths, fairies are said to do so too. In order to find out more about this important category of sprite I knew had to travel further than the end of the garden . . .

CHAPTER SIX

FAIRIES, WITCHES AND WEREWOLVES

I WAS RELIEVED WHEN the door opened to reveal the wildly-bearded face of Eddie Lenihan. He had given me somewhat impressionistic directions to his home over the phone, and I had been driving around the countryside near Ennis, County Clare, in the west of Ireland, unsure about which bungalow to approach.

I was mulling over two key questions: who were the fairies, and, of special interest to my enquiries, what are fairy paths? I had been hunting through the folklore literature on the subject of fairy paths – or 'passes' as they were sometimes called – but had found that little was written about them. Fairies were known in one form or another throughout Old Europe, indeed throughout much of the world, but the tradition survives in rural Ireland possibly better than in most other places (although falling slowly silent even here) and so I felt that this was the place to come to find out more. And this was the man I had been advised by a folklorist colleague in England to speak to.

The Folk Record

Lenihan ushered my wife and me into the parlour where he did his writing, and we all had tea and biscuits around his writing table which was smothered in paperwork. Lenihan is a mythologist and a collector of oral folklore. He has many folklore books and newspaper articles to his name, and is well-know in Ireland as a children's storyteller, in which role he re-told the stories he collected from the Irish countryfolk, so passing on a legacy that would otherwise die off without a sound. He came to particular public attention in 1999, when he successfully mounted a campaign to stop the destruction of a venerable old fairy thorn by contractors building a new road intersection just to the south of Ennis. Lenihan indicated a wall-mounted cupboard behind my wife and asked her to open it. It was a Fort Knox of raw folklore, containing the goldust of tradition he had collected from the mouths of rural people: it was packed with row upon row of audio tape cassettes.

'Some of the people whose folk stories are recorded there are now dead,' Lenihan informed us. 'We are in the last generation that can collect the old country folk knowledge verbatim.' He felt that many academic folklorists did not fully understand the urgency of the situation, or else did not value the collection of oral local lore. Undeterred, Lenihan was energetically pursuing this project, funded solely out of his own pocket, and was now interviewing his rural sources on camera rather than tape recorder.

Fairies and the Dead

While sipping tea and listening to Lenihan tell of his work, and enjoying his frequent digressions into folk tales, my mind made a background check of what I had read about the nature of fairies. Although we are nowadays presented with fairies in films and modern storybooks as being rather twee little winged beings, I knew that in genuine folk tradition fairies could take many forms, from tiny creatures looking like miniature people to very solid humanoid beings the size of tall men. They were all viewed in mediaeval times as powerful, potentially dangerous spirits. The historian Dermot Mac Manus, who hailed originally from County Mayo also in western Ireland, could determine virtually no reliable examples of very tiny fairies in Ireland, but instead found that they principally ranged in size from that of a child of six or seven years of age, to the height of a fully grown adult.[1] There were many fairy races. They all tended to be tricksters, though were generally harmless and sometimes helpful. Nevertheless, despite using epithets such as the Good People, or The Gentry for certain classes of fairy, rural people had a cautious attitude towards them so as not to bring down their wrath, for fairies could get angry, especially if spied upon or disrupted in some way by humans, and certain types could be downright malicious.

There are numerous theories as to what type of spirit fairies represented, but a strong body of opinion holds that they were the spirits of the dead, especially the impersonal, ancient dead. Eva Pocs notes that there is a characteristic fairy mythology connected with the dead, and she also observes that some of the fairies of Europe display qualities almost identical to that of certain types of ecstatic witches. She notes that witches with fairy attributes are mentioned several times in the witchcraft trials' records. Further, during death festivals in Europe, 'the fairies and the dead who seek out humans are practically the same creatures'.[2]

The great American folklorist, W.Y. Evans Wentz, who conducted a personal journey around the Celtic lands at the beginning of the twentieth century collecting first-hand accounts of fairy lore from then elderly people, recorded beliefs in parts of Ireland that 'fairies are the spirits of the departed'.[3] 'These *good people* were the spirits of our dead friends, but I could not recognize them,' one woman told Evans Wentz in Armagh. Another chronicler of Irish fairy lore, Lady Gregory, noted that there was a belief in the west of Ireland that the dead and fairies were different kinds of spirit, but that they mingled with one another, so that when the fairies pass by in a blast of wind we should say some words of blessing, 'for there may be among them some of our own dead'.[4] A faint folk reference here, perhaps, to the Wild Hunt. A similar fairies-and-the-dead link was noted by Robert Kirk, minister of Aberfoyle, who recorded in 1691 that according to the testimony he had gathered from Scottish Highland people those gifted with 'second sight' can see fairies assisting humans in the carrying of the bier or coffin to the grave.[5]

I asked Lenihan whether fairies are the dead in a kind of metamorphosed form. 'Not according to any of the folk sources I have interviewed,' was his surprising reply. He said that people had been quite adamant about this, claiming that the fairies had always inhabited the land, and were part of it. I had to admit that this tallied with the views of Mac Manus. He had noted that the common Gaelic term for fairies, the *Sidhe* (pronounced 'shee'), was actually short for *Sluagh Sidhe*, meaning 'peoples of the mounds'. This was generally understood by folklorists as being a reference to prehistoric burial mounds or barrows, and this had led many of them to the supposition that the fairies were essentially seen as being the spirits of the prehistoric dead. Mac Manus felt this to be mistaken, though, remarking that in every case that fairies were mentioned as living in the ground in witchcraft trials, it was invariably in a small natural hill that they dwelt, and not a barrow. Mac Manus argued that fairies were 'earth elementals'.[6]

I found it interesting that Mac Manus, like Lenihan, collected much of his material from western Ireland. Could it be that in this general region the folk tradition separated the idea of fairies from the idea of ghosts more strongly than some other places? Whatever the truth of that, and I did not raise it with Lenihan, it was unavoidably the case that elsewhere people did make an association between fairies and the dead. Evans Wentz had found this to be strongly so in Brittany. A Breton informant told the American researcher that there the dead were believed to continue inhabiting the same landscape as the living, having a mysterious existence that was a mixture of natural and supernatural, their world mingling with ours.[7] Evans Wentz commented that 'we may now note how much the same are the powers and nature of the dead and spirits in Brittany, and the power and nature of the fairy races in Celtic Britain and Ireland'.

Fairy Paths

Breton fairies wander the Earth on Halloween, just like the spirits of the dead, and Evans Wentz was told that they have their own particular paths or roads over which they travel.[8] And that brought me to my next question, which I had already prepared Lenihan for on the phone. I asked him what the fairy paths were like – straight or crooked. He admitted that he had never yet been able to get a clear statement on this from any of his sources. 'What do you do when you are told that a fairy path passes from one "fairy fort" to another, but your informant is then unsure where it goes, precisely, between these two points?'

I made a grimace of frustration, and we reviewed what we knew about fairy paths. There was indeed a general belief that the fairy paths ran between the fairy forts – or 'forths' as they were often pronounced. Over 2,000 of these raths or ring-forts dot areas of the Irish landscape, and are generally small circular areas delimited by a bank and ditch, now often containing a fringe of thorn bushes. This site type originated in the Iron Age as dwelling places, homesteads, but many of the visible enclosures today date to between AD 500 and 1200, and were used in some cases up until the seventeenth century. Some have underground stone-built chambers or passages, thought by archaeologists to have been for dwelling or storage. To generations of country people these forts were seen as one of the places where the fairies dwelt, living underground, and from which they emerged at night or at special times to travel forth across the countryside. Other dwelling places included rocks and bushes and patches of wild, uncultivated ground. 'Trooping Fairies' were warrior fairies and they would march off in long lines to their fairy battles, and fairies in general were prone to forming processions along their paths when going about their fairy business. For long distances, fairies often flew –

Plate 1: (above) A trail of spirit footprints compared to a human foot, Pony Hills, New Mexico. The tiny prints were carved in the rock about 1000 years ago, and probably represent the track of 'water baby' spirits. See Chapter One.

Plate 2: (left) Ancient shamanic rock markings at Three Rivers petroglyph site, New Mexico. Note the haloed and winged semi-human figure, referring to the shaman's entranced visionary state and soul flight. Bird images can also refer to the out-of-body sensations experienced in shamanic trance. See Chapter One.

Plate 3: (above) A restored segment of a *sacbe* – an ancient Mayan causeway – at Chichen Itza, Yucatan, Mexico. These great 'white ways' cut through the dense rainforest in straight lines, sometimes for many miles. See Chapter Two.

Plate 4: (left) The curious medieval stone path on the summit of Dragon Mountain, Harz, Germany, where it approaches the prehistoric burial site known as the *Ringwall.* See Chapter Three.

Plate 5: Glastonbury Tor, Somerset, marking the Isle of Avalon, where the Wild Hunt brought its retinue of souls for them to enter the underworld, and to where Arthur, and the noble dead of the Bronze Age, sailed on their last journey from Camelot – Cadbury Castle, 12 miles away. See Chapter Five.

Plate 6: John Palmer, scholar of European death roads, stands on a *Doodweg* near Hilversum, Holland. See Chapter Three.

Plate 7: The section of a corpse way near the church at Dyrham, Gloucestershire. Said to be haunted by a 'grey lady' ghost. See Chapter Eight.

Plate 8: Folklorist Eddie Lenihan with the fairy thorn he saved from the roadbuilders. Co. Clare, Ireland. See Chapter Six.

Plate 9: Cecil Williamson, who tried to hug a phantom dog in a graveyard. See Chapter Nine.

Plate 10: Anaesthetist Guy Routh marking the spot alongside a road in Gloucestershire where he saw a ghostly woman standing. See Chapter Ten.

typically flying on the stem of a plant such as ragwort. This is a similar image to that associated with some flying (ecstatic) witches.

To obstruct a fairy path was thought to cause bad luck, poltergeist activity, illness, or even death, and building procedures had to take note of this. Mac Manus recorded several such instances in western Ireland, where it was generally considered unwise to extend a dwelling into an open field area in case it projected onto a fairy path, for such were invisible to normal human eyes. He cited the specific case of one Michael O'Hagan who lived in a cottage just outside Ballyblank. His children were being taken ill and dying, and the doctor, who told Mac Manus of the case, was unable to find a cause, so O'Hagan sought advice from the local wise-woman. She came to his house, and immediately saw that an extension that the man had built to the dwelling 'obtruded into a straight line between two neighbouring fairy forts'.[9] O'Hagan set to at once and demolished the extension. It is said that the mysterious recurring illnesses ceased, and his remaining children grew up bonny and healthy. In another case, Mac Manus describes the problems that beset Paddy Baine's house. This had been built on a patch of land with views towards Sligo's Ox Mountains. But the Baine household was plagued with poltergeist-like disturbances and Paddy had to seek advice from the famed local wise-woman, Mairead ni Heine. She inspected the building and told Paddy that a corner of the house was blocking a fairy path. So he brought in a stonemason and had it removed. The disturbances ceased.

There are numerous houses in the western counties of Ireland with their corners flattened off or otherwise modified in order (it is said) to correct problems resulting from encroachments onto fairy paths. Even when one was being careful such problems could still arise, it seems. Mickey Langan had identified a spot for his dwelling not far from the Baines' place. But he was cautious. 'Carefully, he looked at a few fairy forts,' Mac Manus recounts. 'He was not in a direct line between any two of them, and therefore his new home would in no way hinder the progress of the fairy hosts as they swept back and forth on their nightly expeditions.' So he started digging the foundations. However, as he did so neighbours expressed concern. In the end, local pressure obliged Langan to consult Mairead ni Heine, who came to the site. 'Not here, Mickey,' she said simply, as she looked around. 'Not here.'

Like Mac Manus, Lady Gregory noted how in rural Ireland the building of a dwelling had to take note of the geography of the invisible country. She found locals using the phrase 'in the way' when talking about houses that had bad atmospheres or that seemingly conferred bad luck on their occupants, and cites many instances that were reported to her.[10] The phrase obviously referred to the obstruction of fairy paths.

I wanted to know if fairy paths could only be seen by those with supernatural abilities, or whether their course was revealed by subtle clues visible to anyone who knew what to look for. The twentieth-century Irish nature mystic, 'AE' (George William Russell), told Evans Wentz that he regarded fairy paths 'as actual magnetic arteries, so to speak, through which circulates the earth's magnetism'.[11] If this was the case, then it would suggest that fairy paths would only be visible to supernatural vision. But Russell was not drawing on any documented traditional lore, and seems to have been offering a modern metaphor.

Against the idea of magical paths being visible only to a seer's eyes, there is some evidence that the course of fairy paths were *deduced* from subtle physical signs. This seems evident in the cases concerning fairy forts cited above, but there were also instances involving fairy thorns. Sonny Walsh, an elderly inhabitant of County Clare, told historian Meda Ryan about an incident concerning Biddy Early, the well-known nineteenth-century wise-woman of Clare. She had been called out to visit a sick person in Cahirburley. As she and her companions passed the crossroads there she turned to look at a large thatched house standing alongside.

'Oh, that can't be there, that's in a path,' Biddy Early complained.

One of her companions protested that it was a new house.

'I don't mind,' Biddy retorted, 'that's in a path. That can't be there long.'

The house was indeed pulled down when a new road was constructed there. The whole business had been 'an awful wonder at the time' Sonny Walsh told Ryan. He also mentioned something else: he and his companions were able to trace a row of whitethorns running southeast from the house. Walsh explained that the whitethorns were the mark of a fairy path.[12]

Lenihan was himself investigating a similar situation concerning a building in Kerry, which had once been a dwelling but by now had been relegated to the status of a barn. The original occupant had been plagued with problems, and it took a tinker to explain the reason to him. The gypsy opened the front door of the house, and asked the owner to observe a thorn bush some distance outside. He then went to the back door, opened it, and pointed out another thorn some distance away. The doors and thorn bushes all fell in a straight line: the building was on a fairy path. The owner was advised to either keep his doors open at night (as was the case with the houses on the routes of the Wild Hunt in Germany), or else to build apertures into the doors or alongside their frames to allow the fairies unobstructed passage. The owner had taken the latter course of action, and Lenihan said that he was shortly going off to Kerry to inspect the place. This case reminded me of something Evans Wentz had been told when sojourning in Ireland:

When the house happens to have been built on a fairy track, the doors on the front and back, or the windows if they are in the line of the track, cannot be kept closed at night, for the fairies must march through.[13]

Other informants told the American folklorist about similar fairy 'avenues' through houses. I could not help but liken such accounts to the ideas surrounding the old Chinese landscape tradition of *feng shui*, in which houses and tombs had to be kept off the line of straight roads and other linear features in the landscape. Had the same basic motif of spirit lore extended from China to Ireland, from one end of Eurasia to another? In Ireland, Wales, Brittany, even Albania,[14] the spirits of the land – the fairies or ghosts – had their special routes it was considered dangerous for humans to obstruct.

All the evidence suggested that fairy tracks were straight, but one case in the literature had been cited by doubters to indicate that this was not necessarily so. Evans Wentz was informed that fairies from Rath Ringlestown would form a procession, march forth across the land, and 'pass round certain bushes which have not been disturbed for ages'.[15] But did this actually describe a crooked route? I rather felt the opposite was being described – the fairies were following a direct course marked by fairy bushes which they had to circumvent in order to proceed on the direct course. This fitted with the idea expressed in the other evidence that rows or alignments of bushes marked the course of fairy paths. Both Lenihan and I felt that there may be a mix of different kind of paths, straight and crooked, belonging to the fairies, but it had to be admitted the evidence to hand spoke only of straightness – one of the shamanic hallmarks.

Fairies and Corpse Ways

Fairies sometimes used human roads and paths (like the troublesome spirits of Chinese *feng shui*), and it seems they liked to use the old church ways. The nineteenth-century Irish folklore collector, Thomas Keightley, recorded an account that probably related to this: an informant told of seeing a procession of fairies travelling 'acrass the High Field, in the direction o' the ould church'.[16] There was also a tradition of fairy funerals, and Abergavenny museum curator, Frank Olding, has given a number of examples of these from Monmouthshire in Wales, where it was said that fairies, the *Tylwyth Teg*, in the form of the small lights known as 'corpse candles', 'never fail going the way that the Corps will go to be buried'.[17] A fairy funeral was seen going down Church Lane to the church at Aberystruth, and another to

Llanithel Church. Such accounts link to those of fairy folk assisting at funerals (above), and further strengthen the association between fairies and the dead in many parts of the world. A subtler version of what is probably the same kind of association is attached to Lincoln Cathedral. It is said that when it was decided to build the cathedral, fairies carried the stones from the ancient, Saxon church at Stow 'direct across the fields, where there is still a right of way'.[18]

In Fairy Ways

After our discussions and deliberations, Eddie Lenihan offered to show us some fairy sites in the neighbourhood. We jumped in the car and set out on an impromptu tour that included fairy forts and strange gaps in walls where spirits had passed through, but I particularly wanted to see a site on a fairy path, and this provided the opportunity to visit the old fairy thorn Lenihan's campaign had saved from the road builders. We found the bush standing forlorn on a scarred, muddy area of bulldozed ground, surrounded by loose blocks of concrete and heaps of rocks for hard core packing, and dwarfed by a half-finished fly-over. It was seemingly set in a hollow as we looked down on it from the road, but Lenihan remarked that prior to the roadworks its location was the highest point in what had been a field. When we actually clambered down to the thorn, though, it appeared less forlorn. Catching the last faint golden rays of the setting sun it exuded an air of quiet dignity that spoke of its age and fairy pedigree. Lenihan explained that the bush was traditionally considered to be a marker in a fairy path and a rendezvous point for Kerry fairies on their way to do battle with the Connacht fairies. I asked whether there was any chance of mapping the fairy path through the bush. 'Possibly,' he nodded, patting a gnarled branch of the thorn bush affectionately. He then pointed to a lone thorn in the centre of a field about half a mile away. 'I think that could be another marker on the path, but I'll have to do further field research.'

As we dropped Lenihan home, we agreed to join forces in mapping fairy paths in western Ireland at a later date. Driving back through the town of Ennis, the reality hit home of Ireland being the 'Celtic Tiger' of Europe with its newfound, burgeoning economy. There were building developments going on in every nook and cranny, and tower cranes jabbed up into the sky at every turn. Ireland was riding the wave of the information technology revolution, and while this was good for the standard of living, it was a clear signal that the days of old Ireland were numbered. Eddie Lenihan's warning was true. We are in the last generation that can garner the old lore direct from living oral tradition.

Spirits of the Land

Whether reflections of the dead or elementals in their own right, fairies were most of all a part of the countryside; they were what folklorist Hilda Ellis Davidson has called 'land spirits'. It is a rather archaic concept, and reference to this can be found in numerous old cultures.

Dying into the Hills

The Buryat people of Siberia say their shamans 'become cliffs' – that is, they die into the landscape. There are traditions concerning mythical beings, like King Arthur, who sleep inside hollow hills. Ginzburg notes confessions of individuals recorded in the witchcraft trials in which accounts are given of entering magical mountains such as the 'Venusberg', containing an old sleeping man, 'the *Tonhauser*', and 'Donna Venus', among others.[19] The Norse and Celtic cultures felt their ancestors had died into the hills, literally becoming the very rocks and soil of their native lands. According to an Icelandic saga, Thorstein Thorolfsson was drowned along with his crew while out fishing. Later, he and his dead companions were seen by a shepherd entering the hill of Helgafell. Inside, it was bright with lights and there was a company of people that included Thorstein's father (hills belonged to the ancestral line of families). The connection between land and the ancestral soul was very powerful.

This idea of ancestors dwelling in the hills seems to have transferred or extended to prehistoric burial mounds, and there are legends of beings emerging from such mounds to advise the living, or of people like shepherds falling asleep on the mounds and having inspirational dreams. It was no doubt from these ideas that the tradition of 'sitting out' – divination on burial mounds – developed, and it is thought that they also lie behind the Celtic and Germanic custom of building important sacred places on the sites of former sanctity. As Hilda Ellis Davidson has suggested, there seems to have been an assumption that the impersonal dead of an earlier period could help the living. A case of this seems to be the Hill of Tara in Ireland, where Iron Age pagan Celtic kingship inaugural rites were conducted on a hilltop already sanctified by Stone Age burial mounds.[20] In Norse lore elves were associated with burial mounds although Mac Manus had insisted that it was natural hillocks that were implicated. In one of the old sagas, a witch tells a wounded man that he can be healed if he goes to a certain mound in which elves live, and cover the outside of it with bull's blood, leaving the meat for the elves to feast on. In actuality, this was of course a sacrifice to the ancestors.

Land Spirits

Most land spirits were solitary entities. One Norse pagan, Kodran, resisted baptism into Christianity because he relied on a supernatural being, a *spámadr,* who advised him. This entity lived 'in a big and splendid stone'. The Christians trying to enlist Kodran went at once to the stone and poured holy water on it, much to the consternation of the land spirit dwelling within it. He later appeared to Kodran in a dream, and, shivering, told him that he would have to leave. The land spirits were essentially protective entities who haunted mountains, rivers, streams, forests and fields. It was said that humans with the gift of second sight could see the land-spirits following men as they went off hunting and fishing.[21] How nice it must have been, I thought, to believe that a helpful spirit was following you around. But that is long gone, because Christianity forced these nature spirits out. In one of the old Norse sources tell that Porhallr, a man with second sight, saw 'many hills opening and every living creature getting his baggage ready, both great and small, and making it a day for moving'.

These entities nevertheless hung around, for they became sprites more familiar to us – the Pucks, Robin Goodfellows, brownies, goblins, boggarts and other supernatural entities that inhabited the invisible country of Old Europe. When they were not attached to wild, uncultivated locations like standing stones, rock outcrops, springs, forests, mountain peaks or hilltops and other such places far from the ken of men, they offered their services to human beings. An old Cornish tale furnishes a vivid description of a brownie seen by a human being threshing the corn late at night:

> . . . a little old man, no more than three feet high, covered with only a few rags, and his long hair hung over his shoulders like a bunch of rushes . . . His face was broader than it was long . . . great round owl's eyes . . . shaded by his shaggy eyebrows, from between which his long nose, like a snout, poked out. His mouth reached from ear to ear . . . his teeth were

very long and jagged . . . He had nothing of a chin or neck to speak of, but shoulders broad enow for a man twice his height. His naked arms and legs were out of all proportion, and too long for his squat body; and his splayed feet were more like a quilkan's [frog's] than a man's.[22]

Land spirits inhabited the whole of the Earth: in Nepal, for example, their number included forest spirits known as *ban jhankri*. These were dwarfish entities, with feet facing backwards, possessing enormous strength and intelligence. They lived in caves deep in the forest. For a person prepared to fast and stay out at night in the woods, one of the creatures might appear, and teach the secrets of shamanism. On the other hand, it might simply decide to eat the precocious person.

We know how much they were perceived by rural communities as populating the landscape from at least early mediaeval times because of old place names. To take a few examples in Britain, there is Goblin Combe in the Bristol area, and also Goblin Ledge on the Severn Beach. A large natural rock in Dorset is called the Puckstone. In the same county there was a Puck's Barrow near Winfrith Newburgh, and numeorus other puck names.[23] The piskey or pigsey of Cornwall, and the bucca spirit of that same county, both descend from *pucksey*, itself a derivation of puck (*pwca/bwca*). The Channel Island of Guernsey has a tradition of *pouquelaie* (goblin paths), that run between megalithic sites. *Pouquelaie* also derives from puck/*pwca*. And there are a great many hills, woods, old tracks and other features throughout the land dedicated to puck, goblins, boggarts and demons.

Other distinctive landspirits take the form of strange lights and supernatural animals like black dogs (see Chapter Nine).

Witch Ways

Apart from fairies, nature spirits and the spirits of the dead, I wondered whether there was lore relating to the temporary out-of-body spirits of the trance ecstatics of Old Europe – the witches and magicians, the rural ritual specialists. Surely they too would have been perceived to have had their special 'ways' across the nightside terrain of the invisible country. But I found that the knowledge of such things has become so lost in the fog of amnesia that now shrouds the contours of the invisible landscape of Old Europe that little survives in the documented lore of the land. Most of the knowledge of this kind would by definition have been intimately local, and as is the case with such information most of it would simply have been 'known' locally and never written down, gradually passing from record. This has been compounded by the fact that until recently academics have never really seen the invisible country – the imagined landscape, the geographical dimension of supernatural and mythical lore – as something that needs to be explored. However, we know that witches flew, rode on animals and objects, and travelled 'on narrow paths, crossing bridges, and passing through small gaps'.[24] We would nowadays interpret these as symbolic features but they were projected literally onto their physical surroundings by the ordinary people of mediaeval times, and doubtless of earlier and later epochs too. An old English folksong entitled *The Witches' Death Song* records: 'When the Lord takes old women's senses / He takes them over dykes and fences / Straight away to heaven . . .'.[25] It may have its paganism and Christianity a little confused, but it gets the idea across.

Flight Paths of the Witches

Eva Pocs has written that the European witch trial documents indicate that the 'horizontal flight of the souls of witches above ground and "across the landscape" would have been a general phenomenon'.[26] We get hints of specific geographical remembrances of this in folkloric fragments. On Ewerby Waithe common in Lincolnshire, as one example, there are several coffin-shaped stones lying together. The legend states that a witch was flying over the common carrying the stones when shepherds shot at her with arrows, causing her to drop her load. It was said she had stolen the stones from 'a temple which stood on high ground not very far off'. Local investigations by Bob Dickinson showed that the common lies on a line connecting Dorrington Church and the church and standing stone at the village of Anwick. Dorrington was reputed to have been a witches' meeting place, and one 'Mrs H', a notorious witch in the annals of Dorrington, was said to be seen frequently on the church hill in the form of a hare. So we have a magical flight legend also attached to the standing stones.[27]

There is a particular class of folktale in Britain (at least) that records a supernatural route across the landscape which seems to be the way local witch ways were coded in folk memory. One such tale tells of 'Molly N' who attempted to walk the 12 miles southwards from Bristol market to her home in the Mendip hills. (Molly seems to have been a historical figure who used to dress as a man – it has already been noted that cross-dressing and transsexuality is a sign of the witch and shaman.) Her route took her along an old coaching road that followed the course of a former Roman road. After two miles, she became so tired that she collapsed exhausted by the road where it forked on Bedminster Down. She longed for a cart or horse to take her home. Moments later, a white horse appeared alongside her, and mounting it, the old woman was carried by the steed at a furious pace until reaching the parish boundary at East Harptree, where the horse shied at a stream, the Mollibrook, throwing Molly to the ground and knocking her unconscious. It was noted by local researcher Phil Quinn that the route passed by holy wells, a stone circle, a corpse way and a probable suicide's burial spot at a cross-roads. The ancient road was itself 'suffused' with legends and hauntings, and was also part of a major pilgrimage route.[28] Such folk stories are marked by the allusion to a witch and a mode of supernatural transport.

A more complex example of the same class of tale occurs in Cornwall, and this account was taken by folk scholars directly from unbroken oral tradition in the nineteenth century, when it still survived in the relatively remote region of west Cornwall.[29] It concerns the journey by An' Pee Tregeer ('Aunt' Penelope Tregeer) from Penzance market to her home in Pendeen, a direct distance of six miles. Before she had set out to market, Pee had smeared one of her eyes with an ointment that she found in the home of Jenny Trayer, a Pendeen 'charmer' or witch. She did it out of curiosity, and found that the ointment gave her the 'sight' – she could see the fairy folk. Later at the market, she confronted a fairy man stealing from a stall, and the fairy fellow blinded her eye that had been smeared with the ointment. In a sorry state, Pee started back home. Being half blind, she did not take the direct route for fear of the bogs along it, but instead took a safer but more circuitous one through Castle Horneck fields, to the north of Penzance. Reaching the main highway another four miles further on, the versions of the story vary. In one she mistook a bush for a horse and rider, and then walked on, in another a strange white horse appeared which the weary and bewildered old woman mounted and rode slowly at first till the beast took off like the wind over hedges and ditches. By whichever means of transport, Pee found herself on the bleak moorland known as the Gump beneath the natural rock outcrop of Carn Kenidjeck. This spot is highly mythologised in local Cornish lore, and was notorious as a place where the unwary traveller could be 'pisky led'. On the moor, An' Pee saw the little folk dancing and sporting on a flat green sward illuminated with tiny, brilliant lights. There was a shimmer over every-thing. She saw a fairy couple drinking from a goblet the size and shape of a poppy head or capsule. But she managed to free herself from the enchant-ment 'by reciting the adder-charm' and staggered onwards. As she approached the neighbourhood of her home, she was so keen to reach her bed that she forgot to turn her overcoat inside-out, a sure way to lose any fairies that might be following her, and as a result she got pisky-led in the final few hundred yards to her house. Finally, after a few more adventures, the exhausted woman made it home.

There are various references to the supernatural here – to witchcraft, to magical steeds, to trance-inducing substances like flying ointments and opium (a shorthand way for indicating ecstatic trance, if Eva Pocs is correct in her assumption). Also, the act of wearing clothing inside-out is a specifically shamanic trait, traceable to central Asia. The same basic set of motifs are apparent in both these tales, of Molly N and Pee Treeger, along with geographical references specific to their localities. I had no doubt that many more folk tales using this blueprint could be found around the country, with each one inserting local places into its narrative.

In Spain, a possibly more direct folktale survives. It is associated with the Catalonian dolmen of Piedra de Gentil (The Heathen Stone) at Vallgorguina. There tradition states that the witches of Montseny and Maresma used to assemble at the megalith in order to conjure storms – they were weather magicians. They would jump over the dolmen's capstone, and if they touched it they turned into dark clouds and floated away, dispensing damaging hailstones. There is also a legend that the dolmen is connected to a nearby church by means of a tunnel – often a narrative device in folklore to denote a secret connection or invisible route.[30] That these two legends should be associated with the same place could indicate that a witch route is being dimly recollected.

Vampire Routes

As I now knew, the trance practitioners of Old Europe, the real witches, included among their number those figures that have come down to us as werewolves and vampires. The spirit routes taken by these people simply have not been researched, but a couple of telling hints came to my attention. In the Channel Island of Guernsey, for example, the werewolf is known as *varou*, which originates in the German term, *Varulf* (werewolf), via the Breton *varw*, that relates to both wolves and the dead. There was the tradition of the *Alleren Varouverie* in which a company of eerie revellers would roam the night-time countryside. The name *varou* is still found attached to various places in Guernsey. The Creux des Varous, for instance, is a cavern which is said to extend from Houmet to L'Eree, where a patch of ground near a megalithic site is still known as Le Camp du Varou. In the Balkans, the paths connecting to cemeteries would traditionally be sprinkled with protective whitethorn to dissuade the *vukodlaki* from using them.

The folk memory of the witches' ways still exists, be it underneath a surface grimed with time and waiting to be scraped clear by some enterprising scholar.

Paths of the Shaman

I could not help but wonder if there were fragments of lore indicating the existence of specifically shamanic ways or paths in Eurasia, the original routes through the invisible country, the physical signs of which I had found in the Americas. I discovered that there were, even though in many cases they now amounted to just a faint echo, an archaic whisper.

Nepalese Shamans and Grazing Spirits

One clear, well-documented example in Nepal came to my attention. As scholar Robert Desjarlais explains:

> During their healing ceremonies, Nepali shamans journey on magical flights in pursuit of lost souls or in search of medicinal knowledge concerning their patient. Travelling through a landscape both physical and metaphorical, the shaman's spirit visits several features of the countryside ... On this voyage he may communicate with supernatural beings who inhabit and represent certain geographical domains, such as 'the master spirit of the forest' or 'the spirit of the crossroads.'[31]

A vivid definition of the invisible country. This shamanic journey was typically conducted in trance (though it seems this was not always the case), with the immobile shaman giving a chanted version, a running commentary, of his inner travels to his patient and other tribal members present. The landscape traversed would be known to the shaman's listeners, either directly from first hand experience, or from stories and events linked with it. One recorded chant described a shamanic journey starting from the village where the séance was taking place, successively mentioning a half-dozen hamlets, two river crossings, a cave dwelling, a monastery and a shrine. The shaman's 'flight' (so-called because it sounds more like an earth-bound walk) often followed real-world pathways and trails, but ones that had been granted powerful symbolic aspects over and above their mundane purposes. Sometimes the shaman acted as psychopomp, leading the soul of a dying tribal member or villager through an invisible, symbolic geography 'graphed on the physical landscape' as Desjarlais puts it. These 'journeys' of the newly-deceased often led in mind and soul in a 'more or less straight route' to actual districts that were considered the ancestral home of a tribe.[32] The Nepalese shaman would also call helper spirits who were conceived of as 'grazing' in various localities. These came to the shaman along specified routes in the landscape. This was also the case with the dead: spirits approached the village in which they had lived on the pathways that the forefathers came along when they first settled the community. In short, the countryside of Nepal, apparently to this day, is haunted by ghosts, nature spirits and the souls of its shamans, all of them moving along special routes.

Burying the Buryat Shaman

A vaguely similar idea is associated with the shamans of the Buryat people of Mongolia. The way or path is an 'extremely important shamanic concept' states Cambridge anthropologist Caroline Humphrey.[33] This is also true for the American Indians, where the path is both a powerful metaphor and a literal image.[34] Humphrey stresses that to shamanic societies the realm of the dead is not some other place, it is not located across some void separating life from death, but is nearby, just across the mountains or round the bend in a river, or inside a cliff. It eludes the general population because:

> . . . ordinary human organs of perception are not enough. This explanation is used to account for why shamans must acquire the abilities of their ancestor-spirit and animal helpers, which can see better, track down better, fly or swim underwater. The exercise of such abilities constructs the 'ways' or 'paths' of shamans and spirits. A vision of this kind in effect transforms the landscape.[35]

Buryat shamans prepare their own coffins and choose the site where they want to be buried. At death, a shaman is buried temporarily, then later taken to the designated locale. There, his or her bones and regalia are interred and the shaman's spirit becomes the guardian or presence of the place. The shaman's spirit can turn into a bird or animal and move around the locale; the extent of the 'tracks' it leaves relates to the geographical area involved, and the type of creature the shaman's soul has metamorphosed into.

Shamanic Geography

'In a shamanic culture, mapping one's mental state on to a geography of somewhere outside oneself is not just the privilege of the shaman, but is a basic way of talking about one's emotions and social relationships,' explains anthropologist Piers Vitebsky, a colleague of Humphrey's at Cambridge University. 'This may be a geography of the universe, or it may be a geography of the trees and bus-stops outside someone's house.'[36] The idea of the physical landscape becoming a mindscape is not readily grasped by us today, but it is at the core of the shamanic worldview. We might interpret such imagined landscapes as being metaphorical and mythical, simply providing symbolic tools for the shaman to use, but it is crucial for us to understand that the ordinary people in shamanic societies, and perhaps a good percentage of the shamans themselves, took the mindscaped countryside quite literally as well. That is why it is worthwhile seeking both physical evidence as well as the testimony of folklore and anthropology when investigating the vestiges of ecstatic traditions.

Traffic Jamming

That the inhabitants of Old Europe were utterly fearful of spirits of all kinds flitting through the night-time air is proven by the abundance of what in today's corporate jargon might be referred to as 'spirit management' techniques.

The Labyrinth as a Spirit Trap

Thinking back to the Viking death road and Bronze Age cemetery at Rösaring in Sweden (see Chapter Three), I recalled that there was an ancient labyrinth there laid out in small rocks amidst the burial cairns (Figure 21). If straightness was a deeply ingrained (even if not always clearly articulated) association with the passage of spirits in many cultures, could the complementary theme, that convoluted paths hindered a spirit's progress, have accompanied it? Could the Rösaring labyrinth have been a 'spirit trap' to prevent the souls of those interred in the burial ground from wandering?

There is strong evidence to support this conjecture. One of today's leading authorities on the labyrinth, Jeff Saward, has remarked on 'the world-wide

FIGURE 21: The Rösaring labyrinth. (After Upplands-Bro Kulturhistoriska
Forskninginstitut)

perception that the concentric walls of a labyrinth could somehow serve as a
refuge or trap for spirits and demons'.[37] Saward notes other examples of
labyrinths being associated with prehistoric cemeteries in Sweden and Arctic
Norway and Finland – territory of the ancient Saami people, the Laplanders,
who were a shamanic culture. Further, it was a tradition in Baltic coastal
regions for fishermen to walk round labyrinths immediately prior to setting
off in their boats. A fragment of folklore that survives explaining this practice
comes from Nerderkalix, where the labyrinth was walked in order to entrap
the *smagubbar,* the little people, and prevent them following the fishermen
onto the boats. The labyrinth design is archetypal, for it occurs throughout
the world, and in southeastern India people use flour or powdered chalk to
lay out labyrinthine designs on the doorstep, the threshold of the house, to
protect against unwanted spirits. In a variety of cases, from the Americas to
Europe to Indonesia, the labyrinth was also seen as the abode of mythical or
supernatural beings.

Witch Traps

Old Europe feared both ghosts, the nocturnal wandering souls of the restless dead, and the out-of-body spirits of night-flying witches. People did not want such spirits in their homes, they were thought to be capable of flying in through a keyhole, window or down the chimney or via other apertures. In Bavaria, witch traps took various forms, from small diamond-shaped concentric configurations of threads hung from a beam just inside the main doorway, to a labyrinthine arrangement of pebbles in front of the entrance door, and to spheres of glass filled with tangled threads and other matter outside the front door. These features are now used unknowingly as ornaments. The glass sphere is somewhat similar in concept to the German stoneware witch bottles or jugs found elsewhere in Europe in addition to glass bottles. These variously contained tangled threads, pins, hair or material cut in the shape of a heart, and were placed above a door, beneath the hearth or anywhere else that apotropaic measures were thought necessary. While trapping a spirit in a bottle has echoes of the genie in the lamp, malevolent spirits could also be trapped within other objects, such as boots and shoes – and iron pots. In the folkloric account of a Lincolnshire case, the ghost of a witch that haunted Pilford Bridge, which spans a stream between the villages of Normanby and Toft-next-Newton, was 'laid' by trapping it in an iron pot. (Iron is, of course, the metal that is inimical to fairies.) Other devices protective against the attack of witches included iron knives placed in walls, or naturally-holed stones hung on the door. These were often used in stables and cattle sheds so as to prevent animals from being 'hag ridden' overnight. Iron horseshoes were hung for similar reasons.

To Catch a Spirit . . .

It is interesting that in Siberian shamanic tradition a stretched (and therefore inevitably straight) thread or piece of string was seen as a 'spirit road' and was used thus in both shamanic initiation and healing.[38] A counterpoint to this existed from Asia to Old Europe, in that tangled or more organised webs of thread, string, hair or similar were used for protective purposes so as to hinder the passage of spirits, or, in a more generalised sense, to counter witchcraft and evil spells and influences. In Europe, in addition to tangles in bottles to ensnare the spirit of witches, cat's cradles of thread were placed on the chests of corpses prior to burial to stop their ghosts from wandering during that critical liminal time between death and burial. Also, hoops supporting webs of thread were placed on staves along cemetery paths and other haunted tracks to stop wandering spirits. These European features were remarkably like the American Indian 'dreamcatcher', which is a net of threads woven across a hoop designed to catch bad dreams; a hole in the centre of the net allows the good ones through. In Thailand, people put up stakes topped with circles of interwoven strips of bark at the entrance to their villages, or at crossroads, in order to trap evil spirits.

In Tibet, there is (or was) a complex tradition concerning 'thread-crosses' or *mdos*. Their basic form consists of a cross formed by two sticks, the ends of which are connected with coloured thread 'so that the object assumes finally a shape similar to a cob-web'.[39] These threaded crosses are sometimes very complex and can be up to 11 feet (3.5 m) in height, bizarrely taking on the appearance of modern telecommunications antennae. These objects, whose tradition dates from pre-Buddhist times, have multiple uses, all of them centred on the same basic theme. Weather magicians capture evil spirits by entangling them in thread-crosses like flies in a spider's web, and the crosses are placed above the entrances to houses or on their roofs for the same purpose. In Ladakh, it was customary for huge thread crosses to be placed so as to protect monasteries and the immediately surrounding landscape. Thread-crosses were periodically replaced, the old ones being broken up and burned so as to destroy the evil spirits that had been caught in them. The objects were also used by magician-priests as a kind of cage in which a wrathful deity may be temporarily contained during ritual invocations, or as the temporary abode for a more peaceful god. Similar devices are known to have been used by indigenous peoples in Mongolia, southern Africa, Peru, Australia and Sweden.[40]

Clean Sweep

Another way of disrupting spirit traffic was by mean of sweeping. The idea prevailed from Peru to Europe of sweeping paths or areas in order to clear them of spirits, or, a reflex of that, to turn them into sacred space. In the Andes, the Aymara Indians sweep the squares in front of churches to change them from secular to sacred ground ready for religious parades. They sweep in narrow, path-like strips, and archaeologists suspect that features like the Nazca lines (see Chapter Four) were similarly ritually swept, though for other gods. To this day, the Kogi Indians of northern Colombia ritually clean the ancient stone paths that run through their territory, as they are considered to be the physical traces or counterparts of spirit routes which have to be kept open for the trance usage of the shamanic elite, the *mamas*.

In Old Europe, disused paths or ones that may otherwise have become haunted were 'cleared' by sweeping. Similarly, crossroads would be swept, typically on New Year's Eve or other liminal time. This sweeping tradition is recalled in some folk customs such as the 'Plough Jags', 'Plough Stots' and 'Plough Plays' in parts of Britain. In the Plough Stots of Goathland, Yorkshire, a team of sword dancers proceeds to a crossroads. They are accompanied by a 'Betty', a man dressed as a woman, who symbolically sweeps the road. In the Plough Play at the neighbouring villages of Normanby and Burton Stather, Humberside, 'Besom Betty' has to sweep 'all I can see' before the mummers' play begins, as if to create sacred space. She does this before she is killed by 'Beelzebub'. But this 'death' turns out to be trance, as the mummers' song explains:

> I should have thought an old fool like you would know
> This gal's not dead, but in a trance . . .
> Why, she's been living on boiled green worzel tops three weeks, without water . . .

The references to ecstatic practice and the echoes of shamanism revealed in such folk performances are self-evident.

CHAPTER SEVEN

THE MYSTERIOUS WAYS OF THE GODS

I T HAD BECOME overwhelmingly apparent to me that the former inhabitants of Eurasia thought of themselves as living amid a great deal of spectral traffic, most of which was feared. But I learned that the same folk principles that were believed to govern its passage appear to have been adapted for religious purposes – for the use of gods.

Church Lines

In the way that the Christian Church often sought cultural advantage by placing its holy places on sites of former pagan sanctity, it seems that in medi-aeval and early modern times it may also have appropriated some of the pagan beliefs about wandering spirits being confined to specific routes, for it co-opted them to the service of the Holy Spirit, Christianity's own spectral presence. The subtle practice of what Ulrich Magin has called 'church lines' has been noted in Continental Europe. In Worms, Germany, for instance, there are seven churches on a line only two miles long, with a third of the distance marked by a road. This very precise alignment passes at right angles through Worms Cathedral.[1] Such alignments apparently evolved from the concept of 'cathedral crosses' in which churches were located at cardinal points relative to a central cathedral or main church, thus placing the invisible imprint of a cross over a city – and sometimes, where major roads also helped mark out the configuration, it was quite visible.

This form of Christian sacred geography can be seen in many mediaeval cities, such as Zurich, Speyer, Paderborn and Goslar, where the four mediaeval parish churches and the mediaeval main, market church of SS. Cosmas and Damian mark out a Latin cross with its arms pointing towards the cardinal directions.[2] (In this case the cathedral is not part of the configuration because it was built after the period in which the cross had been planned.) Utrecht has a perfect cross configuration. Magin dates the cathedral crosses to the Ottonian (AD 900–1000) and Salien (AD 1000–1100) periods, and the church lines from Staufer times (AD 1200–1300). These church patterns are not accidental occurrences, but represent quite deliberate spiritual (we might even say magical) power play by the mediaeval Church, and Magin cites the work of various historians on the subject.[3]

Most research on this topic seems to have been conducted in Germany, but there are hints elsewhere. John Palmer has noted references to cathedral crosses in Holland, and in Britain researcher Brian Larkman noted an extraordinary alignment of all York's mediaeval churches and chapels: in the distance of little more than 700 yards/metres, five of them align to the seventh-century heart of York Minster and on to another chapel beyond.[4] Larkman has referred to it as a 'corridor of sanctity'.

Folklore may also hold references to such sacred geography. This is often couched in the imagery of supposed tunnels. Philip Heselton has researched a number of tunnel legends in the Holderness district of Yorkshire, and some of these relate to alignments between churches. A supposed tunnel links Beverley Minster with Meaux Abbey, and another was said to run from Swine Church towards Sutton Church. Hesleton found that if he extended this implied alignment it involved two other churches as well.[5]

Lines of the Gods

Vaguely similar ideas to 'church lines' are associated with non-Christian deities, too. As we have seen, the 'land spirits' had their special paths, and some of these spirits were actually evolutions of local Celtic deities. Traditions elsewhere speak of travelling gods. When Telipinu, a Hittite 'missing god', went wandering from his shrine he tended to blight the land, so it was important to persuade him to return. It was believed the other gods sent out a bee to sting him to urge him back to his temple (a beeline?). The people then laid 'paths' decked with honey, oil, and incense for the god to return along. In some instances he is then 'pulled' along the paths, perhaps physically in the form of an image, though the sense is uncertain.[6]

A more comprehensive example, involving architectural modifications, occurs in Nepal with regard to the Newar god, Nasa Dyo, who is closely related to the dancing god, Shiva. This deity, too, leaves his shrine on a regular basis. It is believed that he can travel 'only in straight lines'.[7] As a consequence of this, old Newar towns are threaded with a network of holes or slits in walls so as to allow his progress. Indeed, he is represented in his temple simply as an aperture at the focal point of the shrine.

Gathering at the Crossroads

It became increasingly obvious from countless references I picked up as I went through the literature and spoke with researchers that the meeting and parting of ways were key locations in the invisible country as well as in the physical world. I had seen that they were the places where vampires and witches gathered, where spirits could be summoned, where ghosts haunted, where the shamanic 'spirit of the crossroads' resided. The theme was found in virtually every culture in every era: crossroads were viewed as 'dimensional gateways' as we might say nowadays, where this world and the otherworld briefly interacted.

The scholar Martin Puhvel has made what is probably the definitive study of the worldwide belief in the haunted nature of crossroads.[8] 'The meeting and parting of ways . . . has left its imprint on the mind of man at various levels of cultural development,' he writes. Ancient Hindu religious rules forbade the obstruction or defilement of crossroads, and instructed anyone passing a place where four roads met to make a sunwise (clockwise) movement, for in India crossroads were considered the haunt of various gods and supernatural beings, including Rudra, lord of the dead. The ancient Greeks associated Hecate, a goddess of sorcery and necromancy, with crossroads, and statues depicting her facing in three ways were sometimes placed at them. These images were venerated with nocturnal rites and offerings of certain foods like cakes, eggs and honey in order to avert evil. These offerings, made at full-moon, were known as 'Hecate's suppers' and were for both the goddess and her ghostly retinue. Hermes, the Greek god of roads and travellers also naturally became associated with crossways. In the Christian era, the age-old veneration of crossroads was continued in the erection of crosses and crucifixes at them, and for the dispersal of evil influences so readily caught by the unwary traveller passing through such places. Crossroad cults were one of the signs of paganism that the mediaeval Church sermonised against. In Japan, phallic and vulvic deities were erected at crossroads. One was known as Yachimata-hiko, 'eight-road-fork prince', and another was Dosojin, 'road ancestor deity'. Divination was often conducted at these images by travellers. The east African Yao tribe used to leave flowers at crossroads as an offering to Mulungu, an important deity associated with such places.

In some cultures, crossroads could become objects of veneration in their own right – in ancient Persia sacrifices were made to 'the fording of rivers, and to the forking of the highways, and to the meeting of the roads', while Mexican Indians used to leave offerings of their own blood and that of poultry at rough stone and clay altars at cross-track locations. In a wider context, American Indians generally linked cross-tracks to the concept of the 'four winds', a version of the powerful Four Directions and Centre Place motifs in ancient American Indian thought.

Raising the Spirits

As well as deities, all the supernatural creatures of the night were associated with crossroads. Demonic spirits were supposedly raised at them – as indicated in the sixteenth-century story of Dr Faustus, in which Mephistopheles was conjured at a crossroads. The old magical text, *Clavicula Salomonis (The Key of Solomon the King)* instructed that a crossroads is 'the best place of all' at which to conduct magical operations. In the 1760s, the magician Thomas Parkes conjured spirits at the Staples Hill crossroads, now in built-up Mangotsfield near Bristol. At this site, which has its roads radiating out in the four cardinal directions, he drew a chalk circle and raised spirits that were 'in ye shape of little girls about a foot & half high'. They had shrill voices, and went behind a bush to sing, producing 'a perfect consort of such music'. Eventually, though, Parkes brought forth less savoury spirits – 'dismal shapes . . . and Balls of fire' – which severely frightened him.[9] According to a Tyrolean tradition, it was possible to meet the devil himself if one went just before midnight on Christmas Eve to a crossroads 'over which funeral processions used to pass' (presumably on a corpse way) and lay down there. The devil would eventually appear in the guise of a huntsman provided the would-be seer could muster the stoicism not to laugh, cry or utter a word no matter what spectral apparition passed by beforehand. The devil would then confer various abilities on the person.

Fairies and other sprites also frequented crossroads. In a 1940 Irish account, a man in Kerry let his dog loose on a group of cavorting figures at a crossroads, not realising they were fairies. The spirits vanished instantly, and the dog dropped dead on the spot.[10] An old Irish belief maintained that processions of fairies would become visible on certain nights of the year at crossroads, but in Denmark it was understood that trolls could not pass through a road intersection. In Iceland, it was thought that elves could not pass a person sitting at a crossroads. If they did encounter such a hindrance to their progress, they would offer the person various gifts in order to persuade them to move out of the way.

I recalled that Icelandic seers would visit crossroads on St John's Eve to conduct divination from spirits summoned down straight roads from cemeteries (see Chapter Four), and a similar practice is recorded in the Faroe Islands. There, the diviner had to go on Twelfth Night to a crossroads from where one of the roads leads to a church (again an allusion to a church way or corpse way). He or she had to sit on a grey calfskin with its tail pointing down the road towards the church, while looking in the opposite direction. The diviner must stare fixedly at an axe, which has to be constantly sharpened. The spirits would then appear from all directions, howling, capering and grimacing around the diviner who must not be distracted. They would leave precious objects, but the diviner was not to look at them either. Finally, the sprites would make an attempt to tug the calfskin from under the seer, who must at once cut off the tail with the sharpened axe, at which point the elves would vanish. Failure in the performance of any of these tasks on the part of the diviner would result in the treasures being lost, and the person falling under the spell of the elves and trolls for ever thereafter.

Crossroads Burials

Considering the rich skein of associations that link the denizens of the invisible country, it is not surprising that crossroads became strongly associated with the dead, particularly in the form of burial and ghosts. Crossroads were favoured locations for burial grounds in numerous old cultures, such as in ancient India, Greece and in Slavic societies, but the best-known burial association with crossroads was the interment of suicides at them.

In Germany, the corpse of a suicide would be taken to a crossroads on a harrow, and there buried, with the harrow placed on top of the grave covered by earth except for three spikes left protruding, thus signalling the nature of the interment. A custom developed in Britain of burying a suicide at a crossroads with a stake driven through the corpse, to stop its ghost wandering. In Ellesmere, Shropshire, a man was buried at a 'four-lane end' with a forked stake through his body 'to keep it down'. Nevertheless, the place was always

thereafter considered a 'frittening' (frightening) one, with unpleasant apparitions being seen there from time to time. The origins of this staking custom
are lost, but it was outlawed in Britain by legal decree only as recently as
1823.[11] A similar custom took place in Uganda, where the Baganda tribe
would burn a suicide's body at a crossroads. Also, if a child was born feet first,
the Baganda would strangle it and bury it at a crossroads. A similar fate befell
light-coloured people, as their ghosts were especially feared. In Old Europe,
criminals as well as suicides were sometimes buried at crossroads, where,
indeed, gallows were typically erected.

Haunted Crossroads

In all these cases, the underlying principle seems to have been that the crossroads were a good place for burial in order to 'fix' what were considered to be
particularly dangerous ghosts. It is not surprising therefore that crossroads
became closely linked with ghosts in general. There is an abundance of beliefs.
At Halloween in Wales it was believed that ghosts could be seen at midnight
at every crossroads. In the Abruzzi Mountains of Italy, processions of ghosts
could be seen by anyone resting their chin on a forked stick at a crossroads. In
northern Germany and Poland there was a fear among travellers that if a shadowy figure was encountered at a crossroads after sunset it would follow the
person home and haunt his house for days afterwards. In the eventuality of
such an encounter, the remedy was for the traveller to escort the spook to a
cemetery and say some prayers for it. (Once more, there is an echo in this of
corpse way customs – crossroads were, after all, typical resting places for funeral processions.) In Hessen, Germany, it was a custom to take crockery belonging to a deceased person and smash it at a crossroads, to prevent the return of
the person's ghost. In Russia, there was an unpleasant belief that animated
corpses lurked at crossroads ready to pounce on and devour unwary travellers.
In southeastern Africa, the Wadschagga people would sacrifice at crossroads
for the benefit of the *varimu varekye* (the lost spirits). These were the ghosts of
people who had left no descendants to honour or propitiate them. They wandered the forests and countryside, gathering at crossroads at night. The sacrifices were to stop them from causing trouble. Because crossroads were haunted, it was a Chinese custom to burn paper money at them whenever a funeral procession passed through, to stop the ghosts there from interfering with the
spirit of the recently deceased. In some cultures, such as the Mexican Indians,
it was thought that crossroads were haunted by particular categories of ghosts,
such as women who died in childbirth.

Crossroads, Witches and the Wild Hunt

The Wild Hunt is also associated with crossroads. In Saxony, one armoured Wild Huntsman rode a fiery-red horse through forests and across heaths at the head of a pack of baying spectral hounds. When he encountered a crossroads, this fearsome rider tumbled to the ground, and had to crawl across to the other side before continuing on his wild way. Another German Wild Hunt tradition had the spectral horde being led by Frau Gauden in a wagon. She tried to avoid crossroads, but if she happened on one, the wagon invariably broke down. A hapless human was then abducted in order to repair the vehicle. A similar tradition attached to Frau Holda, another leader of the Wild Hunt. In Holland by contrast, crossroads were understood to be sanctuaries from the Wild Hunt.

It had already become apparent to me that the crossroads were special haunts of the travelling spirits of ecstatic witches and werewolves, and Puhvel's work provides copious further evidence of this. For instance at certain crossroads in the German province of Oldenburg on given nights one could see the witches pass by on their flight path to the 'Brocksberg' (the Brocken in the Harz Mountains). Puhvel also makes a perceptive connection between mandrake, witches and crossroads in Germany. Because of its vaguely anthropomorphic appearance, mandrake root was thought of as personifying a tiny imp-like being and was often used as a kind of doll-idol known as Alraun in Germany. Jacob Grimm identified this name as an old generic term for wise-woman or witch, and there are some early modern references to Alraun as being a goddess associated with crossroads. Puhvel thinks she may be a descendant of Hecate.[12] Mandrake was associated with crossroads in Welsh tradition too.

In symbolic terms, that crossroads should attract such attention is explained partially by their liminal characteristics, but in terms of spirit lore there is an underlying motif that crossroads seem in general to hinder the passage of spirits – that's why they congregate there. This seemed to complement the idea that straight, open and unfettered paths, roads or 'ways' encourage the passage of spirits. This I feel to be one of the deepest motifs embedded in the whole concept of the haunted land.

I KNEW I was only scratching the surface of the full spirit lore of old Europe and Asia, but it was sufficient for me to understand that many spirit ways involved the physical world in one way or another, such as the existence of special paths, ordinary roads, lines of sight, architectural modifications, rows of bushes and the like. Even when there were no physical traces, the courses of invisible paths and roads were located geographically in the landscape by the folk mind. The invisible and visible countries interacted. But in the end all this spirit lore and mythical geography simply boiled down to the folklore and superstitions of past times. But did it? An encounter I had on a modern highway pushed me into an investigation that was to cause me to question that assumption.

It was time to face some disturbing fellow travellers in the modern world . . .

PART FOUR

THE LAND IS STILL HAUNTED

CHAPTER EIGHT

ROAD HAUNTINGS

I SPED ALONG THE motorway luxuriating in the freedom of driving in the virtually traffic-free conditions of the early morning hours. It was a little before 5 a.m., and I was travelling southwards towards London on the M6 motorway near Birmingham. It was a trip I had made dozens of times before at this hour of the morning, and everything seemed much the same. But that was about to change.

Except for a large white van on the inside lane some distance up ahead, I had the motorway to myself. Then I noticed a mini-pickup truck coming along a slip-road ramp onto the highway, so I pulled over into the central lane to allow it to join the main carriageway smoothly without slowing. I was going faster, so I glided past the slightly shabby-looking pickup. As I did so, I glanced idly sideways at the driver's cab. It looked empty – I was looking right through the cab's windows at the motorway embankment beyond. I was puzzled as to what sort of posture the driver must be sitting in so his or her head and shoulders would not be visible through the side window of the cab. I peered more intently but there was no glimpse of a profile, a hand on the wheel or the hint of a person's silhouette. I sped on until I was level with the white van. Out of instinct I glanced in my rearview mirror and saw a completely empty motorway behind me. Although my view was unimpeded, I nevertheless dropped well back behind the white van once more and looked all around. There simply was no other vehicle in sight, nor any exit points where the mini-pickup could have left the carriageway. Only then did I realise that I had seen a phantom vehicle. I experienced a chilling sense of primal fear, and I floored the accelerator instantly wanting to be in London, surrounded by lots of people, and the noise and bustle of normal, everyday life.

On the Road

I came to understand that the investigation of such happenings in modern times was a natural and essential continuation of the research into shamanic archaeology and the ancient spirit lore of the land. But there was a crucial difference in this phase of the work – dealing with reports that purported to be *actual experiences*: it was still folklore, but it was *our* folklore and it was being presented as real encounters by people from the beginning of the early modern era to the present time. My M6 experience had taught me that we still inhabited a haunted land, and its study was not simply an academic exercise.

Phantom Vehicles

Although it could have been any country, for convenience I started to explore records primarily in Britain – the Isle of the Dead in antiquity – for other examples of road ghosts so as to put my own modest, and what I considered slightly oddball, spectral experience in a wider context. As I scoured the libraries and poured over reports of road hauntings, I learned that my personal experience had not been so oddball after all, for accounts of the appearance of ghostly vehicles were not uncommon.

The A428 road linking Rugby and Coventry in the English Midlands has produced reports of a ghostly lorry over a long period of time[1]. The vague form of a lorry travelling eastwards towards Rugby occasionally alarmed drivers out in the wee hours for it bore down on them with such swiftness that there was no time for avoiding action. An impact always seemed inevitable, but it never came – the lorry simply faded away. The minor road leading west through Bayham from Lamberhurst in Kent, just off the A21 road from London to Hastings on the south coast, has been repeatedly haunted in daylight by what seems to be an old-fashioned black limousine – also described as 'resembling a motor coach'.[2] The 'unusually straight'[3] road allows distant views of cars parked along its verge. The phantom limousine, though, disappears when drivers are within about 100 yards (90m) of it. Another daylight

spectral vehicle has been reported on the A4 road west of Hungerford in
Hampshire. It is a car seen near a rise in the road. On one occasion three
drivers saw it at the same time crossing the road ahead of them, and then disappearing.[4]

A stretch of the A57 Manchester to Sheffield road near Mottram-in-
Longdendale was reported as being haunted by a phantom truck during the
1920s. This spectral vehicle was blamed for three deaths and more than 20
serious accidents.[5] A little further north, where the A6024 rises out of the
Longdendale valley over the bleak moorland of Holme Moss, an old-fashioned black car 'in mint condition' appeared out of nowhere behind motorist
Andrew Sylvester in 1999. Sylvester reported a 'static type of smell and a very
cold sensation'.[6] On glancing again in his rearview mirror, the vehicle had
vanished. At around 7.30 p.m. one July evening in 1964, on the road between
Modbury and Gara Bridge near Dartmouth in Devon, Stephen Bale and his
wife had an encounter with a ghost car travelling towards them as they
motored in the direction of Gara Bridge. 'Being lovers of cars we both saw
what appeared to be an early 1920s Daimler Laundelette, coloured black, with
a wire-netting roof rack on,' Bale reported to folklorist Theo Brown.[7] The car
vanished. The Bales were to see the same apparition three or four times afterwards at the same spot. Such reports are almost endless. I now knew that my
encounter had not by any means been the only one of its kind.

Many of the hauntings were explained away by people as being spectral
images of cars that had met with accidents, but it was hard to understand why
relatively few such incidents had lodged a record in the ether when there were
hundreds of road traffic accidents every week if not every day. One thing I
did notice as I went through the accounts, however, was the recurring image
of an old-fashioned black car being described in widely disparate reports.
Almost the archetype of a car, if such a thing could be (it could, as I was to
find out later, see Chapter Twelve). It also occurred to me that a stretch of
road consistently haunted by a daylight ghost vehicle might be put down to
some kind of mirage effect caused by the conditions along that particular part
of the road. But I was reluctant to dismiss too many of the reports in this
manner, being only too acutely aware that my own 1980 sighting had been
no trick of the light.

The predecessors of ghostly motorised vehicles were phantom horse-
drawn stagecoaches, a celebrated supernatural motif associated with roads. A
ghost coach has been seen on repeated occasions in the countryside around
Aylsham in Norfolk, for example. 'A notable feature of the reports is the way
the coach sometimes follows existing roads and sometimes goes straight
through hedges and across streams,' author John Harries has noted. 'Old

maps indicate that in Tudor times the land was not enclosed and the hedges
did not exist, and streams had a ford or even a bridge.'[8] A phantom coach-
and-horses with a headless driver is said to haunt Coach Lane, near Hambury
Farm, West Lulworth, in Dorset. A stretch of road between the Bear of
Rodborough Hotel and Woodchester on Rodborough Common just south
of Stroud in Gloucestershire has produced several sightings of phantom
coaches and headless horsemen. In the early 1970s, a young couple saw 'the
outline of a stagecoach' on the lane, and in 1977, a man reported that 'about
five years' earlier he had been walking his dog just after midnight when he
suddenly saw 'a horse and rider who was headless. It was very frightening and
the dog was barking.'[9]

Headlessness is a persistent feature of these kinds of sighting, folklorist
Edward Waring has noted.[10] It is this often incomplete nature of such apparitions that seems to have driven local people to drum up legends to explain
them, such as drivers being decapitated by tree branches, but there is rarely
any solid foundation to the stories told. Sometimes, the incompleteness takes
the form of coaches being heard rather than seen. On Rodborough Common
mentioned above, inhabitants of apartments that had been built in the
grounds of Rodborough Manor reported hearing horses hooves sounding on
cobblestones, though there was never anything to be seen, and any cobblestones had long been removed.[11]

As well as horsedrawn coaches, I found a noteworthy set of reports in the
ghost literature referring to apparitions of more humble carts.

Spectral Figures

Lonely spectres treading the dark highways of the otherworld also appear in
our world on our roads. That venerable ghost hunter, the late Elliott
O'Donnell, described a particularly eerie road haunting he personally experienced. He encountered the supernatural on two successive evenings while
walking on a country road in the Scottish Highlands. On the first occasion
he just heard footsteps behind him, but on the second night he swung round
and saw the dark shape of man trailing him at some distance. The shadow
seemed to be the source of the footsteps and was advancing towards him.
O'Donnell was terrified, and looked around for some mundane explanation,
but there was none. The famed ghost hunter stood stock still, and the shadow passed him as though oblivious to his presence. O'Donnell felt a transient
'icy chill'. The shadow was like the silhouette of a short, stout man, but the
nerve-racking detail that caught O'Donnell's attention the most was that the

figure was headless. 'There was a well-defined neck, but beyond it, where a head should have been, nothing!'[12]

The A23 road that has long linked London with Brighton on the south coast of England appears to be a particularly haunted route – especially along its southern extent between Crawley and Brighton. A particularly haunted spot is around the village of Pycombe, close by the junction of the A23 with the A281 – indeed ghost hunter Andrew Green considers this locale to be among the most haunted in south-east England. A well-reported case here involved Patrick and June Geary who were driving north on the A23 one dark rainy evening in 1976. They saw a girl in a light-coloured raincoat running along the central reservation ahead of them. She had no hands or feet that the witnesses could discern. Suddenly, the figure turned and ran into the road ahead of the Gearys' car. A terrible accident seemed unavoidable, but the figure seemed to glide along the top of the car bonnet (hood) without impact. Eight years earlier, another couple reported that they had seen a figure in a white trenchcoat run across the A23 from the central reservation and simply fade away. Other motorists have similarly reported a tall slender woman wearing a cape and hood at the spot. She was sometimes seen with a child. One man even claims to have encountered a ghostly figure attired in cricketer's clothes!

Other reports along this southern stretch of the A23 include that of Dave and Joan Wright. A man in shirt-sleeves staggered into their headlight beams and Mr Wright felt sure he must have hit the man, though no impact was heard or felt. Stopping the car, Wright went back to search but found nothing. One summer evening in the late 1970s, Joe and Sheila Harper joined the A23 from the A27 Shoreham road. They saw two figures wearing light-coloured clothes crossing the road a short distance ahead of them. Mr Harper flashed his headlights to warn the figures, but they instantly vanished.

A woman in grey has haunted the stretch of the A23 near the village of Bolney for many years. In the early 1990s three young men were driving along it when a woman wearing a grey dress appeared suddenly in front of their car. The driver braked hard, causing the vehicle to skid into a low wall in front of a pub. Clambering out of the car, the youngsters could find no trace of the woman, but two other witnesses standing nearby said they had seen the woman appear as if out of nowhere and then vanish as the car hit her. Police breathalysed the young driver, and found that he had not been drinking. Some miles further north, between the village of Handcross and Crawley, close to the junction of the A23 with the M23, a youngish woman in a red coat is sometimes reported being seen by the roadside. When a motorist stops to offer her a lift, she seems to vanish.[13] From the perspective of the individual witness the A23 apparition seems specific enough, but taken over time, the haunted zone appears to throw up an indeterminate, generalised and usually pale human-like form (see Chapter Eleven).

Sightings such as these A23 phantoms are typical of many along stretches of road throughout Britain, and doubtless many other countries as well, though only a few highways are as densely populated with ghosts as the southern A23. While the heart-stopping encounters between such spectral figures and motorists usually involve the sighting of or a collision with a non-material entity, road ghosts can occasionally display more solid characteristics – as in the case concerning 53-year-old driver, Keith Scales, described in the introduction. Scales ran into a woman standing in the middle of the road. She bounced over the bonnet and then disappeared. Scales got out of his slightly damaged car and looked all around for the woman, but couldn't find her. The police searched the entire area around the accident spot but could find no trace of the woman nor any spillage of blood on the road. Local people in the area, however, previously reported seeing a ghostly white female figure in the area.[14]

Ghost Cyclists

Some road ghosts take to their bikes rather than simply standing around on the verge like lost souls. A Mr Liddicott told folklore authors Florence Jackson and Gordon Ottewell about an experience had by his father at some point during the years 1918–25, when he used to cycle from Stroud to Bisley in Gloucestershire on Saturday nights on a regular errand. On his way home one night he could see someone pushing a bicycle near the top of Stroud Hill. No matter how hard Mr Liddicott senior tried to catch up with the fellow, he always seemed to stay the same distance ahead – rather like a mirage. Reaching the top of the hill, Liddicott got on his bike, as did the figure ahead of him. As if going out of control, the mysterious cyclist sped towards a tall hedge and went right over the top if it. On reaching the spot, Liddicott searched all around, expecting to find the man injured, but there was no trace of him or his bicycle. A few weeks later, a rather shaken man came into the pub at Bisley saying he had witnessed a similar bizarre happening.[15]

Mr Andrew Lucas told me about a curiously similar experience around the same time involving his grandfather, W.H. Lucas, who was a bus driver during World War I. He was driving his vehicle late at night along a lane near Mablethorpe, Lincolnshire. In the dim beams of his wartime shaded headlights he caught sight of a young woman on a bicycle ahead of him. He

slowed down behind her waiting for an opportunity to pass, as the road was
narrow. The cyclist speeded up and suddenly veered off into the roadside
hedge. Lucas stopped his bus immediately, and he and the handful of pas-
sengers he had on board got out to see if the girl was injured, but no trace of
her or her bicycle could be found.[16]

Figures from the past

Rather than appearing as contemporary figures, some road apparitions have
a strange time-warp quality about them. Shortly before 8.00 one October
morning in 1999, driver Lee Fellick was approaching Midhurst in West
Sussex along the A286 from the south. Suddenly a figure stepped out into the
roadway a short distance ahead of his car. It was wearing a long waistcoat,
baggy trousers, boots and a Quaker-style hat. 'I braked instinctively,' Fellick
reported. 'By the time I had slowed right down I was about fifteen feet away
from him and I realised it was a transparency – I could see right through it.'
The apparition crossed the road and 'just dissolved' into some trees.[17]

Another 'time-warp' apparition, this time on the Cornwall-Devon border,
was described for me by Cheryl Straffon, who edits *Meyn Mamvro*, a Cornish
magazine dealing with the county's many prehistoric monuments. The incident took place 'probably between 1976–1979' when Cheryl and a friend were
driving late one evening on the 'lower road' from Gunnislake towards
Calstock where her father lived. It is a quiet road and there was no other traffic on it. This is her own account of what happened:

At some point along the road both my friend and I saw ahead of us in the
car headlights a line of men crossing the road. This was unusual on two
counts: one, they had on their heads old-fashioned miners' helmets with
candles as lights, and two, they seemed to cross the road and 'disappear'
into the wall beside the road. They were crossing in an east to west direction. I remember saying to my friend 'What was that?' and she said something about it being very strange. As I drove past, I looked in my rearview
mirror but saw nothing behind me . . .

After that, I mentioned it to a few people over the years, but it was not
until some years later that I received a startling confirmation of my sighting. My father used to send me regularly copies of the weekly local paper
The East Cornwall Times. One day when I received it (I regret that I have
no idea of which issue it was in or even which year) I was amazed to see a
headline that a Gunnislake woman had seen the ghosts of miners walking

across a road. As far as I recall, this was the same road where I had seen my 'vision'. The following week two other local women wrote to the paper to say that they too had witnessed the same sighting ...[18]

Other 'time-warp' phantom figures reported along roads or in fields often include English Civil War soldiers, highwaymen, and World War II airmen. But occasionally the observed figure comes from remoter times. A classic case in this regard is the sighting by prehistorian R.C.C. Clay during the winter of 1927–8. He was driving on the B3081 road that crosses Bottlebush Down between Cranborne and Sixpenny Handley in Dorset. It also crosses the Dorset Cursus – a Neolithic earthwork (see Chapter Four) six miles in length. As he drove along Clay became aware of a horseman riding on the downs in the same direction as himself. Clay was fascinated, and slowed his car down. At one point the horseman was galloping parallel to Clay's car at a distance of only 50 yards (45 m). Clay saw that his legs were bare and that he wore a long, loose cloak. The horse had a long mane and tail, but apparently was not fitted with a bridle or stirrups. The horseman turned his face towards Clay periodically – though the prehistorian could not make out any features – and waved an implement or weapon threateningly above his head. With a shockwave of astonishment, Clay realised that he was looking at a prehistoric man. After about 100 yards (90 m), the horse and rider abruptly disappeared. Clay stopped his car and went over to the spot where the apparition had vanished, and found the trace of a round barrow (a Bronze Age burial mound) that he had never before noticed.

Although he drove along that road many times afterwards, Clay never again saw what seems to have been the ghost of a Bronze Age warrior, but his enquiries among shepherds who used Bottlebush Down and other local folk revealed that the figure had been seen at the same place from time to time by other witnesses, and other apparitions near round barrows on the downland had also been reported.[19] What seems clear from Clay's sighting is that the prehistoric phantom saw *him*.

Strange Spooks

Certain road ghost reports describe apparitions that have distinctive 'hallucinatory' properties, in that they possess especially bizarre or out-of-place aspects to their appearance or behaviour. For example, osteopath Nigel Jones passed on to me the account one of his patients had given him. The fellow had cut short a fishing trip on the Littlehampton coast to the west of

Brighton due to the onset of a thunderstorm. Driving home on the outskirts of Arundel, West Sussex, he caught sight of a figure in his headlights. It was standing by the road in the pouring rain and looking at the man's car as if with an air of curiosity. The witness brought his car to a halt and observed closely. The figure was male, tall, very muscular and completely naked but covered in hair. 'Like an ape's?' Jones had asked his patient. 'No, it was more dog-like,' the man had replied. Appreciating just how bizarre this figure was, the man became alarmed that he was perhaps the target of some kind of set-up, so he drove off in a hurry. However, his curiosity got the better of him, and after a few minutes he turned back to revisit the scene of the sighting. Nothing was visible – the figure had vanished.

Bob Prowse (brother of Dave Prowse who played Darth Vader in *Star Wars*) glimpsed a strange roadside figure in his headlights when driving through the Kent village of Hartley on the A229 in the early hours of 26 June, 1999. The figure was that of a tall, blond male. It had a 'bluish' cast to it, and had its arms to its side as if standing to attention. Prowse was adamant that he did not imagine the figure.[20] Reports of such bizarre 'hallucinatory' figures surface frequently in localised areas that are subject to outbreaks of unusual light phenomena (see below).

Phantom Hitch-hikers

A specific and celebrated sub-category of road ghosts is the 'phantom hitch-hiker'. The basic pattern of this type of phantom is that a motorist picks up a hitch-hiker (usually, but not always, female) who mysteriously disappears while the car is in motion, much to the puzzlement and alarm of the driver. There are a range of variations on this basic theme such as the hitch-hiker might give an address, which when checked later by the mystified driver reveals that the hitch-hiker had been dead for some time; the hitch-hiker leaves some item behind in the car that is later found on that person's grave or body; the hitch-hiker issues a prophecy, or warns the driver of a forth-coming danger such as specific bend in the road, just before disappearing. The phantom hitch-hiker story recurs worldwide, and Michael Goss, in writing one of the classic works on this subject,[21] was readily able to present over 100 separate accounts to illustrate the theme. The story occurs throughout the United States, and the 'vanishing hitch-hiker' legend is often associated with that country. In fact, not only does it occur everywhere, it has versions that long precede the automobile: a Swedish case was recorded as occurring in 1602, when the vehicle involved was a sleigh.[22]

Goss comes to some conflicting conclusions himself in his book, pointing out that a good part of the phantom hitch-hiker phenomenon is undoubtedly folklore, yet it is sprinkled with some incidents that adhere to the theme of the legend yet which appear to be authentic happenings. He also notes that in the more legendary, folkloric accounts the hitch-hiking ghost always seems to have a purpose, but in claimed actual incidents the phantom often appears and disappears without any apparent rhyme or reason. This half-folklore, half-incident ambiguity I was to gradually learn was a characteristic of a good many types of haunting.

Phantom Funerals

Another sub-category of the road ghost genre is the 'phantom funeral'. These spectral processions also seem to occupy the borderline between legend and reported actual event. In some cases, they may be the folk memory of the use of a road as part of a corpse way (see Chapter Three). An old folklore-style account is exemplified by the story of a man who around 1900 saw a brilliantly illuminated, driverless 'mourning coach' being pulled by two horses late one night on the road near the village of Lytchett Matravers, Dorset. In more recent times in the same county there was the report of a motorist who saw a coffin fall onto the road from a cart in a ghostly horse-drawn funeral procession near Gillingham. A spectral coffin was also seen lying in the road a mile north of Wimborne in the county. Dorset folklorist Edward Waring has found accounts of phantom walking funerals in Milborne St Andrew, on Sackmore Lane in Marnhull, and on the Lytchett Minster to Poole road, among others.[23]

A claimed actual observation of a phantom funeral in Wales was collected from the family of the eyewitness, Margaret Lewis, who died in 1958, by country-walks author Laurence Main who is local to the area where it supposedly took place. The woman was walking home one moonlit night northwards on the country road to Llanymawddwy from Troed-y-rhiw near Dinas Mawddwy, Dolgellau, where she had been visiting a sick neighbour, when she saw two robed clergymen leading a funeral cortege ahead of her. The procession stayed in sight until it reached the ford (now bridged) across a stream, the Nant Efall-fach, where it vanished. Margaret Lewis heard the next morning that the sick woman she had visited had died in the night. Her funeral took place as Lewis had seen it, including the detail that two clergymen led the procession – the local vicar happened to have another clergyman visiting him at the time who elected to take part in the burial service.[24] Margaret Lewis also saw the dreaded 'corpse candle' death light on another occasion along this same stretch of road (see below).

Crossroads Ghosts

Crossroads were considered important supernatural places in the nightside history of Old Europe, as I had discovered, and they also figure in modern accounts of the haunted land. One cold, clear night in October, 1947, Don Cottrell was travelling south on his motorcycle along the A24 Horsham to Worthing road in West Sussex. At Buck Barn Crossroads, where the A272 crosses the A24, Cottrell noticed an elderly man sitting on an old milepost on the roadside. The old man got up and walked out into the road immediately in front of Cottrell's motorcycle which unavoidably ran straight into him. Cottrell felt an impact yet continued on a short distance until he could turn the bike around. Returning to the scene, the road and surroundings were completely empty. Apparently, numerous other motorists have experienced similar mysterious incidents at this place.[25]

Where the A641 and A58 roads meet between Bradford and Brighouse in West Yorkshire is known as Hell Fire Corner. People today assume this name relates to the fact that numerous accidents have occurred at the spot, but it had that name prior to motorised transport.[26] The crossroads is said to be haunted by spectral horsemen and cars, usually seen prior to accidents. Judy Wood, a group of trees behind the crossroads, is also haunted, and eyewitness accounts tell of inexplicable lights and 'hideous white shapes' there.

Much further south, in Gloucestershire, there is Prestbury, said to be the second most haunted village in England. On a number of occasions the sound of an invisible horse's hooves have been reported at the crossways here, where Mill Street joins the exceptionally haunted Burbage, the oldest street in the village. Tradition has it that the ghostly galloping belongs to the horse carrying a Royalist despatch rider during the English Civil War. Prestbury was occupied by Cromwell's men, and they brought the rider's horse down at the crossroads, and the poor fellow was executed on the spot. A skeleton uncovered at the crossways last century was thought to be that of the doomed cavalier. The title of the most haunted village in England goes to Pluckley in Kent. The crossroads here is known as Fright Corner, and is reputedly the scene of multiple hauntings – the figure of a woman, a ghostly glow and a spectral highwayman.

The list of haunted crossroads could extend indefinitely, and it could be that many of the ghostly traditions associated with them are folkloric reworkings of the former general superstitions associated with such places. Yet once more, as this brief sample has shown, while some stories seem to be legends, other accounts tell of what were seemingly actual incidents. The record flickers from folklore to fact, and back again.

Up the Alley, Down the Path

It is not just main roads that are haunted – byways, paths, tracks and lanes in town and country also have their share of ghosts. Indeed, they may be *more* haunted than the relatively major roads, but because less people use them in modern times there are less reports to go on.

Haunted Corpse Ways

From what I could see and was told, it looked as if a good proportion of reputedly haunted paths were either definitely or probably old corpse ways, and that infuriating mix of legends and reported actual events was also evident in this category of reports.

The Lych Way is one of Britain's best-known corpse paths, cutting across the wastes of northern Dartmoor to Lydford churchyard. Now a recreational rambler's route, it has long been reputed to be haunted by white monks and phantom funeral processions. In Dorset, a corpse way ran up from the hamlet of Plush over Church Hill and down towards the church at Buckland Newton, in which a special door accommodated the terminus of the route. The ghostly creaking and jingling of coffin carts are said to be still audible on Church Hill.[27] Another acoustic haunting is found on a path linking the haunted village of Lychett Matravers (above) in Dorset with its church: there is a place called Whispering Corner where disembodied, subdued voices can at times be heard as if in urgent conversation.[28] Researcher Phil Quinn found two haunted corpse ways in south Gloucestershire. One linked the hamlet of Hinton to St Peter's Church, Dyrham. Where its course follows Church Lane through Hinton the corpse way passes the site of an old chapel where a ghost has been reported 'on a number of occasions'. At the other end of the corpse way, a 'grey lady' spectre has been reportedly seen walking the final stretch of the way through the churchyard at Dyrham Church. A few miles further north, a corpse way extended from the village of Hillsley to the church at Hawksbury. Its course passes through a crossroads called Coldchange Hill where coffins were rested and prayers said. The ghosts of monks are said to haunt this spot.

Despite these two haunted examples, Quinn remarks that his study of 25 funeral paths in the greater Bristol region, in which these two paths fall, has revealed that most do not have haunting legends attached to them.[29] This could be due simply to the vagaries affecting the survival of tales associated with them, or it could mean that examples with such legends relate to actual sightings. (This latter suggestion is strengthened if Quinn's observations are representative, for it suggests that the idea of haunted corpse ways cannot automatically be assumed to be just folk memories of a route's former use, otherwise such tales would be more widespread.) Two other Gloucestershire cases do seem to relate to claimed actual sightings, both come from the town of Tewkesbury. In the late 1980s two women reported seeing a coffin being carried 'in a secretive manner' along Mill Street from the Abbey towards St Mary's Lane. Interestingly, there did use to be a burial ground in St Mary's Lane, and there is a legend concerning a midnight burial in the immediate area.[30]

A stronger report comes from a couple who in July or August of 1982 saw two young boys on crutches playing together late one warm evening in Church Street. The wife noted that they were dressed in rather old-fashioned clothes – knickerbockers. The crutches had arm-pads, and similarly seemed to be old-fashioned. She also thought it odd that these young lads should be out so late. When one of the boys noticed the married couple, he and his companion scuttled off down a nearby alleyway. The wife was in the area some weeks later, and asked a local shopkeeper if he had ever seen two crippled boys playing in the area. He had not, but commented that the alleyway led to a seventeenth-century graveyard. She saw that it was now bordered by a high wall that disabled children could hardly have scaled. This was not the end of the curious incident: in December 1982 the woman recounted her experience at a dinner party, where one of the guests listened particularly attentively. He later explained that he had been born in Tewkesbury, and three times in his life he had heard exactly the same story.[31]

Path to the Place of Dread

A classic case of a spirit encountered on an ancient ghost path was reported by Arthur Grimble in his *A Pattern of Islands*. In the early years of the twentieth century, Grimble was a District Officer of the British Colonial Administrative Service in the Gilbert Islands, an archipelago in the western Pacific. The islanders had an age-old belief that the spirit of a person who died would travel northwards along the chain of islands to a promontory, the Place of Dread, on the northern tip of the northernmost island, Makin-Meang. From this promontory, the spirit departed over the ocean to the heavenly lands. Seated at this promontory was Nakaa, the Lord of Death, ready to ensnare unwary souls. For the spirit to avoid Nakaa's traps, a specific ceremony called *Te Kaetikawai* (The Straightening of the Way), had to be conducted over the body of the recently deceased so as to ensure the spirit's safe route through the islands to the Place of Dread. The ghosts of those who died on any of the other islands proceeded northwards 'by the road above the western beach', but those who died on Makin-Meang itself proceeded along a path running along the eastern shore. Anyone coming back from the promontory had to do so only via the eastern path, and then only after ensuring that no local death was expected, for travelling south one would meet the ghost of anyone who had just died, and that would signal misfortune. (The western path was more populated by travelling ghosts, so that was why no one went south along it.) When Grimble visited Makin-Meang he insisted on going to see the Place of Dread in the face of the strenuous arguments of the locals. In the end, and most unwillingly, a village constable took him to the site – an unremarkable spit of land. It was just after 2.00 p.m when Grimble with his guide now trailing behind him set off back down the eastern path. After a few miles, he saw a man approaching him:

> He walked with a strong limp . . . He was a stocky, grizzled man of about 50, clad rather ceremoniously in a fine mat belted about his middle . . . As he came up on my left, I noticed that his left cheek was scored by a scar from jawbone to temple, and that his limp came from a twisted left foot and ankle . . .
>
> He totally ignored the greeting I gave him. He did not even turn his eyes towards me. He went by as if I didn't exist . . . It was so grossly unlike the infallible courtesy of the islanders.[32]

When Grimble asked the constable who the man was, the islander screamed in fear and ran off ahead down the path – the fellow had apparently seen nothing. When Grimble reached the village he had initially set off from, he found the constable and the headman in animated conversation. Grimble told of his encounter, and he was informed by the headman that what had passed him on the path had been the ghost of Na Biria, who had died shortly

before 3.00 p.m. In disbelief, Grimble was taken there and then to the man's
hut, where the Straightening of the Way ritual was still being conducted
around the man's corpse.

Spectres of the Civil War

Another claimed actual ghostly encounter, this time in an alleyway in the less
exotic setting of an Essex village, was reported to me by Sandra Maddox. The
alley, in Newport, near Saffron Walden, may have been on the course of a
former corpse way. The incident took place around 9.00 one October
evening in 1978. Mrs Maddox and two friends were returning home from the
village youth club:

> We decided to take a shortcut from Wicker Road up an alleyway leading
> to Church Street. There were street lights at the bottom of the alley and
> also at the top, so it was quite dark and had a slight bend so it was not
> possible to see from one end of the alley to the other. As we neared the
> bend, we became aware of someone walking toward us dressed as a cava-
> lier – I say 'walking', the 'person' drifted towards us. We couldn't see his
> features as he was silhouetted against the light in the church entrance, but
> he wore a large hat with a plume, and a cape – full attire for a cavalier! I
> remember saying, 'Look, it's Guy Fawkes!', but as the figure neared us we
> had an overwhelming need to press ourselves against the wall until 'he'
> had passed. None of us were brave enough to look directly at the figure as
> it passed.
>
> When we reached the end of the alley we all felt a lot braver and decid-
> ed to run back and catch a glimpse of this person who we at first thought
> had been in fancy dress. But he was nowhere to be found.[33]

Royalist cavaliers are a curiously recurring image in ghost accounts. A mounted one is said to haunt a lane called the Knights Ride at Uplyme in Dorset,
and another has been seen to materialise near Hound Tor on Dartmoor, to
take just two of many other examples. But their adversaries in the English
Civil War, Cromwell's roundheads, appear almost as frequently in reports.
An intriguing case concerns the church at Crondall, in Hampshire, which
was vandalised by Cromwell's men. In 1899, the antiquary Stephen Darby
was sketching parts of the building's interior, when he noticed a person enter
the church dressed as a roundhead soldier would have been. As Darby stealth-
ily trailed the curious visitor around the building, the figure vanished.

Enquiries made of the vicar revealed that the ghost quite often appeared. In 1940, two cyclists were resting by Crondall church when they saw a misty shape heading towards the building. It clarified into the figure of a rider in Cromwellian dress 'who passed through the churchyard wall, up the avenue, and into the building'.[34]

Pathway Spirits

Other things haunt alleys and lanes too. Ghostly footfalls are heard in a passageway linking Shaftesbury Avenue and Banner Road in the inner city district of St Pauls in Bristol,[35] a boggart or goblin in spectral animal form terrified a man on a path leading into fields from Shatton Lane between Shatton and Offerton in the Peak District,[36] and fairies were sometimes seen accompanying funerals on burial roads in Wales (see Chapter Six). Indeed, the routes of funeral processions along Welsh corpse ways (known usually as 'burying lanes' or 'death roads' in Wales) were traditionally swept, to rid them of haunting spirits.

From at least Anglo-Saxon times, certain lanes like various other features in the landscape were thought to be haunted by 'land spirits' of one kind or another, as I have already noted (see Chapter Six). In Oxfordshire alone there are Puck Lanes in Eynsham and Witney, and a presumed track in the village of Steeple Barton is remembered in the old field name of Demnesweye, 'Demon's Way'.[37]

CHAPTER NINE

NON-HUMAN
SHADES OF THE LAND

PILGRIM'S WAY, THE mediaeval pilgrimage route from Winchester to Canterbury, and formerly a prehistoric track, has for centuries been reported to be haunted by the sound of invisible galloping hooves on the section between Hollingbourne and Charing, just north of Ashford in Kent. Ghostly galloping sounds occur quite often in the ghost report literature, and point to the fact that accounts of animal spirits form a major strand in the matter of landscape hauntings. One of the most important is the 'Black Dog'.

Black Dogs

This is known by different names in various parts of the country: Black Shuck, Barguest, Skriker, Gytrash and various other appellations, but it is still essentially the same beast. Stereotypically, it appears as a giant hound with glowing red eyes 'as big as saucers', but in most actual accounts it tends to appear as a more normal-looking dog – at least at first glance. Traditionally, the phantom Black Dog is associated with stretches of certain roads and paths, with parish boundaries and other borderline or liminal locations like bridges and coastal areas, with death (often as a portent), and sometimes with the devil and witchcraft. The association with death may derive in a pragmatic sense from the role of dogs as corpse-eating scavengers in some ancient societies, and in a mythical sense with them being guides of souls to the otherworld and protectors of tombs, as was Anubis in ancient Egypt. In Norse lore there was the image of the Helhound – a poem in the Norse *Edda* tells how the shamanic hero-god Odin 'met a hound that came from Hel', that is, the underworld.

Just how normal a phantom Black Dog can initially appear is well revealed in a personal account given by the late Cecil Williamson, the former owner-curator of the witchcraft museum at Boscastle in Cornwall. Living nearby at the time, and prompted by his interests, Williamson decided one night in 1972 to visit the grave of Richard Capel in the churchyard at Buckfastleigh, on the southern edge of Dartmoor in Devon. Capel, a great huntsman, was reputed to have sold his soul to the devil. When he was buried in 1677, he was placed in a tomb which is in effect a small roofed building, surrounded by wrought-iron railings, near the church porch. It is said this was paid for by local people to prevent his tortured soul from escaping. If so, it is not completely successful, for legend has it that on stormy nights Squire Capel sets off with the phantom black hounds said to surround his tomb and goes a-hunting out on the moor along the ancient Abbot's Way. This is of course an echo of the Wild Hunt, and the legend supposedly inspired Sir Arthur Conan Doyle's Sherlock Holmes story, *The Hound of the Baskervilles*. What happened to Williamson, though, was an actual experience. He arrived at the tomb around 3.00 a.m., and sat on a grave covering for about half an hour, when:

. . . a big, black, long-haired labrador dog came padding by. It spotted me, stopped, did a stare and a sniff. Decided I was kosher and came to rest its head in my lap. It was warm, solid and I felt its warm breath on the back of my hand. I asked what it was doing out on its own at this time of night. This sort of dog-lover's chat went on for about fifteen minutes, then it suddenly got up, put its paws on my lap and gave my face a big lick or kiss. Yes, it was warm and wet, and my first reaction was to put my arms around the beast and give it a big hug. This resulted in another 'kiss' and I hugged it again. This time my two arms went through the dog! It was like crushing a blown-up paper bag. My two arms were still clasped around me – but the dog had vanished into thin air![1]

Other spectral hound legends that relate to the Wild Hunt mythos include a phantom pack of dogs known as 'Gabrielle's Hounds' reported as being heard at various places across the Peak District, including the areas around Bradfield, Hathersage, Eyam and Offerton, where a man reported encountering a phantom dog-like creature (see above). The aerial barking of

'Gabbygammies' are said to haunt the sky over the Ashmore area in Dorset, while on Dartmoor the ancient copse of Wistman's Wood is associated with the periodic appearance of a pack of black dogs known as the Whisht Hounds – 'whisht' being a local term for spooky, derived from 'Wisc', a regional name for Odin.

The cases concerning phantom hounds that reputedly haunt specific lanes and paths are legion. A Black Dog phantom is said to haunt Godly Lane which leads from the churchyard in Burnley, Lancashire; Boggart Lanes at Charlesworth, near Glossop, and in Oughtbridge on the outskirts of Sheffield refer to the Barguest; in northern Somerset, a stretch of road between St Audrie's Farm and Perry Farm near Watchet on Bridgewater Bay is haunted by a Black Dog, while an author and his companion were literally dogged by a black hound as they walked home one moonlit night from Chideock towards Morecombelake near Lyme Regis on Dorset's coastline. They reached an old graveyard where the road from Seatown crosses the A35, and, dumbstruck, watched 'the hound pad its way towards an enormous grave-stone and disappear before our eyes'.[2] And there are a great many more such examples.

Devon is said to harbour at least 50 Black Dog haunts, according to folk-lorist Theo Brown.[3] A phantom dog haunted Dog Lane, now Haye Lane, which leads to the Y-junction known as Copplestone Cross at Uplyme on the borders of Devon and Dorset where stands the Black Dog Inn. The ghostly dog is said to have knocked down the corner of the inn at one time. Another Devon building which had its corner supposedly damaged by a ghost dog is a schoolhouse at Down St Mary near Copplestone. (The damage is of a phantom nature, because though masonry is heard to fall, no visible, physi-cal damage occurs.)

This is just one Black Dog haunt of about a dozen that Barbara Carbonell plotted in mid-Devon between Copplestone and Great Torrington roughly 20 miles to the northwest.[4] Carbonell was a follower of Alfred Watkins's 'ley' (alignments-of-sites) theory, and she saw this line of Black Dog hauntings in the context of that. It is an intriguing coincidence that the Black Dog pub with its supernaturally damaged corner stands at Copplestone Cross, Uplyme, while this schoolhouse is close to the village of Copplestone – and Carbonell took her alignment as starting at 'Coplestone Cross' there. The two locations are about 30 miles apart.

Theo Brown has suggested alignments of Black Dog hauntings in the county herself. One extended from Doccombe near Mortonhampstead west-wards across Dartmoor, through Postbridge and on to Roborough on the west side of the moor, where a ghost dog is said to attack travellers. Another of her lines 'continues into a Cornish system' and ends near Liskeard.[5] The Dorset folklorist Edward Waring noted an alignment characteristic of Black Dog haunts on the Isle of Portland off Weymouth. The phantom hound there is known as Row Dog; it is shaggy, as high as a man, with large fiery eyes. It doesn't attack people, but will bar their way. 'Occasionally . . . one is given two definite points between which the dog runs,' Waring notes.[6] Claimed Row Dog runs on the island occur between Grove Point and the Bill, from Wakenham to Perryfield Corner, and along Avalanche Road in Southwell. But long alignments do not seem to be the norm with Black Dog haunts, or hauntings in general for that matter, and are usually located in one area or on a short stretch of road or pathway.

Not all Black Dogs are black. In the Scottish Highlands and Islands there is the fairy dog, the cu-sith, which is white or green. In September, 1949, Morag MacCartney and two companions encountered the Fairy Dog on the island of South Uist. As they were making their way one dark night round the upper end of Lochnan Eilean they saw a white dog approaching. It bounded straight towards the group, passing between Morag and one of her friends, a local teacher. The animal was 'white all over, and had a small black head'. Its full tail was coiled up over its back. Morag spun round as the creature passed her, but it had vanished. Mentioning the encounter in general terms when she got back home, Morag's aunt asked her: 'Was it a white dog?' The spectral creature was well known to those who had lived long thereabouts. The Fairy Dog always moves in a straight line.[7]

Dark Horses

Although phantom dogs make up a large category of animals haunting the land, there are other creatures also. Martin Puhvel has noted that crossroads traditionally harboured 'spectral animals'.[8] These were usually monstrous-looking, and included not only ghostly dogs, but also horned beasts, and grey cats among other phantom creatures. Horses figure quite prominently in the land-haunting stakes as well. One correspondent to *The Ley Hunter* journal recalled a youthful encounter with a literal dark horse when he was setting off one morning on a hike from a youth hostel in Litton Chaney, Dorset. He was walking along a quite narrow and very steep road:

I was approaching a gap in the thick hedge to my right when I became aware of the sound of horses' hooves (probably one horse, in fact) galloping aggressively towards me through the gap. I must have stopped

walking to locate the horse as it was not in sight, when quite suddenly a
dark horse-sized shape began to materialise in the gap in front of me . . .
All this scarcely took a few seconds but I felt under severe menace from
this shaking, thundering shape rapidly assuming solid form in front of me.
A sense of self-preservation made me feel that I must not let it 'fully
become real', so I shouted at it as aggressively as I could, and it just vanished away into nothing, in the same place. Believe it or not, I waited a
few minutes to see if anything else was going to happen, then I went on
my way.[9]

Sometimes, the spectral creature is totally bizarre. This report comes from a
'Mr K', a North Sea oil rig worker, and refers to an incident that happened
in Lincolnshire:

I was driving down the back road from Great Yarmouth to Lincoln. It was
very dark and quite rural in that area . . . As I drove down the road I
noticed a shape in the fields at the righthand side . . . as I got closer it
moved nearer towards the road and I got the shock of my life – it had the
body and legs of a horse but a man's face! It was very scary and unpleasant. I didn't hang around, but put my foot down hard on the accelerator
and 'got the hell' out of there!
        When I got home I told my wife and friends about it, but most peo-
ple just laughed at me . . . I kept quiet about it after that, but I am convinced about what I saw. I know it seems impossible, but I *did* see it and
it wasn't just a horse or deer.[10]

The compiler of the report, Alison Downes, noted that this apparition bore
a strong resemblance to a spectral manifestation reported in 1966 near
Drogheda, County Louth, Ireland, which was described as a 'huge horse with
a man's face and horrible bulging eyes'. Interestingly, Eva Pocs has commented that ecstatic practitioners of Old Europe (see Chapter Four) who
were believed to transform into animals often chose the form of dogs, cats
and horses. The witches might also cast a spell on a victim and change his or
her form into that of an animal. 'We have numerous documents referring to
victims who were turned into horses,' she remarks. 'Riding or galloping on
the animal alter ego of a transformed human was a characteristic attribute of
European witch beliefs, and remained one of the most characteristic motifs
of witch legends.'[11]
        But didn't these creatures result from body-image hallucinations in
trance states? I then recalled Professor Brian Bates of Sussex University

once describing a disturbing incident he witnessed in full waking consciousness in an Austrian forest. He saw a female ritualist's head flickeringly transform into that of a wolf.[12] Could hallucinations somehow 'escape' into common reality, or, at least, into someone else's mind? Such ideas were among the deliberations I would later have on a far-away hilltop (see Chapter Eleven).

Gleamings in the Gloaming

The distant lights caught my attention out of the corners of my eyes. It was a warm and pleasant July evening in 1989, and dusk was beginning to gather. I was walking past the upstairs windows of our then home. They afforded an unimpeded view out across the rooftops of the Welsh town of Brecon to the peaks of the Brecon Beacons. I stopped and stared intently. Lights were seemingly moving around on the lower slopes of the Beacons. I considered it to be a curious time of day for people to be out climbing the mountains – in the five years we had lived in the house, I had never seen such a thing. Then I realised the lights were simply too big and bright to be the flashlights of ramblers or climbers. I called my wife's attention to the lights, and while she watched went to get the binoculars. Looking through these I saw that in the dusk my naked eyes had deceived me: the lights were not on the mountain slopes but on top of a group of pine trees lying between Brecon and the lower slopes of the Beacons. The lights were white or yellow-white orbs up to 3 feet (1 metre) across; one would shine out intensely atop one tree then extinguish itself, only for another to gleam out on top of another pine. This stunning ballet of lights lasted a full 15 minutes.

The remarkable display particularly excited me because I knew I was witnessing one manifestation of the rare phenomenon I had been calling 'earth lights' for almost a decade and which had been the subject of some of my books.[13] I had seen such things only a few times in my life, but my research had shown they had been witnessed around the world for centuries and perhaps millennia. In our modern culture they were inevitably bound up with notions concerning 'UFOs', and most people interested in that subject were looking for craft from beyond Earth, not little-understood phenomena issuing from our own planet, which is what the evidence had led me to understand earth lights to be. Most (though not all) scientists do not bother much with them due to this association with what they perceive as the lunatic fringe. As a consequence, the whole range of earth-light phenomena tends to slip between two stools, and reports ends up, if anywhere, in the files of folklorists.

Earth lights seem to be a range of little-understood natural phenomena that are related to the family of lightforms that include earthquake lights and ball lightning. The evidence suggests that they are produced within the matrix of the vast forces that are in play in tectonic stress and strain within the Earth's crust, which in turn perhaps interact with the equally awesome electrical energies loose within the atmosphere. Energy nodes or foci are formed that result in glowing and often shape-shifting lights. This is not to be taken as some glib 'explaining away' of puzzling phenomena, for the lights produced are unquestionably exotic, with strange characteristics that will demand a great deal of study before we will properly understand them. There is no need to go into the detailed arguments and evidence surrounding the subject here, as that has been presented in depth not only in my own books but also in the works of others.[14] A few earth-light examples will be sufficient to illustrate the phenomena in general. This is necessary, because I found to my amazement that pursuit of the subject leads directly to the matters of spirits, of the haunted land, of shamanism – a convergence of research interests that I never dreamt possible when I started out on what I believed to be totally separate lines of enquiry.

An extraordinary occurrence aptly illustrates at least some kinds of earth lights. I was involved in the production of a television documentary on the subject in 1996. It had its first network screening in Britain on a Sunday evening in November of that year.[15] Within a few hours of the transmission reports were coming in of strange lights being seen in the skies over Cornwall. The reports continued throughout the following week: there were rectangles of light 'moving jerkily' through the heavens, spheres of light looking 'like the moon' that slowly dissolved, and slow, silent flashes of light in the sky. Local papers wondered if it was a mass psychological reaction to the documentary, and I must admit I, too, wondered much the same thing. But why only in Cornwall? The answer was forthcoming exactly a week after the programme's transmission when Cornwall experienced its largest earthquake of the twentieth century. It was not big by international standards, but it was significant none the less. It transpired that similar strange lights had been documented prior to earlier quakes in Cornwall going back a century or more. I then recalled that I and three other witnesses had seen beautiful but highly mysterious golden balls of light dropping silently out of clouds only a couple of miles from the epicentre – but two years earlier. I had also collected reports from long-time residents of Cornwall's Land's End district of seeing football-sized spheres of purple light near some of the old tin mines that dot the land-scape. I was told they often appear after rain – perhaps due to electrical changes in the atmosphere, I reasoned, or variations in atmospheric pressure on a faulted and tectonically sensitive landscape.

Haunted by Lights

There are numerous places in Britain where concentrations of light phenom-ena have been reported in the past or continue to occur today, such as parts of the Pennines in Derbyshire and Yorkshire,[16] the Elan Valley in central Wales, and the Barmouth coastal area of Wales near the Lleyn Peninsula – the epicentre of many British earthquakes, including one in 1984 registering 5.5 on the Richter scale and the arena for an extraordinary outbreak of lights in 1904 and 1905, witnessed by London journalists as well as by locals. Scotland has had balls of light appear over certain of its lochs, especially Loch Leven, and in areas such as the Moray Firth. Many other locations have pro-duced reports of strange lights from time to time. One witness described an encounter while on the prehistoric Ridgeway path near Wantage: 'To my left, about three yards away from me just above the fence surrounding the field, I saw a ball of light about one inch bigger than a cricket ball. The light was intense and white, but not a drop of this light issued outwards from this ball'.[17] (This lack of radiated light is a characteristic of earth-light phenome-na, and is frequently reported.) The light made a figure-of-eight movement before disappearing, then reappeared and disappeared in different locations before finally vanishing. The A684 road across the Yorkshire Dales in the West Witton area has long been the site of a moving light phenomenon, repeatedly reported by motorists,[18] but here is a specific account of an encounter from a woman who with three companions rented a cottage in West Witton in August, 1970:

> One night I woke up to find an enormously bright light reflected on the wall beside my bed. I turned over, thinking that the curtains were open, but they were tight shut. In any case, there was no light source outside the back of the house, as the ground sloped down to the valley and the near-est road in that direction was miles away. The only way I can describe the light is being like a great headlight on a car, but seen through the bare branches of a tree, causing a fragmented appearance. The light seemed to waver . . .[19]

The witness saw the light again the following week, but this time with her friend, who became very agitated. At the same time, unexplained bangings erupted briefly in the cottage. This poltergeist-type of effect has been widely noted around the world in association with earth lights, and especially in localised areas subject to high-incidence periods of light phenomena. One such instance was the outbreak of sightings in the Yakima Indian reservation near the Cascade mountain range in Washington State, USA. Various kinds of effects were seen (and in some cases photographed and triangulated by reservation fire wardens) ranging from glowing clouds at night to small dancing lights and large-scale aerial lightballs. The outbreak lasted in waves between 1972 and 1978, and was accompanied at times by ghostly crunching sounds on gravel paths leading up to fire lookout points, disembodied voices calling the fire wardens, and there was also a report of a wild-looking, seven-foot-tall humanoid entity appearing fleetingly on a reservation road, terrifying two witnesses in a car.

My search for the lights has taken me to all kinds of remote places. One is the Hessdalen Valley near Trondheim in Norway, where a tremendous outbreak of light phenomena was witnessed and to some extent monitored in the 1980s. Recently, an automatic station has been set up there with a webcam so remote observers can monitor the valley for strange phenomena in the comfort of their own homes and computer keyboard.[20] I also helped to conduct monitoring sessions at various 'spooklight' sites in the United States, often revealing that reported light phenomena were in fact distorted refractions of distant vehicle lights. One of the main American spooklight locations is around Marfa in the Big Bend country of Texas where it meets the Rio Grande. Most of the currently-reported lights seen here, especially from the designated roadside observation point, proved to be distorted vehicle lights seen over 30 miles (48 km) away across the undulating semi-arid landscape known as Mitchell Flats. But lights have been reported across the vast region for a century, and in the Chisos Mountains, where a local teacher had told us she had seen at close quarters a three-foot-wide ball of white light slowly bouncing along by a road, I did witness an unexplained white flickering light near the foot of a mountain. It lasted for about ten seconds. The area is totally uninhabited, and it was in the early hours of the morning.

With Erling Strand, who heads up the Hessdalen Project, and a TV producer, I also spent long nights out in the utter wilderness of the Kimberley region of Western Australia. Strange lights were seen and photographed there too – transient, gleaming moments in endless hours of darkness broken only by the stars and visible galaxies of the southern sky. One sighting coincided with exceptional geomagnetic disturbance. Earth lights in Australia are

sometimes referred to as 'Min-Min' lights, as they were first recorded by settlers in the vicinity of the Min Min Hotel between Winton and Boulia in
western Queensland – though it is unclear whether the lights were named
after the hotel, or vice versa. I recall sitting out in a tiny and remote
Aboriginal encampment at twilight drinking tea from a tin cup listening to
my hosts telling about lights they had encountered in the bush. The
Aborigines believed that the lights were accompanied by invisible but incred-
ibly powerful spirits. One man showed me where he had been thrown as if
by invisible hands when a light had floated in and out of the surrounding
desert and hovered around the edge of the encampment. Again that 'poltergeist' effect. Another fellow said he had witnessed the incident.

Corpse Candles

This only confirmed what I was already at the time coming to appreciate –
ancient and traditional peoples thought of the lights in terms of spirits. In
Wales, this was manifested in the belief of the *canwyll corfe* (corpse candle),
which was viewed as being a harbinger of death. A description of a typical
corpse candle was given to author Alasdair MacGregor in Carmarthen by the
daughters of John Thomas, who had died in 1946. Thomas and a friend were
out for an evening walk when they saw a strange light travelling towards them
from the small village of Francis Well. 'It looked like a bright candle flame,
without the candle; and it kept on coming nearer and nearer to us,' Thomas
had told his daughters. 'It passed by us, on the other side of the hedge, just
where the footpath came up from the valley. It went on, hopping along a few
inches from the ground, and then vanished in the distance.'[21] Though the
event was remarkable in itself, it particularly stuck in Thomas's memory
because just three days later a funeral procession came up that very pathway
from Francis Well.

In similar vein, Margaret Lewis who saw a phantom funeral on a small
Welsh road near Dinas Mawddwy, saw a corpse candle on another occasion
when walking that same road. The light travelled between a cottage and an
outlying barn: two days later, Lewis maintained, a woman had died during
childbirth in the cottage, and her body had been rested in the barn prior to
the funeral. At the turn of the twentieth century, an old Welshwoman who
spoke no English told W.Y. Evans-Wentz about supernatural lights seen in
and around the small village of Nevern, in Preseli, south-west Wales. She
claimed that corpse candles appeared like 'a patch of light' usually about 'as
big as a pot', and were not a flame 'but a luminous mass'. A pale green one

was seen in Nevern just before the death of the local doctor.

But is all this just old folklore? Apparently not, if a 1991 incident in Nevern is anything to go by. In March that year, builder Paul Ladd was on his way home through the hamlet from his usual stop at the pub, when he was accosted by a light. It came up off the river when the builder was crossing the ancient bridge. He described it as being a little under three feet (90 cm) in diameter, and silver-grey in colour. 'It was like a torch with no beam, a shimmering, glowing thing, only about as tenth as bright as a streetlight.' As Ladd walked on, the light tagged along after him. It began to unnerve the man, and he lit a cigarette; as his match flared, the light shrank back, just like an animal would when confronted with a flame. Ladd walked on past the ancient church and then tried to hide in a hedge under a tree to get away from the thing which had started stalking him once more. 'It came into the tree then shot out again. Came in, shot out – this happened about eight times, then it just vanished.'

Paul Ladd is a straightforward working man, giving a palpably honest account, and was totally unaware of any history of corpse candles at Nevern. Sceptics could claim he was having a (rather pointless) lark after being in the pub, but in fact other residents of Nevern also saw a strange light that evening. One young woman told a local radio reporter that a hovering light had apparently tried to enter her house when she was saying goodnight to her boyfriend, but she managed to slam the door shut in time to prevent it doing so.

Spirit Lights

The lights were known of throughout Old Europe, and various cultural explanations were built around them. In Ireland, such lights were associated with the fairies. In Hungary, strange nocturnal lights were thought to be the *liderc*, or werewolf, out and about.[22] In mediaeval Switzerland, mysterious lights were considered to be ghosts.[23] In Dutch legend, the 'lights of the heath' (possibly marsh gas) were said to indicate buried treasure. In Lapland, the Saami saw lights flying through the night sky as the spirits of shamans going about their nocturnal business. In England, the lights had various associations: amongst other things, they could be fiery dragons, corpse-candles, fairies and 'hobb lanterns' – 'hobb' being one old term for a goblin. In some parts they were known as 'the Devil's eye' with obvious connotations. Sometimes, they were just a plain mystery: the nineteenth-century 'Peasant Poet', John Clare, admitted to being 'robbed . . . of the little philosophic reasoning I had about them' when he along with others saw unexplained lights moving back and forth over Eastwell Green and Deadmoor in Helpston, Cambridgeshire. He later had a particularly close encounter with a lightform 'of a mysterious terrific hue', and confessed to being 'frit'.

People made various sorts of 'spirit' associations with earth lights all around the world. To the Chinese Buddhists they were expressions of the *Dharma*, and within the precincts of a temple on the southernmost summit of the lights-haunted holy mountain of Wu Tai Shan they built a tower from which to observe the 'Bodhisattva Lights'. British Buddhist John Blofeld wrote of seeing from it 'fluffy balls of orange-coloured fire, moving through space, unhurried and majestic'.[24] In India, curious lights seen around Darjeeling were said to be the lanterns of the *chota-admis* (little men), while a temple was built on the sacred Purnagiri Mountain in northern India because lights were regularly seen there, and reported by Westerners in the 1930s. The phenomena were understood by local people to be ghostly votive lamps for the Goddess Bhagbatti. Lights seen around the Rajmahal Hills in Bengal are called *Bhutni*, a reference to goblins, or else are thought to be borne by ghosts.[25]

In Brazil, the earth light is known as *Mae de Ouro* (Mother of Gold), and is thought to lead to buried treasure – probably a concept brought over from Europe. In 1895, Sir George Maxwell, a government official at Tanjong Malim in Malyasia, had a close-up view of numerous 'fiery globes the size of a man's head' on the local sacred hill of Changkat Asah: the people there thought them to be the spectral heads of women who had died in childbirth.

Africa, too, has its spirit lights. In her *Travels in West Africa*, author Mary Kingsley tells of exploring Lake Ncovi in Gabon in 1895 where she saw a violet lightball 'the size of a small orange' coming out of a forest on the lakeside. It floated down to the sand beach where it hovered until joined by another light. They circled each other as Kingsley set off towards them in a canoe, but as she approached they split up, one light disappearing into foliage and the other floating off across the water. Kingsley followed that one and when she had almost caught up with it, it sank into the water. The writer could see it glowing as it descended. Local people later told her that such phenomena were *aku* or devil lights. The Azande of the Congo believed that weird nocturnal nights were magical phenomena produced by witch-doctors. In Togo, between Dahomey and Ghana on the Gulf of Guinea, mysterious moving lights are said by the Konkomba people to be sorcerers flying by night. They refer to them as 'sorcerer fire'.[26]

Perhaps a spectrum of mercurial luminous phenomena, 'earth lights' can in general be seen as quintessential 'land spirits'. They expose the rift in worldviews between the modern world and the former traditional peoples of the Earth: we have aliens, they had spirits; we have UFOs, they had flying sorcerers.

Comings and Goings

A smaller but distinctive category of landscape haunting concerns the apparitions of features in the witness's surroundings.

Spectral Houses

One of the classic cases of this kind is that of the woman who was visiting friends in the Camel villages near Cadbury Castle (see Chapter Five) in the 1920s. She was out walking alone when she saw a large house standing in a field. A man and a small boy came to the door and their old-fashioned dress intrigued her, so she walked towards them. Suddenly, the house and figures vanished before her eyes. She later mentioned the incident to her hostess who was puzzled by it for she had never heard of any house standing in that location. Later enquiries are said to have revealed references to a secret house built somewhere in the area centuries ago to house the young Henry II during troubled times.

Elliot O'Donnell collected a number of reports about such ghost houses: at the Penley crossroads near the Forest of Dean two witnesses saw a house and occupants that later disappeared, while in Chagford, Devon, there was a rumour that certain ghostly cottages manifested themselves every ten or twelve years. Theo Brown tells of a friend riding through Doccombe near Moretonhampstead on the edge of Dartmoor who fleetingly saw a large manor house behind an ordinary-looking fieldgate. Later research produced no evidence of there ever having been a building there.

A woman told Theo Brown of a curious experience she had one damp and misty November afternoon in 1939, when living at Start House near the village of Slapton, Devon. She and her sister were walking a small lane to Kingsbridge about five miles away when they saw a great manor house with arched doors set amidst trees. 'I knew the country so well, having walked there dozens of times, and I knew there was no house there,' the woman told Brown. 'Also it did not *look* real. It is difficult to explain, for although the house was perfect, yet it had no substance. That is the best description that I can give.'[27] The house gradually faded away after about five minutes. Interestingly, a completely independent report described a whole spectral landscape in the same immediate area – on the coast a few miles away near Churston Ferrers, Brixham. It happened just over 18 months earlier, in March, 1938, when a man walking on the cliff path climbed over a stile beyond which lay a vista of fields only to find himself almost falling over the edge of the cliff. The fields – and presumably the stile – had vanished.[28]

Other reported ghost buildings include a farmhouse in a village near Bridgnorth, Shropshire; two cottages in Wallington, Surrey; a Georgian house in (or not in) Bradfield St George, near Bury St Edmunds, Suffolk, and a mansion near a wood at Leigh-on-Sea in Essex, among numerous other examples.

It is perhaps too easy to dismiss these sightings as some bizarre kind of hallucination. From Norway comes apparent evidence that spectral buildings can be photographed. Photographer Lillian Lyngstad took a picture of a group of houses by a lakeside near Engan, in Nord-Trondelag, for use in a local newspaper. When it was published, astonished readers wrote in to say that one of the houses in the photograph had indeed stood there 90 years ago, but had long since been demolished. When Lyngstad went back to take several more photos she captured the same scene – except for the ghost house. On one of these subsequent photos, though, there was a smudge of colours where the house had been, as if it could not quite register on the film emulsion on this occasion.

Slips in Time?

A celebrated coming-and-going was a fairground seen by the writer Edith Oliver in the huge megalithic complex of Avebury in Wiltshire. On a rainy late afternoon in 1916 she saw coconut shies, swingboats, crowds of people and torches and flares amidst fairground booths. Because of failing light and the rain, she did not bother with it any further and left the area. It was some years later that she learned that though the Avebury fair had been an annual event, the last one had been held over half a century prior to the time she had seen the fairground. It seems that she also saw standing stones around which the fairground was situated that are no longer extant.

Another apparent 'time-slip' type of apparition was seen by Ingrid Johnson one evening shortly after the great storm that blasted Britain in 1987. Ingrid was driving along Ripe Lane towards the village of Ripe in West Sussex when her car stopped suddenly and all the lights went out. Unable to restart the engine immediately, she decided to leave it for a few minutes before trying again. While waiting she glanced across the road towards a hedgerow and farm gate and saw the figure of a German airman sitting on the top rung. She thought that there must be some filming going on in the area, but as she looked the man faded and disappeared. Intrigued, she got out of the car to look around for an explanation, only to realise that even the gate had vanished and in its place was a dense hedge. She later learned that other people had also seen the figure at the same spot, and it was assumed that he is the spectre of a German pilot who crashed in the field during World War II. But even if that was true, it does not explain the ghostly gate.[29]

A further 'time-slip' apparition in the same county occurred in the early 1930s when Mrs Stevie Hobbs was four years old. She had been taken by her foster mother to the Devil's Dyke, a dry valley beneath an Iron Age hillfort, just north of Brighton. The young Stevie asked her mother what had happened to 'the train on a rope', because it had been there when she had visited the site earlier with someone else, but now it was nowhere to be seen. The foster mother told Stevie not to be silly, but many years later Mrs Hobbs came across a book that gave the history of the area and documented a cable car that had been in operation at the site from 1894 to 1909, when it was dismantled because it was no longer financially viable.[30]

CHAPTER TEN

WHITE LADY AND BLACK MONK

THE WHITE LADY type of apparition is one of the most ubiquitous landscape spirits in the literature. A typical instance of it is illustrated by the White Lady of Castle Gresley, Derbyshire, who is a ghostly woman dressed in white who supposedly occasionally appears in a wooded area on the outskirts of the village. The apparition's haunt is close to a reservoir which is supplied by a spring near the spot where it is said a woman was drowned many years ago. The name of the pool is White Lady Springs. Folklorist David Clarke points out that this begs the question of whether the story arose as a result of the curious name itself, or whether the spring was so named because of the female apparition that haunted it. 'What is not in doubt is the connection between this kind of ghost and liminal places in the landscape such as rivers and springs especially where waters meet and merge and at bridges and fords which symbolize boundaries between life and death,' Clarke further comments.[1]

Folklore or Fact?

As with so much of what I was learning in perusing and collecting reports, the White Lady apparition sometimes retreats into pure folklore, yet at other times comes forward to present reportedly direct encounters with modern people. Two Welsh instances illustrate the dichotomy. Every county of Wales has several haunts of the White Lady, or *Ladi Wen*. Mythically, she is probably the vestige of a pagan goddess, but in folklore there are stories to explain her appearance. So, for example, when people as late as 1863 were still claiming to see a spectral but elegant white lady haunting a particular spot near the village of St Athan in the Vale of Glamorgan, the story was that that was where she had been buried alive many years before by her enraged husband who wrongly thought she had been unfaithful to him.[2]

But *Ladi Wen* can become more than mere folklore. Amateur folklorist and archaeological researcher Dewi Bowen happened to overhear a young surfer, 'C.P.', telling some friends in a pub about a frightening encounter he had undergone early in the morning when he had been driving to catch the 'Atlantic roll' at Rhossili Bay at the end of the Gower Peninsula on the coast of South Wales near Swansea. The young surfer had been on his way to the beach through the village of Llangennith shortly after 6.30 a.m. He was driving as quietly as possible so as not to disturb the villagers, when, cresting a hill, he almost hit a mysterious young woman who seemed to be covered from head to foot in diaphanous white material. She was apparently oblivious of C.P. and he lost sight of her.[3] C.P. did not know it but Bowen did – where the surfer had seen the lady in white was on a stretch of road close by an ancient holy well. Celtic holy wells are associated with saints, most often female, who are as a rule Christianised versions of Celtic deities, themselves probably anthropomorphisations of earlier spirits of place. Moreover, as Bowen was aware, the Gower Peninsula (and Glamorgan in general) is particularly well endowed with *Ladi Wen* traditions.

Similar sightings have been reported on the B4068 road near the Cotswold village of Naunton in Gloucestershire. Around 10.00 p.m. on 26 August 1998, hospital anaesthetist Guy Routh was driving along the road when his headlights illuminated a woman in a cream-coloured dress standing on the verge. He slowed in case she was in trouble, and she smiled at him and gave a slight wave. He stopped to make sure she was all right, but she had vanished when he looked back. A smell of wood smoke suddenly filled his car, and he got out to find the smell was not perceptible outside. He looked around for the woman in the pale dress, but she was nowhere in sight. 'There were just two trees and a field,' he said. 'There was nowhere she could have been hiding.' He insisted that he was not at all tired at the time nor had he been drinking.

On another late evening, this time in April 2000, a security guard was driving to work on the same stretch of road. 'A figure all in white appeared in front of the car out of nowhere,' he reported. 'It looked like a monk and was six feet tall.' Too late to brake, the man drove right through the figure. When he stopped and went to look, there was nothing to be seen. He reported the incident to the police. Another report on that stretch of road described a car stopping inexplicably, and its occupants feeling as if water was seeping up over their feet, though there was nothing to be seen.[4]

When I read these reports, I was put in mind of the variable appearance of the pale ghost of the A23 (above) which also took on many forms, from a woman in a pale trenchcoat to a cricketer and shirt-sleeved men. Again I could not resist the notion that it was almost as if the appearances of the ghosts were variable presentations based on some basic blueprint or *idea* of a figure (see Chapter Twelve).

Like Black Dogs, White Lady ghosts can be of many colours, though when not white, grey, black and green predominate. Here is a previously unpublished account of the grey variety. One October weekend in 2000, Claudia Copestake was staying over with friends at the village of Cranham, near Painswick, Gloucestershire. On the Saturday night, after having 'stuffed our faces full of food' the group of friends decided to go for a walk around the village. It was about 9.00 p.m., and very dark, but they had two flashlights with them. After about half an hour into their excursion, over fields and hedges, and along dirt tracks, they found what seemed to be a bridleway. As they set out along it, one of the two torches ran low on battery power, and with only one decent beam of light it was difficult to see where they were walking. Claudia and a friend were in the lead when the ground suddenly gave way, and both fell into a deep hole. Claudia was dragged out by the others, but the friend lay injured at the bottom of the hole:

It just so happened the treacherous hole was adjacent to a cottage, with large iron gates. We looked up, and saw the hazy silhouette of a figure standing just behind the iron gates staring directly at us, so Bryony shouted to the figure: 'Can you help us please? My friend has fallen down this hole and we can't get him out!' At that point, the person in the hole screamed in pain, so we attended to him . . . We looked back to see if the person was still there . . . but the figure had disappeared. We looked around the area . . . hoping to find the person, because we were in serious need of help . . . our friend's head was now bleeding quite severely, and he kept passing out. We gave up . . . and concentrated on getting the trapped person out, and finding the way back home, in the pitch black . . .

Once we had got home safely, we dressed our friend's wounds, and he was fine in no time . . . The next morning we informed the father of the girl we were staying with of the previous night's events, and told him of the figure that had just walked away when we asked for help. The dad started asking lots of questions about the figure we had seen. Was it male or female? Where was it? Did we see its face? Because it was dark, we couldn't really come up with any detailed answers, we weren't able to tell the gender of the figure, because it was too dark. The father simply said 'Oh, you must have seen the Grey Lady of Cranham' . . . it all made sense now – when the figure suddenly disappeared and didn't show any sign of emotion or even movement when we shouted for help. We were all quite shocked, and a bit chilled, to think that we had been so close to a ghost, and that we had even talked to it! At the time we just thought it was a rude neighbour![5]

Though most white and grey lady spectres are hazy, vaguely anthropomorphic forms that are assumed to be female figures, some seemingly take on a distinct appearance. This was the case in July, 1956, when a Mr Stocker was acting as wireless operator in a Land Rover during a Territorial Army summer camp on the Otterburn military ranges in Northumberland. Stocker was sitting in the front passenger seat, with the driver as his sole companion. It was an overcast day and they were travelling through open moorland on a single-track road. As they crossed a bridge and ascended a slight hill, Stocker saw 'what looked like an elderly woman dressed in a long, grey coat and a shawl'. She was standing on a sandy area on the lefthand side of the road beneath a hawthorn tree. After they passed her, Stocker glanced in one of the vehicle's rearview mirrors, but now could see no one beneath the thorn tree. He told the driver he had seen an old woman, and the driver confirmed that he, too, had seen her. They went back, but there was nobody visible anywhere on the open moor around, and there were no footprints in the sandy ground at the spot.[6]

It is easy to see this roadside apparition as a witch-like figure, especially given its location alongside a lone thorn tree. Mythically speaking, this would be the 'hag' aspect of the land goddess (who has a triple form: virgin, mother, hag), if the category of 'Lady' spectres relate to that. But can myths be seen standing by the road in broad daylight?

The Hooded Ones

The Black Dog and the White Lady are two of the most prominent forms of landscape spirit as reported in relatively modern times, but there is a third type – the Black Monk. He, too, can be white or grey as well as black. (In cases like those on the B40681 near Naunton, above, the 'White Lady' and a white monk apparition seem to have become blended.) 'Black Monk' reports come in a variety of related forms, as a brief, representative sample can illustrate.

Near Spy Lane on the main road in Loxwood, West Sussex, motorists occasionally report seeing a figure 'resembling a black monk'. It sometimes walks into oncoming traffic and then promptly vanishes. Local explanations range from the spirit belonging to a monastery that once stood nearby, or of it being the ghost of a member of the Cokelers sect that once lived in the village.[7] A caped figure is sometimes seen gliding rapidly along the side of the A1 road between Scotch Corner and Boroughbridge in Yorkshire. A dull glow about it is sometimes noted. A ghostly procession of monks is said to periodically haunt the valley between Hartland Abbey and the ancient church at Stoke in north Devon.

An 1872 sighting of another spectral procession of monks was reported near Buckfast Abbey, also in Devon. The monks wore a habit of 'either white or grey' according to the witness, and walked in Indian file amongst some bushes before dissolving from view. Theo Brown remarks that monks returned to Buckfast Abbey only in 1882, and they were Benedictines who wear black. Before them, in the early twelfth century, there were Savigny Monks, known as the 'Grey Friars' because of the colour of their robes, and following them, in 1148, came Cistercians, who wear white. After the Dissolution in the sixteenth century there were no monks at Buckfast until the arrival of the Benedictines.[8]

Haunts of the Cucullati

The Cotswolds, a north-south escarpment of honey-gold limestone containing many picturesque 'Olde English' villages and towns and extending east-west between Oxford and Gloucester, seems to be an area especially prone to monk-like ghosts. Among the examples from the region are the occasional sightings made of spectral monks in the aptly-named Cowl Lane near the Abbey in the ancient town of Winchcombe, Gloucestershire. One report was submitted in 1993 by a man who had been walking past the side entrance to the Abbey a little before midnight and noticed a figure walking in front of him in 'a long robe and flat type of hat'. The witness glanced at the ground momentarily, but on looking up the figure had vanished.[9] Other Cowl Lane reports sometimes mention that the legs of the ghosts cannot be seen, giving the appearance that they are floating or else walking on a surface lower than the modern one.

Another lane in Winchcombe, The Monk's Walk, has also been associated with monk-like ghosts: one witness on his way home one summer's night felt a sudden, cold breeze spring up, and a hooded figure appeared from nowhere walking down the lane towards him.[10] Monkish ghosts have also been reported on roads immediately around and about Winchcombe, including a smiling one near Postlip Hall, where apparently there used to be a chapel in mediaeval times. Another habit-haunted place in the region is the town of Tewkesbury, whose origins go back to Roman times. A spectral monk in a black habit has been seen by numerous witnesses in and around the ancient Abbey there. One of the star spooks in the much-haunted Prestbury a dozen miles to the south is a 'Black Abbott'. He has appeared in the churchyard on numerous occasions, and a former vicar recalled once seeing a monk sitting on a tombstone and, intrigued, went over to talk to him but he 'faded slowly away in front of my eyes'.[11] The Black Abbott has also been seen in Mill Street.

Yet again, like the other categories of landscape spirits, the monk-like apparitions seem to slip between a generalised folklore and reported specific incidents. A previously unpublished and commendably detailed account concerning an actual experience is given below in the words of the witness herself. It is given almost in full, as such detail is fairly rare in the ghost report literature. The witness is Paula Copestake (the mother of Claudia, who had the 'Grey Lady' encounter, above) and the place was the Neolithic long barrow of Belas Knap, an isolated site in the Cotswolds barely two miles south of Winchcombe. Mrs Copestake, her husband Philip, and eight-year-old son Edward were visiting the site on a crisp, clear afternoon in early February, 1998. While Mr Copestake was busying himself taking photographs of the forecourt area of the long barrow, Paula Copestake climbed to the top of the mound in order to take in the panoramic view and to enjoy the solitude. She was therefore disappointed to see a group of people moving towards the site from the northwest, across an adjacent field.

I told my husband to hurry up with his activities before they could reach us. At first sight there seemed to be about five people, one smaller in front and the others in two pairs, walking quickly towards Belas Knap along the field boundary which forms part of the Cotswold Way. They faced forwards and were all dressed alike in dark, greyish-black clothes with pale, oval, translucent faces beneath pointed hoods. They were only a few hundred yards away and I initially thought perhaps they were a family group or a group of friends on a walk.

I was distracted by my son and when I looked back again I was startled by the emergence of more figures in the group. I told my husband that 'hundreds' of people were coming and I impatiently again urged him to hurry because there seemed at least a dozen people walking purposefully towards where we stood. They seemed to emerge from the dark shadows of the overhanging evergreen trees and bushes along the boundary between the two nearby fields. (I told myself they must all be ramblers wearing green waxed jackets with their hoods up because I thought that at a distance dark green could easily be mistaken for dark greyish black.) Every figure was hooded and they still followed the smaller figure at the front. I assumed that he must have been a child of about 12 because he was half the height of the others. I could not see any part of their bodies below knee level so I thought they must be walking through long pale dead grass that obscured their lower limbs. They walked closely along the hedge-line in silence, never turning to their companions but all walking at a vigorous pace, so I was surprised on looking for a second time to see that they appeared to be in the same position as before in the field. They did not appear to have made any progress in reaching the long barrow, despite their fairly rapid pace . . . They appeared to walk down a slope and up again as if going down into a ditch and up the other side. This was my second visit to Belas Knap and I didn't recall seeing a ditch before but I accounted for this by [assuming] that I was previously mistaken and reasoned that there must have been a fairly deep dip in the land to account for their partial disappearance and re-emergence.

I was annoyed that so many people were coming to disturb our peace and so with a third and final look at them, I then deliberately turned my back and walked to the other end of the mound. Disturbingly, they had seemed to be even further away than ever although still moving as purposefully towards us. I felt exposed silhouetted against the skyline in full view of so many people and so I joined my son who was exploring the side chambers of the barrow.

Finishing his activities in the barrow forecourt, my husband Philip had meanwhile climbed to the top of the barrow and was surprised to see no one at all. We all sat inside the side burial chamber facing the direction in which I had seen the walkers but no one ever arrived or crossed the ploughed field in front of us. I felt extremely uneasy inside the chamber, like an intruder, a violator of something esoteric, private and precious, and that we shouldn't have been there. I felt that some ill fortune might befall us if we didn't leave quickly, but, strangely, I forgot totally about the hooded figures until we reached the car.

In the days that followed, I repeatedly awoke early with flashbacks. It was like seeing a film being replayed back, frame by frame, accompanied by every split second thought that I'd had with each image. There were anomalies in what I had seen that my rational brain had tried to explain away, but the images did not fit my explanations somehow. Something felt wrong and so to satisfy my own curiosity, we revisited the site some three weeks later. Despite my husband's assurances to the contrary, I could not accept that I had seen something supernatural. We re-enacted everything we had said or done initially on our previous visit and established that my sightings had taken place within two to three minutes. From his elevated viewpoint, Philip should have been able to see anyone walking in the landscape. But what convinced me above all was the change in the topography of the landscape itself. The green overhanging canopy was gone. The field boundary was different to my previous memory of it, there were now far fewer trees and the stone wall was more exposed and dominant. Even the line of the boundary wall looked subtly altered. The long grass and large ditch were not there and the present path was much wider, flatter and further away from the edge of the field. There was also only a faint undulation in the ploughed field close to where I had seen the figures sink down into the now vanished slope. As we watched a young couple approach us along the present-day path from the same direction as the hooded figures, I finally accepted that I had witnessed a scene not of this time.[12]

Philip Copestake, a geologist by profession, speeded up his activities on being informed by Paula that some people were quickly approaching the barrow. He was not able to look in the direction that they were said to be approaching from due to the presence of undergrowth at the front of the barrow. 'I was surprised, on climbing to the top of the barrow, that no one was visible,' Philip said. ' I immediately thought that the walkers must have passed by the barrow without stopping to view it – unusual as it is a major point of interest on the Cotswold Way. However, on looking in all directions from the elevated position at the top of the barrow there was no one in sight in any direction, neither was there enough time for the people to pass out of view into the distance. Our son had seen nothing at all during this time, however, he had been busy investigating the side chambers of the tomb.'

This is clearly one of those sightings in which ghostly figures along with spectral landscape features appear superimposed on the present-day scene, and seems to have been a 'time-slip' type of apparition.[13] I was particularly intrigued by Paula's curious but potentially valuable observation that the figures did not seem to be making headway through space, despite apparently walking ahead vigorously: I suspect there is a significant clue here.

Over and above such theoretical considerations, this case, as with all the other 'black monk' type of reports, puzzled me. Why should ancient monks have left such an impression on the ether or whatever-it-is so that their spectres should be perceptible so many centuries after their passing? After all, a great many other people, farm workers and visitors, must have been active around Belas Knap over the centuries, not to mention the people who built and used the place as a temple of the ancestors.

I got what may be the first glimmerings of an answer (although one that begs greater questions) when I escaped from the rain one afternoon by ducking inside the museum in the Cotswold town of Cirencester. It is full of

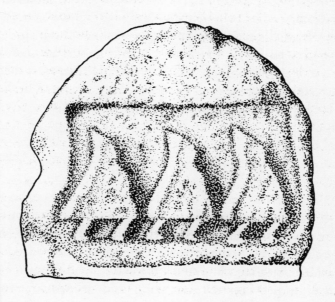

FIGURE 22: Romano-British stone relief showing the *Genii Cucullati*. Corinium Museum, Cirencester. (Drawing: Eileen Aldworth)

archaeological finds made in the region. As I sauntered through a room displaying Roman remains, my attention was drawn to a semi-circular slab of rock about 1 foot across that had three hooded figures carved in relief on it. They were striding purposefully from left to right. Hooded figures? What did they represent? It turned out they were Romano-British depictions of *Genii Cucullati*, 'hooded spirits'. These were cult images that appeared in locations

around Europe, where they appear as single individuals, and seemed to relate
to some pagan tradition. In Britain, they tended to be depicted in triple form,
revealing a Celtic gloss. The two main centres of distribution were around
Hadrian's Wall in northern England and the Cotswolds.

'The cult of the Genii Cucullati appears to have embraced profound and
sophisticated belief systems,' Celtic scholar Miranda Green has written.[14]
Hilda Ellis Davidson unequivocally designates them as land spirits. She notes
that 'belief in them evidently flourished among the Celtic people of Britain
. . . Such traditions did not wholly die after the coming of Christianity'.[15]
Elsewhere, she remarks that the images of these hooded figures 'leave an
impression of inevitability and supernatural power'.[16]

As I gazed at the small stone relief carving in front of me, I wondered if it
was possible – if I dare even think it – that the supposed monkish spectres
seen by people today were actually much older wraiths, these *Genii Cucullati?*
Perhaps we were seeing the phantoms as figures we could explain, mediaeval
monks, when they were in fact something far more archaic? Had the
Cotswolds become a centre of the cult because people there saw them particularly often, as seems to be the case to this day? My guess was that the hooded
spirits were simply part of the haunted land.

I FELT THOROUGHLY confused by the time I finished my enquiries into road
ghosts and all the other land spirits of one kind and another. The data consisted of primarily anecdotal material (except for my sightings, of course),
which does not make good science, for scholars always view anecdote with a
measure of disdain, kicking it into touch as folklore. There was some wisdom
in this: as I had learned from my forays into 'ufology' people's observations
simply cannot always be taken at face value. Yet many of these reports seemed
to be sincere, and, much more importantly, an underlying sense of cohesion
seemed to underpin them. There were recurring details, and many of the
apparitions were nonsensical fragments like the disconnected scenes of a
dream, not the sort of thing people invent just for pointless mischief.
Furthermore, I had personally witnessed ghostly or anomalous phenomena.
Something is being seen. Yet, nevertheless, I had a gnawing feeling that we
weren't dealing exactly with black monks or dogs, white, grey or green ladies,
cavaliers and roundheads, or 'mint condition' black cars. So what was it
exactly that was haunting the land?

I had another trip to America coming up, during which I hoped to be able to search for ancient shamanic rock art depicting spirit footprints that I had heard rumours about. I promised myself that during the fieldwork I would find some spot sufficiently atmospheric where I could sit down and ponder the deeper mysteries of the haunted land . . .

PART FIVE

SEEKING SOLUTIONS

CHAPTER ELEVEN

BETWEEN A ROCK
AND A HARD PLACE

A S I GAZED out over the urban sprawl of Albuquerque I saw it as symbolic of the way in which our culture is eclipsing all former knowledge, for it looked like an encroaching tide eating hungrily away at the foot of West Mesa, and it made me understand why I felt a sense of urgency in trying to make a coherent picture – a snapshot at least – of the ancient and virtually universal idea of a haunted land . . .

I had learned that the haunted land was an extremely deep-rooted concept and had taken numerous forms in various cultures and ages. The common denominator was that everyone in the world before our modern culture emerged three centuries or so ago believed spectral entities shared the land with them. People saw, feared and learned how to control the great company of spirits who roamed the landscape, a company that included ancestral spirits, ghosts of the recent dead, the out-of-body spirits of shamans, witches and sorcerers, deities and the mercurial spectral forms of elemental sprites.

Could this all be nothing but superstition? Much of it was just that, I felt sure, yet I had the sense it was based on something fundamental in the human mind on the one hand, and perhaps something unsuspected in our relationship to our surroundings on the other. After all, we still lived in a haunted land today, for members of my own culture report the seeing of spirits in the landscape, and there seemed to be an overall internal consistency in the body of that recorded testimony. Have we, as a culture, missed something? Have we had a blind spot in our worldview?

The View from the West Mesa

I sat down on a low rock perched on the edge of West Mesa from where I was still afforded a view of the roads and buildings stretching away across the desert below. I felt myself to be on the boundary between two worlds: behind me the rock carvings and ghost paths of archaic American Indians, before me the spreading tentacles of today's hi-tech world. This place fitted what I had in mind when promising myself a few hour's contemplation on the puzzles my inquiries into the haunted land had presented me with.

I was pretty sure that the historical record of the haunted land had different sources, and the picture was muddied with superstitions, folk tales and a wide range of rote belief systems. I had visited shamanic landscapes that physically mapped out the unseen contours of an invisible dimension of the land, had traced the routes of all manner of spirits and souls through the physical environments of numerous countries, and I had explored the folk beliefs of many peoples. However, it seemed that shamanism was the first human spiritual system to have left a physical trace of what was perceived as a spirit geography. It was the old shamans who could see the realm of the ancestors, and visit it in ecstasy, in trance. In the shamanic worldview, the supernatural otherworld was considered to interact with the physical surroundings.

At the core of all this, I wondered, did the shamans, those strange, lonely figures in the first watchtowers of the supernatural, experience phenomena that were in some sense or other objective? The answer had to be 'yes' if it was to be accepted that modern people were also witnessing phantoms in the landscape. I decided from the evidence I had collected and my own experiences that at least some apparitions were genuine phenomena of some kind. The tough question was, of what kind? As no one else had been able to explain this I hardly expected to come up with the solutions myself, but as my study of the history of the haunted land was effectively at an end as a project in itself, I figured that it was perhaps worth following a few lines of thought about the implications of ghosts and haunting to see where they led in order to get an idea of where future research should head.

Getting in the Spirit

There tends to be two prevailing, highly polarised views about ghosts: either they are spirits of the dead, or that accounts of them result from a mix of hallucination, misperception and hoax. My sense was that there could be some truth in both positions, but that neither fully described the true situation.

Taking the basic 'spirit model', that apparitions are the ghosts of the dead, was the easy option because at first glance it seems the most persuasive approach, apparently explaining most of the manifestations of haunting. Many people can think of some anecdote that seems to bear it out, as I could myself. I recalled the nurse who with a colleague saw the ghost of a young man in the corner of the ward while his corpse, still warm, lay on the bed.

More specifically, because I knew it to be certainly the truth, I remembered an experience my brother, Michael, had told me about. A woodworker, he had been restoring oak panelling in an old house in our home village in the English Midlands. As the owner of the house had given him the key to go in and get on with the work, Mike had locked himself in the house while he worked on the panelling. Suddenly, a voice behind him said, 'You're doing a really fine job there.' Mike turned round to see an elderly gentlemen admiring the panels. 'Thanks – I do my best,' Mike had smilingly replied, and returned to his task. Then he suddenly realised he had locked himself in the room: how had the old fellow got in? My brother turned round again but there was nobody there. The man had seemed perfectly solid, the only unusual thing about him that Mike had noticed was that he was wearing slightly old-fashioned clothes. Later, when he returned the key, Mike told the houseowner about the mysterious old man. 'Oh, we've seen him around the place, too – we call him Fred,' the man laughed. 'We don't bother about him – he's harmless.' It was assumed he must have been some previous owner.

In many ways, this was a classic ghost encounter, but there are problems. What about the old-fashioned clothes? Since when did clothes have a soul that could survive death? The stock answer from those who believe in the spirit model is that the dress of a ghost is the product of thought-forms. But whose thought-forms – the witness's, or the ghost's? And if clothing can be a thought-form, what about the appearance of the ghost itself? The problem extends further. My phantom mini-pickup truck, for example: the apparition was just of a vehicle. There was no driver. And what about all the other phantom trucks and automobiles, or the spectral stagecoaches and carts? Do vehicles have souls? And what about the ghost houses, or the gate on which the phantom German airman sat (see Chapter Nine)? It was clear to me that all was not so neat, tidy and straightforward as first appears with even this most basic and popular of haunting explanations.

Play It Again

Another idea is that some apparitions are not actually spirits, but kinds of recording or place-memory images, replaying some habitual or emotion-charged action time and again until their energy is all used up. But on what medium is the recording imprinted, and how or why is it accessed?[1] And why should only a relatively few habitual or emotion-charged actions from the whole history of human activity at a particular place replay themselves? Such a theory does not in any case account for the apparitions of objects and scenes.

An associated explanation for some apparitions is that they are less emotionally-charged time-slip phenomena. Just for a few passing moments, someone in this time for unknown reasons obtains a glimpse of a person, object or scene of some other time. There were accounts I noted in the record that seemed to fit this pattern, especially the ghost houses, spectral landscapes, and phantoms in old-fashioned dress, particularly when they seem to be walking on an earlier ground level. But is it 'only' past time that is involved? Some of the possible time-slip instances, such as my brother's experience, or Clay's sighting of a Bronze Age horseman, involved apparent interaction with the witness. If the subject that is the apparition in this time is in turn seeing an apparition of the witness in his or her time, then that would mean future ghosts are possible – an idea briefly toyed with in the film *The Man Who Fell to Earth*, starring David Bowie. Yet we don't seem to see those; it had struck me in going through the literature and hearing people's accounts that as far as one could tell there didn't seem to be future ghosts, just past ones.

This brings up another question: what is the 'half-life' of a ghost? In private discussion, historian and folklorist Jeremy Harte had pointed out to me that accounts of ghosts of people from a period of history previous to that of the witness are not found in the record before about 1680, and came into being slowly over the following two centuries. 'For instance, nobody saw the ghosts of Roman soldiers in Dorset until the arrival of mass education taught the public that there had been such things as Roman soldiers, and then they started popping up all over the place,' he had remarked. Most ghosts seen in mediaeval times were those of recently-dead persons known to the witness, or monstrous spirits and demons. (Spectral buildings such as castles were, however, reported occasionally in the mediaeval era.) Ghosts seen today appear from their dress to date any time from the modern era up to 500 years or so ago – unless, like R.C.C. Clay, the witness is a prehistorian. So we have a lot of cavaliers and roundheads or Elizabethan ladies in England, or all-purpose monks and white and grey ladies. Most of these spectres seem to be going about, or repeating, their business in their own time like a film loop. They are disengaged from us, unlike the mediaeval ghost that still held a personal significance for the witness. Harte commented to me that reports of this type of simply observed, impersonal apparition have existed probably only as long as there have been movies.

The implications of this are that ghosts are only able to appear in a form that is accessible to the information held in the mind of the witness. This hits the idea of ghosts being place-memory images pretty firmly on the head, as it does the notion of them being time-lapse phenomena. I had to admit it begs the question whether ghosts are simply hallucinations, after misperceptions and hoaxes are taken out of the equation, as sceptics maintain.

All in the Mind

The dictionary definition of a hallucination is that it is a sensory perception (using any or all of the visual, auditory, tactile or other modalities) with all the compelling attributes of normal perceptions of the objectively real world but without the normal physical stimuli. (Technically, a hallucination is only that if the person experiencing it thinks it is real; if the person knows it to be of a hallucinatory nature than it is called a 'pseudo-hallucination'.) Hallucinations tell us that the brain can conjure up the likeness, the verisimilitude, of what we take to be physical reality. It is rarely realised that our normal, everyday experience of reality is conjured by similar brain processes – we never know what the external world is truly like, because we never directly experience it.

The limited amount we perceive of the vast flux of energies that constitutes what we consider as being 'out there' comes to us through the doorways of our senses – light through the eyes, soundwaves through the ears, and so forth. Whatever the energies are that strike our retinas, ear drums and nerve endings, they are not what we consciously perceive because those external energies are changed, *transduced*, at the sensory doorways into electro-chemical impulses or signals that zip though nerve circuitry to their designated parts of the brain. There, a process that is not yet understood, assembles and transforms them into a show that lights up our minds – the cognitive auditorium within our skulls known by specialists as the *sensorium*. It is here that the miracle of consciousness and perception takes place every millisecond of our waking lives. When we go to sleep or enter a trance, the same 'stagehands' in our brain put on another show for us, so our sensorium flickers with dreams and visions, some of them as indistinguishably 'real' as the data assembled from the signals coming via our physical senses. So whether awake, asleep or entranced we perceive only hallucinations – or, more accurately, displays within the sensorium produced by similar brain mechanisms. Seen in this way, our perceptions of reality are as much a mental product as any vision.

According to researchers like Celia Green and Charles McCreery ghosts are 'metachoric hallucinations'.[2] They point out that apparitions can graft themselves onto a person's perceived environment, as in the cases when parts of non-physical landscapes suddenly appear in front of a witness, or the hallucination of a figure and some object in its vicinity is patched into the actually-seen scenery, as with the German airman sitting on a gate. Hallucinatory imagery can also briefly entirely replace a person's perceived surroundings. Green and McCreery described one case in which a man working at his office desk suddenly found himself in a room at his home; he seemed perfectly awake and normal, and the surroundings seemed as real as his office. Within a few moments, he was 'back' at his desk.[3] In another case, the witness looked out of a college window where the red brick buildings, normally, visible had disappeared to be replaced by large rhododendron bushes of apparent complete solidity. Out of them bounded 'the biggest black dog I'd ever really seen, very fierce with a small piece of either chain or leather attached to its neck'.[4] If the whole scene had not changed, then the hallucination would have been identical to a Black Dog apparition.

The idea of metachoric hallucinations might appear to stretch credibility, but we do know the human brain can indeed create effects of this kind. Psychiatrist Morton Schatzman, for example, had a patient, Ruth, who was troubled by the apparition of her father. She could see him and talk with him as if he were really there, even though he was invisible to others who were present. Eventually, she learned how to control these appearances. Schatzman, who wrote a book on his patient (*The Story of Ruth*, 1980), recorded the EEG patterns from Ruth's visual cortex in response to standard visual test stimuli. Ruth was able to alter these recordings by producing an apparition that acted like a real person intervening between her and the visual stimuli. Further tests confirmed that the apparition did not originate in Ruth's retinas. Commenting on these experiments, neuropsychological researchers Laughlin, McManus and d'Aquili remark:

> It would appear that Ruth is now able to construct, probably largely within the cortex, the hallucinated alterations of perceptions she desires . . . This ability is not unlike the demands of certain visualization practices that form the heart of Tibetan tantric yoga.[5]

Hallucination Triggers

Apart from mental illness, hallucinations can be triggered by a great variety of mental and physiological conditions, ranging from meditational and yogic states and drug visions to spontaneous trances that can occur when a person is fatigued or stressed, falling asleep or waking up from sleep, food or sleep deprived, having an allergic response to something (even – or perhaps especially – electro-magnetic fields), and so forth.

One curious mind-change condition called sleep paralysis can occur while someone is sleeping. Typically, the person awakes to find themselves temporarily paralysed and aware of a being standing over them or pressing down on them. In mediaeval times this was known as the incubus or succubus phenomenon, and was considered to be a visitation by an impure, sexual demon. The apparitions experienced in the sleep paralysis state are notoriously vivid and real, with the senses of touch and even smell often being involved.[6] People experience these phenomena today just as much as in mediaeval times, and certain types of apparition seem to recur, to judge by the accounts I had read on an Internet list dealing with experiences associated with sleep paralysis.

One such apparition is a hooded figure. Danielle described one of her sleep paralysis 'visitors' as being a man under five feet in height: 'He looked like a gnome and was wearing a striped green robe and as I looked at him he pulled off his mask and I don't remember what his face looked like . . . I have [also] seen a man in a white glowing robe, with a hood. He is usually positioned at the foot of my bed . . . when I tried to take his mask off he had a black face.' Vicki, a 'happily married attorney', saw 'a short, little evil monk . . . dressed in a coarse, maroon robe tied around his waist with a rope. The hood was pulled up over his head and down over his face. I couldn't see his face, it was total darkness.' Julilla, on the other hand, was visited by a hooded figure who 'just wears black'.

Environmental hallucination triggers might also be implicated in people who are suitably neurophysiologically 'primed', for whatever reason. One fairly common environmental effect is 'road hypnosis' which is particularly potent during long car journeys at night when the focus of a driver's attention on the pool of light cast by the headlights on a forever oncoming road can induce light trance states. A recently discovered environmental effect in cases of haunting is infrasonic sound. Engineer Vic Tandy has found that reported hauntings in two places, a factory and a fourteenth-century cellar, could be put down to the neurophysiological effects created in susceptible witnesses by a prevailing low-frequency sound in the environment, specifically around 19

Hertz (cycles per minute) in the cases investigated.[7] Such sounds can be produced by a wide range of sources, such as faulty machinery or even the wind blowing within certain confined places. While Tandy's work has involved interior locations, there is no reason why outdoor locales cannot also at times be subjected to infrasound – perhaps from roaring water, wind and other natural sources.

More bizarrely, certain places develop a reputation for inducing weird experiences – a coastal rock outcrop on the Scottish island of Islay in one example, and Hound Tor on Dartmoor in Devon is another. The reasons why such places should have these effects is unknown, but there could possibly be geophysical explanations, such as the rocks being particularly radioactive or magnetic (see Chapter One). I had thought that a specific geophysical explanation might be a candidate for certain road ghosts because of findings I made in 1980.[8]

During a period of a few weeks when intensive work was going on at the Rollright stone circle near Oxford, I had three people independently report seeing apparitions on 100-yard stretch of the county road that passes close by the monument. One witness, now a county archaeologist, saw a huge dog with short, dark grey hair pass alongside his parked van before vanishing; another, a now retired Oxford University surveyor, saw a car with two people in it approaching as he left the monument to go to his own car parked by the roadside. He turned his eyes away for a brief moment to unlock his car, and on looking up found the oncoming vehicle had disappeared without trace. There was nowhere it could have turned off. In a third instance, a woman reported the brief apparition of a traditional gypsy caravan moving along the road. What I knew but these witnesses did not, was that the stretch of road in question, and that stretch alone, exhibited a high level of natural radioactivity (presumably due to energetic rocks such as granite in the road's foundation). Radiation levels on that piece of road were three times higher than the ambient background level, or levels elsewhere along the road.

Armed with this knowledge, I had taken a radiation monitoring instrument to check out two other sites that had come up in my research into modern road ghost accounts – the B4068 near Naunton in Gloucestershire (see Chapter Ten), and the haunted Nunney-Frome road in Somerset (see below). In the Naunton case, one witness, Guy Routh, was able to show me the exact spot where the roadside apparition he saw had stood, so I was able to undertake precisely located radiation readings. There was nothing unusual in radiation terms about the spot, nor the point along the road where the witness had first seen the spectral woman up ahead. This was also true for a spot radiation check I conducted on the Nunney-Frome road, though, of course, this may not have been one of the precise locations where witnesses had seen the road ghost. There were no clear-cut patterns in terms of radioactivity. Nevertheless, I still felt that if the research resources could be mustered it would be good for detailed radiation (and magnetic anomaly) checks to be made on all roads associated with recurring road ghost reports in case there is a geophysical element involved in at least some apparition appearances, which, on the strength of the Rollright road example, there seems to be.

Place-related

While the ability of the human brain to hallucinate exceedingly real-looking apparitions is beyond doubt, and that they could likely be provoked by physiological or environmental factors (or the two combined), there are aspects of the haunting phenomenon that remain unexplained by the hallucination model. For instance, while hallucinations may well be what many road ghosts are, why should people have hallucinations of such similar kinds on specific lengths of road? The nub of the puzzle is that ghosts are *place-related* hallucinations.

In a brilliant study of over 70 haunted road locations in Dorset, Jeremy Harte found that up to 54 per cent of his cases occurred next to parish boundaries – typical 'liminal' locations (see Chapter Three). This is far beyond chance. Harte comments:

> What is curious is that these sightings took place, not in the days of Gospel Oaks and beating the bounds, but in the present [twentieth] century, when boundaries are no longer common knowledge. I doubt if the bus driver who stopped on Wool Bridge to let the phantom coach go by, or the motorist who saw a white car skid off Dancing Hill and vanish (Sherbourne) knew that they were on the edge of mediaeval parishes.
>
> The existence of a boundary was one of the predispositions for a sighting, even though it had no material existence and was not known to the percipient. Who was it known to – the ghost? Now there's a thought . . . [9]

Because of this and other factors resulting from his survey, Harte decided that the distribution of haunted roads in Dorset was not random. 'Some places have repeated hauntings, others are quiet at night,' he comments. 'Is this simply a reaction of psychology – an acknowledgement that some places feel spookier than others? The evidence suggests not.' As an example, he refers to a White Lady haunting that was reported for over 50 years at a place called Washer's Pit, and notes that many other places in the parish were as dark and lonely as Washer's Pit yet no one credited them with a ghost. It is just that some places produce hauntings and others do not. 'It is strange that people should see ghosts at all, but that they should always see them in the same place is very strange indeed,' says Harte. 'After all ghosts are spiritual things, while location is a property of matter.'

This, I felt, neatly encapsulated the subjective-objective conundrum ghostly hauntings present.

Zones of Disturbance

Looking more closely at haunted places, I noted that there is some preliminary evidence that certain haunted roads appear to run through what can only be termed 'zones of disturbance' – as if there is something about the area rather than the road itself that caused the haunting. To my knowledge, there have been no formal studies of this phenomenon, but a few researchers have occasionally touched on it in passing.

The Road of Horrors

A fine example is folklorist David Clarke's study of the A616 Stocksbridge bypass on the edge of moorlands in South Yorkshire, near Sheffield.[10] The bypass was opened in 1988. Despite being so relatively new, it has been the scene of many road traffic accidents resulting in numerous fatalities and hundreds of injuries, and boasts some rather eerie hauntings. In 1997, for example, Paul Ford and his wife encountered a figure on the road. As they got nearer they could see it was a man in a long cloak. 'Then I realised it had no face and it was just hovering above the road,' Ford recalled.[11]

Phantoms started to be reported even while the bypass was under construction in 1987. A truck driver working at a depot close to the bypass route reported that he and his workmates often heard 'small voices' singing late at night, though they could never find out the source of the singing or make out what the song was. In September, two night security guards patrolling the unfinished bypass saw what they described as 'young children in mediaeval clothing' dancing in a ring around an electricity pylon near a bridge. By the time the men stopped their vehicle to investigate, the little figures had vanished, leaving no footprints in the muddy ground. On another occasion, in the small hours, these same security men observed a figure on a newly-built bridge over the bypass. They directed the full beams of their patrol car's headlights on the figure. It was wearing a long cloak, appeared to have no head, and the headlights shone straight through the body. The phantom then disappeared. Both men, fit and strong, one a rugby football player and weightlifter, admitted to being reduced to terror, a state confirmed by their boss who they called out in panic. Two police officers were patrolling the unfinished road on the night of 11 September. They stopped their patrol car, quietly observing the road workings for any signs of thieves or vandals. Police Constable Dick Ellis suddenly felt cold and uneasy, and then glimpsed a figure standing by his side of the car. In an instant, it was standing by the other side of the car, pressing itself up against the window. Ellis's companion, Special Constable John Beet, let out a yell of surprised alarm. The figure looked to him 'like something out of Dickens' time', wearing a cravat and waistcoat. It stared at him and then was gone in a split second. The police officers immediately searched the area but found no trace of anyone. The sightings of apparitions continued.

Clarke points out that the bypass was carved through hillsides that were already haunted. He has traced local lore concerning sightings of a ghostly monk in a long hooded cowl going back many decades prior to the construction of the bypass.[12] He has also collected verbatim accounts of sightings made on the older roads near to the course of the new bypass. On the B6088 near the village of Wortley, for example, Judy Simpson and her businessman husband David saw a figure running through a field next to the road. It was 'just a grey outline of a person' and was not quite touching the ground. It leapt from the field over an embankment landing on the road in front of the Simpson's car. They screeched to a halt too late to avoid impact, but the figure 'just seemed to melt into the car'.[13] On another occasion, Graham Brooke and his then (1987) young teenage son were jogging along the same stretch of road. Up the road he saw a figure wearing a dark-brown hood with a cape covering his body walking towards him. It was walking on a level a little lower than the existing surface of the road. Brooke's son also saw the figure. They came within 50 yards (45 m) of it and both had the sensation of the hairs rising on their necks, and could smell 'something really musty'. Brooke noted the figure's 'blank face' and every detail on its cloak before it simply vanished.

Clarke observes that there were also reports of a spectral woman in white and mysterious fairy-like dancing children in existing local lore, but a story explaining that the ghostly monk appeared because the bypass had disturbed his grave seems to have been an after-the-fact tale, a piece of modern folklore unsupported by any historical evidence.

The Haunted Lane

Another example of a 'zone of disturbance' would seem to be the reputedly haunted lane linking the village of Nunney with the Somerset town of Frome three miles to its northeast. The haunted nature of the road began to emerge in the local press in 1977 on account of the experience of a motorist who picked up a hitch-hiker on the lane. The passenger, a man, got in the back seat of the car, commented how cold it was, and shortly afterwards vanished. The motorist did not hear the car door open or close. Somewhat perturbed, he reported the matter to the Frome police. This may have stayed as simply an apocryphal 'phantom hitch-hiker' story, were it not for the fact that the same motorist, a local man, encountered the same apparition in the same place some time afterwards. The figure appeared in the middle of the road, causing the motorist to take avoiding action which resulted in his car colliding with a lamppost. A number of local people came forward to comment that they experienced an eerie sense of a presence when driving alone at night along the lane.

Another claim the news reports elicited came from lorry driver George Gardiner regarding stories he had heard some 30 years earlier from fellow hauliers who had seen a ghost-like figure on the road. Investigating the location, author Michael Goss found that there had indeed been a number of reports made to the local police from passing motorists claiming that they had picked up hitch-hikers who promptly vanished.[14] A duty police officer told Goss that they had had people come into the station in states of 'virtual hysteria' claiming encounters on the road. One result of the publicity was that the people of Nunney mounted 'ghost patrols' – vigilantes of the supernatural.

By further probing, Goss found accounts of the Nunney-Frome lane ghost dating to the years before the first press reports had appeared, and went on to discover that the rumour of the haunted road receded ever deeper into 'the impenetrable depth of time and folk-memory'.[15] It may have gone back much further than even Goss supposed, because an area of land adjacent to the lane was known as 'Pook Fields', suggesting that the old land spirit, Puck, had been known to haunt there from at least Anglo-Saxon times.[16] Interestingly, that impression still persists. Scientist Mark Spurlock, who lives

on the road, has found from his own research that 'the road and the surrounding area has perhaps a disproportionate amount of such [ghost] tales
associated with it'.[17] Although he has not seen the road ghost himself, he did
observe what appeared to be 'a large black cat' while walking his dog in local
fields. He saw the big cat's outline clearly, and observed it prowling around
for at least ten minutes before it slipped away. It was much bigger than a
domestic cat, yet it did not disturb sheep that were in the field. On returning
home Spurlock joked with his wife that they may soon hear tales of the 'Black
Cat of Nunney'. As it turned out, later that year, 1999, a batch of reports
of a puma-like creature being seen around the area did appear in a local newspaper.

So is it the roads that are haunted, or the tracts of land they run through?
Until there are more detailed, closely-textured studies of haunted roads, it
will be hard to tell. It could be that roads act like channels collecting up the
spirits that haunted certain areas. It is also by means of roads that most
people move through the landscape, so 'road ghosts' could be more a func-
tion of the availability of witnesses than an indicator of a special type of
haunting. But perhaps that is too glib.

CHAPTER TWELVE

THE MAGIC THEATRE

T HE REASON THE idea of ghosts being place-related hallucinations is a
conundrum is because it means ghosts display both objective and subjective qualities simultaneously. The old shamans who had once experienced their visions among the rocks where I was sitting might have handled
that without any problems, but for my culture it was a supremely awkward
(not to say heretical) concept. The models created by shamanism or any other
former spiritual tradition would not be satisfactory for most of us today, in
the sense that there had to be a model and language dealing with them that
would get across the issues embedded in the haunting phenomenon in terms
that fitted in with the scientific worldview of the present-day culture.
Otherwise, this important part of human experience will remain shamefully
excluded from the mainstream intellectual discourse of our times, languish-
ing as it currently does as a slightly jokey sideshow of spooky titillation for
entertainment purposes at Halloween or Christmas time. While many people believe in ghosts, the actuality of such phenomena is not 'official' in cultural terms, and their potential for advancing our understanding of ourselves
and the world we inhabit is consistently disregarded at mainstream level. I felt
passionately that as long as the virtually universal experience of apparitions,
of haunting, remains ignored at a serious level, our modern worldview is
incomplete. That ignorance is a stain on the scientific tradition that our culture supposedly extols.

If a ghost is a mental image being conjured by the hallucinatory mechanisms of our brains in response to some real but non-physical stimuli and

being pasted onto the mental image, the 'hallucination', of the physical world presented within the sensorium, how does it get there if the physical senses are not involved? Could there be a 'back door' into the magic theatre of the mind? I recalled that there are some controversial stirrings of thought around the fringes of quantum physics, psychology and brain science that hold the potential to breach the existing divide between what we consider to be inner and outer realities. For that was the problem: we assume what goes on in our head is locked inside the skull, and what goes on outside in the 'real world' is entirely separate. I racked my unscientific brain for what little I knew of the current ideas.

All is Illusion

First the physics. The physical world, as we know from the textbooks, only *appears* to be solid. That is an illusion, because under increasingly closer inspection it breaks down into ever-smaller parts – into elements and molecules which in turn are comprised of collections of atoms. Atoms themselves are variously made up of subatomic particles, such as protons, neutrons and electrons, among other very weird particles. At this level of the very small – the subatomic *quantum* level where things cannot be directly perceived but only detected – matter, which seems so solid and secure on a large-scale, breaks down into a shimmer of energy. Subatomic particles behave as both particles and waves at the same time: the basis of the real world is thus a curious state which quantum physicists recognise as being governed by what they term 'uncertainty'. Ultimately, the energy that gives rise to subatomic wave-particles and thus atomic structures and matter itself emerges from empty space, nothingness – what is known in quantum physics as 'the vacuum'. The catch is that it is not really empty; it seethes with something known as 'zero-point energy', a quantum-level activity. 'Virtual particles' blip temporarily into existence from it, then vanish back into it. For my purposes it was not necessary to delve into the complicated technicalities of this, it was enough to visualise the quantum field as being like a boiling and bubbling cosmic sea out of which appears all matter, the whole manifest universe, like some continent emerging from the deeps. Quantum mechanics facilitated an endless cycle of becoming, of continuous creation 'out of the everywhere and into here'.

It is one thing to understand that the world around us ultimately breaks down into subatomic energies, but we can too easily overlook that we do so too. Ultimately, the human body (and that means the brain as well) is comprised of elements, molecules, atoms and subatomic quantum states just like the world around it. We emerge from and ultimately dissolve back into the same bubbling 'quantum sea'[1] like everything else in the universe. We are stardust, as the song puts it. Less poetically, it has been estimated that the average adult human being is comprised of enough carbon to make 10,000 lead pencils, enough iron to make a large nail, and enough water to fill a five-gallon drum. But our human matter adds up to something different to the other matter surrounding us – *consciousness*.

The Inside of the Outside

That brings us to the psychology. 'Inside' the physical brain is the non-physical mind – though in fact the two are so indivisible that mind is to brain what the grasp is to the hand. Brain-mind. Using a simplistic picture, we could think of consciousness as being like the 'inside' of what the physicists are studying the outside of. Or to put it another way, consciousness, the mind, is the shadow of the physical. So we all have our normal, 'individuated', separate, waking minds that are what we think of as our conscious selves and identify with our physical bodies. Each of us feels as if we carry our mind around in our brain which is in our body. We tend to think of it as a more or less sealed system. But when we fall asleep, as we all know, our sense of self-awareness diminishes, and we drift into dreams which are scenes and actions being generated by the brain-mind. When in the dream state we are wallowing in the shallows of the *unconscious mind*. This shades off into deeper and older levels of the psyche that the psychologist C.G.Jung referred to as the *collective unconscious* – a level of mind that we each inherit from the vast databank of all humanity that has preceded us. The unconscious mind and the collective unconscious lie like strata beneath the waking conscious awareness. If one sinks down deeply enough into this unconscious realm of mind, Jung argued, it eventually 'passes over into the physiology of the organism and thus merges with its chemical and physical conditions'.[2] Such a structure of the psyche or mind echoes the physics of the body: there is the individual, physical person just as there is an individuated level of consciousness, but as we go deeper into the mind, just as we go deeper into the structure of the body, that individual sum we call a person dissolves into components, so that the unconscious mind roughly correlates with the level of organs and autonomic functions within the body, and the yet deeper collective unconscious is mind at the transpersonal level of molecules, atoms and the quantum sea. The deeper we go, both physically and mentally, the further removed from the individual we become, the more impersonal things are.

In terms of this model, the vacuum, the quantum sea underpinning matter, is in consciousness terms what mystics through the ages have variously described from the 'inside' as the Void, nirvana, the Tao (Dao), cosmic consciousness, the 'abysmal void of beatific knowing', and so forth. At that level of mind the sense of self is transcended; it is an ego-less state where our mind merges with the universe at the all-pervading quantum level.

Through the Back Door

This is where the brain science (or, more exactly, consciousness studies, which is a mixture of neuroscience, psychology and philosophy) comes in. There is currently a great debate taking place in this area. One school broadly argues that consciousness is just a product of the neurological processes going on in the brain – it is an 'epiphenomenon', that is, it is an effect produced by the interactions of parts of the physical brain. Critics of this argument brand it as an excessively materialist, reductionist approach to the nature of consciousness. Other schools argue in various ways that there cannot suddenly appear in the universe a property that was not inherent in it from the start, and that 'consciousness' or 'mind' must be a something – a field, a force, a quality – that the brain draws on, uses, manipulates and shapes but does not exactly produce. Such proponents are dismissed in turn by their critics as 'dualists', the charge being that this approach reintroduces old and discredited notions of a mind–matter split – the very issue I was facing in my deliberations on the haunted land.

However, there is a developing third approach that to some extent combines both positions: some researchers are seeking structures in the brain that could be linking neurological processes to the quantum field.[3] In other words, they are seeking the back door to the magic theatre of the mind. While this is a highly technical area of research that is not of direct relevance to ghosts and haunting, I felt it was important to know that some brain structures and processes that are candidates for such a role are being researched by brain scientists and was not some wacky new age notion. An informed idea of the 'quantum brain' could be on its way.

If this approach proves correct, if the springs of consciousness are indeed in the quantum sea, then it means both mind and matter ultimately have the same roots if probed deeply enough. I sensed that there might be the hint of a bridge here on which to approach the subjective-objective nature of the phantom phenomenon. But how did it actually work? What was the 'inside' of the interface between mind and the quantum sea? In other words, what was the consciousness experience of that transduction like? I glimpsed a clue that gave some leads, a clue that eventually led back to another of Jung's key psychological insights – namely, the existence of what he called *archetypes*.

Out of the Depths

C.G. Jung's concept of the archetype was many-layered. At the simplest level of explanation, an archetype is a primordial structure or pattern embedded deep in the human collective unconscious, a mental prototype that generates fundamental images and concepts such as the hero, the king, the queen, the old wise man or woman, the virgin, the lover, the pilgrim or traveller, and all the myriad prototypes upon which our conscious mental activities embroider onward their ever more complex patterns. Jung arrived at his concept of the archetype as a result of his observations of essentially similar patterns and motifs underlying the recurring dreams and imaginative imagery of the many patients who consulted him as a psychologist, and by the long and close inspection of his own dreams and imaginative processes. While each of us builds up our own personal store of mental images and patterns through our lives, archetypes are archaic and universal, transcending time and culture.

Archetypes are such extraordinarily stable and enduring structures that they can evolve without losing their inherent integrity. They inform myths, which are expressions of archetypal motifs. This task is largely taken on these days by the cinema and television. Some movies that strike deep chords in audiences worldwide, like the *Star Wars* series, employ mythic themes and have casts of archetypal characters – heroes, princesses, wise elders, magicians, demonic villains, and so forth. Archetypes are the distillations of all the experiences of humanity across countless generations and across all cultural boundaries, and they even encode experiential material from our pre-human, animal origins. Archetypes themselves are forever unconscious entities – we can never know them directly, Jung argued, but only through the images, ideas and symbolism they generate. They are living forces within our minds, present with us and active throughout our lives from earliest childhood. Archetypal images are especially powerful because they carry with them a profound aura of awe-inspiring mystery brought from the deepest levels of mind: they are spiritually potent. They are haunting.

The relevance of archetypes to the haunted land dilemma I was contemplating is that, like a few other researchers before me, I had become aware of a persistent archetypal element in the record of testimony I had been inspecting concerning spirits in the landscape. One aspect of this was that some apparitions seemed more like *ideas* than actual entities. The A23 as one example in the material I had examined, or the Naunton road in Gloucestershire as another, seemed to me to be haunted by the generalised concept of a pale human figure whether expressed as a man, a woman, an individual or more than one figure. I suspected that these generalised ideas – the White Lady, the Black Monk, the Black Dog, the lonely roadside figure, the spirit wandering the border between this world and the next, the elemental sprites of nature haunting the fields, woods or rocks – are all essentially archetypal images.

While I knew it would take a Jungian psychologist to properly tease out the exact archetypal characteristics of the main types of recurring land spirits, it had already struck me that the White Lady type of ghost, for instance, was a reflection of the 'Earth Mother' goddess image that had appeared in the mythologies of civilisations from the earliest times. The archetypal nature of the image is shown by its appearance worldwide, in both the Old and New Worlds, in civilisations that had no direct contact with one another. The goddess is often associated with whiteness – assumed to be a reference to the moon, though it is probably a more complex association than this alone, and may also link with death. Albion, the ancient Roman name for Britain, was derived from the goddess Albina, the White Goddess. Interestingly, the poet Robert Graves noted that Albina derives from etymological roots that are found in the Germanic words elf and elven (elf-woman) and also in *alpdrücken*, nightmare or incubus (see above for the association of this with sleep paralysis).[4] The ancient barley goddesses Demeter and Perspehone are associated with the Argos region of Greece, a name which means 'shimmering white'. Graves traces the barley goddess also in Io, in Greek myth the nurse of the infant god Dionysus. Io was sometimes represented as a white cow, white mare, or white sow.

Mother-goddesses were a very important fertility image in pagan Celtic culture, and some of these too were associated with the moon and its links with whiteness and death. The moon also symbolises change, with its cycle of waxing and waning, as in human life, and so in myth the goddess can appear as a young virginal woman, a mother, or an old crone – in just the way the White Lady type of ghost appears in several guises, because both mythic figure and apparition operate on similar archetypal dynamics. The deities of the old myths are like ghosts themselves – capable of shape-shifting forms at will.

The goddesses associated with leading the Wild Hunt also come from this same archetypal mould, so we have the huntress Diana with her lunar associations, and I had already learned that she was simply a gloss of earlier goddesses like Bendis, Epona, Artemis, Hecate and many more (see Chapter

Four). Epona, the goddess associated with horses, was also linked, like White Lady apparitions often are, with water, and with death, as well as fertility. She 'reflected the deep mysteries of life, death and rebirth' Celtic Scholar Miranda Green notes.[5] Hecate was associated with the fertility of the earth, and with the night and ghosts. In later Greek myth, she became the moon goddess.

There were images associated with some of the representations of the Earth Mother goddess that seemed to relate to other types of landscape spirits too. I recalled from my walk around the museum in Cirencester that Roman carvings sometimes depicted the *Genii Cucullati* in association with the Mother Goddess. So did the hooded spirits also associate in the Celtic mind with this fertility image? It seems likely, because some Celtic statues of *Genii Cucullati* can be taken apart to reveal a penis. Others are shown carrying scrolls, thought to be symbolic of knowledge or wisdom.

Dogs, also, were associated with some manifestations of the goddess. Hecate, for example, was portrayed as a figure with three heads, one of a lion, one of a horse and one of a dog. Epona, too, was frequently depicted as being accompanied by a dog, 'which could reflect either healing or death' in the Celtic mind, Green observes.[6] The dog Cerberus in Greek myth was, of course, associated with death, being the guardian of Styx, the dark river separating life and death.

I began to see that much of the company of landscape spirits archetypally reflected in varying aspects not only themes of death, healing and fertility, but the very land, which was after all the stage, indeed the matrix, for the whole life cycle, vegetable, animal and human, from fertilisation, through birth and growth, to death. From the earth and back to the earth. Seen in a collective way, the spirits of the land comprised a spectral play of archetypal images that was the land displaying itself to our mythic or archetypal levels of mind. It is because these levels of our consciousness have become so unfamiliar to us in the present cultural climate that we do not recognise this. Jung himself noted:

It not infrequently happens that the archetype appears in the form of a *spirit* in dreams or fantasy-products, or even comports itself like a ghost.[7]

But how do cars and other vehicles fit into this archetypal context? I figured that death associations were involved, for in early steppe, Celtic, and Norse tombs, wagons were buried with the corpse. It was obviously thought that the vehicle could have a spirit form able to transport the dead person on the road leading from the grave to the afterlife realm. (A similar idea obviously attached itself to boat burials.) Researcher Alby Stone argues that this is the deeply-rooted archetypal-symbolic foundation for phantom coaches.[8] Certainly, wheeled transport has been with us for sufficient millennia for an archetype to have been formed in the human unconscious. It is an archetype as old as the wheel. Phantom lorries and automobiles (and mini-pickup trucks) are simply evolutions of the archetype.

And what was this road that led to the otherworld? The concept of the death road in Indo-European cultures goes back at least to the Anatolia (Turkey) of the second millennium BC, where a cuneiform inscription refers to 'the great road – the road that makes things disappear' in a funerary context. Things disappeared on it because it was the road of the dead. The image of such a road was maintained in Indo-European tradition in varying forms right through to the mediaeval period. So the dead walking paths to the otherworld is a deeply embedded psychic motif, an archetype in itself, and this could be why roads figure so prominently in the haunted land. Stone suggests that the phantom hitch-hiker may be a version, however unconsciously appropriated by the modern mind, of the doomed traveller on the road to the otherworld of the dead. This idea could probably be extended to many forms of road ghosts.

I could not fail to notice that people in sleep paralysis states or otherwise experiencing spontaneous forms of 'metachoric hallucination' could also see hooded figures and black dogs, indicating that such images do indeed result from primordial, formless forces occurring within the collective unconscious. I also now understood that it was this archetypal nature of ghosts that caused landscape spirits to slip back and forth across the limbo zone between folk-myth and reported actual experience. They live in both realms, for archetypes were considered by Jung to be the confluence of spirit and matter.

At the Meeting of Mind and Matter

'In archetypal conceptions and instinctual perceptions, spirit and matter confront one another on the psychic plane,' the great psychologist wrote.[9] To Jung, the psychic and material were two sides of the same coin. The exact nature of archetypes was nevertheless left vague by Jung because the neuroscience of his day had not advanced sufficiently to accommodate his great insight, nor had concepts about quantum physics matured.[10] Jung would almost certainly have latched onto the latest approaches in quantum physics with great enthusiasm. In a prescient work on apparitions written in 1957, Aniela Jaffé, Jung's personal secretary and herself a Jungian scholar, commented that the concept of the archetype 'does justice both to the psychical and to the physical realm' and noted in passing 'that this approach shows significant parallels with atomic physics'. She continues: 'The psychic and physical are no longer fundamentally separate, but emerge as two different aspects of the same background reality'.[11]

If the collective unconscious is the shadow or the 'inside' of the quantum sea, and archetypes are its denizens as Jung maintained, then whatever archetypes are, they exist at that quantum level. The appearance of spirit forms could be one of the ways we experience at a conscious level the strange dynamics involved in the energetic conversion of quantum events into mind and matter. While they more commonly manifest in creativity in its myriad forms, whether great music, art, poetry or inspired thought, the purest emanations of those shadowy, unformed pre-structures that are archetypes may indeed be phantoms, briefly and simultaneously partaking of the mythic qualities of the unconscious mind and the manifestation of physical reality, and shown to our conscious awareness through the brain mechanics that give us hallucinations and that conjure the images we have of the physical world.[12]

I could see, though only dimly, that the archetypal nature of land spirits revealed that the haunting of a place was taking place at a level where the structure of mind and physical reality merged, because the nature of both mind and land were rooted in those dark and mysterious mechanics constantly taking place at the quantum levels. Perhaps haunted places, 'zones of disturbance', are ripples or currents within the quantum sea that disgorge their archetypal contents at various times in response to the action of strange tides beyond our current understanding. The witness is metaphorically like a beachcomber who comes along at the right moment to see what has been washed up on the sands of conscious awareness.

Within this framework, an approach to the mystery of haunting could be that three systems – ghost, place, and mind – deriving from the same quantum roots briefly interact: an intersection of mind and matter we simply do not (yet) have the information to truly understand. The whole show is put together in the magic theatre of the witness's mind, in the sensorium. It would be one unified event in which the old idea of objective and subjective realities disappear. However this can be properly expressed only in the mathematical language of quantum physics on the one hand, or the direct experience of mystics on the other.

Degrees of Manifestation

It was apparent from my study of witnesses' accounts that spirit types like the White Lady could appear in various forms, from glowing blobs of vaguely human-like appearance right through the spectrum of manifestation to fully detailed, 'individuated', figures – the same sort of range as shown in the contrast between the dreamy edge of the unconscious to fully focused waking, individuated consciousness. Often, though, even quite detailed apparitions had missing arms, hands or faces – as had been reported in some of the A23 examples.

One of the most fully formed of the roadside 'ladies' in the sample of testimonies I had studied was the figure that appeared on the Gloucestershire road near Naunton. I asked witness Guy Routh to describe the woman to me in detail. He told me she had average-coloured mousy-dark hair, neither short nor long, was neither young nor old, her facial looks were more or less average in terms of attractiveness, and her cream dress was calf length, so not particularly long or short, and was not of any distinctive style, but rather a simple, classical cut. So even at this level of detailed structure, the figure was noticeably non-distinctive, like a stereotype, a norm, an *idea*. On another occasion on that same length of road, as the record had shown, another witness had seen a much less structured white figure that he interpreted as being like a monk in a white habit.

Beyond Time and Space

Pushing speculation further, this archetypal-quantum approach may also allow for the time-slip elements seemingly apparent in some hauntings, in that the quantum sea like the transcendental realm of consciousness it also is, exists beyond time as well as space. It could also possibly account for ghosts of the recent dead appearing, for it could be that human consciousness actually does survive what we know as death as some patterned structure within the quantum sea. So maybe some apparitions are indeed the 'spirits' of those who had died, briefly riding the waves of the quantum sea back into perceptual reality before dissolving away into the heart of all things.

Framing the Right Questions

There were a lot of ifs and maybes, and my head was spinning (not for the first time) on my journey through the haunted land. Nevertheless, my instincts told me that as unfamiliar as the ideas and language related to quantum physics, neuroscience and Jungian psychology were to normal thinking, at least to my normal thinking, they offered a way to go in the understanding of the kind of phenomena I had been encountering in the haunted land. It was important to frame the right questions if meaningful answers were to be forthcoming. The hidden agenda of my quest back through the ages in both the Old and New Worlds had been for a clearer grasp of the remarkable heritage of the ancient mind, for former ways of seeing that we might yet come to understand and appreciate in a new way, and that may even influence our future perceptions of reality. I had to accept that such a process of reclamation was yet in its infancy and that a wholly unexpected area of research was only just beginning to open up.

In the final analysis, what haunts the land is mind-at-large – the spirit in the landscape is consciousness itself. When the mystery as to how that takes place is fully solved, as it will be, the modern world-view will shift irrevocably.

THE AFTERNOON WAS drawing to a close, and lights had begun to twinkle here and there among the urban sprawl below me. The rock I was sitting on was beginning to feel very hard – it was time to get up and make my way back to Albuquerque. As I picked my way down through the anciently-inscribed rocks of Boca Negro Canyon I acknowledged the spirits of the old shamans, those archaic technicians of consciousness who knew how to navigate the mysterious, shadowy reaches of the otherworld, the quantum sea. They had their models to guide them, and our embryonic scientific concepts were simply another way of trying to deal with the same old truths. I had started out with shamanism and ended up with quantum physics, with something like a fairground ghost-train ride in between. Each culture had to find its own way of understanding. I thanked the shades of those old sailors of the quantum seas for helping to direct my thoughts.[13]

I drove off towards Albuquerque and back into the fold of my own globalised, modern culture, leaving the strange and ancient world of West Mesa behind. Yet today's cities and highways exist in a land haunted just as much now as in any former era. The spirits of the land would continue to wait for us along the roadside until we learned how to allow them back into our worldview. They had something to tell us, and I suspected that was why they still haunted us.

I switched on my headlights to help me spot anything strange that might be standing on the side of the road. Maybe there would be an archetype hitching a ride . . .

References and Notes

(Dates in parenthesis after a title indicate year of first publication.)

CHAPTER ONE: Signs of the Spirits

1. Schaafsma, Polly, *Indian Rock Art of the Southwest*, School of American Research/University of New Mexico Press, Santa Fe/Albuquerque, 1980, pp. 193–5
2. Bradley, Richard, *An Archaeology of Natural Places*, Routledge, London, 2000
3. Coles, John, *Patterns in a Rocky Land: Rock Carvings in South-West Uppland, Sweden*, Vols 1 and 2, Uppsala University, Uppsala, 2000, p. 47
4. Ellis, Hilda Roderick, *The Road to Hel*, Cambridge University Press, Cambridge, 1943, p. 75
5. Whitley, David S., *A Guide to Rock Art Sites, Southern California and Southern Nevada*, Mountain Press, Missoula, 1996
6. Slifer, Dennis, *Signs of Life: Rock Art of the Upper Rio Grande*, Ancient City Press, Santa Fe, 1998
7. Schaafsma, Polly, *Rock Art in New Mexico*, Museum of New Mexico Press, Santa Fe, 1992
8. Halifax, Joan, *Shaman*, Crossroad, New York, 1982, p. 90
9. Devereux, Paul, *Places of Power*, (1990), Blandford Press, London, 1999; Devereux, Paul, *The Illustrated Encyclopedia of Ancient Earth Mysteries*, Cassell, London, 2000
10. For examples: Persinger, M.A., Richards, P.M, and Koren, S.A., 'Differential ratings of pleasantness following right and left hemispheric application of low energy magnetic fields that stimulate long-term potentiation', *Intern. J. Neuroscience*, Vol.79 (1994), pp. 191–7; Persinger, M.A., 'Out-of-body-like experiences are more probable in people with elevated complex partial epileptic-like signs during periods of enhanced geomagnetic activity: A nonlinear effect', *Perceptual and Motor Skills*, Vol. 80, (1995), pp.

563–9; Healey, F., Persinger, M.A., and Koren, S.A., 'Enhanced hypnotic suggestibility following application of burst-firing magnetic fields over the right temporoparietal lobes: A replication', *Intern. J. Neuro-science*, Vol. 87, (1996), pp. 201–7; Persinger, M.A., Richards, P.M, and Koren, S.A., 'Differential entrainment of electroencephalographic activity by weak complex electromagnetic fields', *Perceptual and Motor Skills*, Vol. 84 (1997), pp. 527–36

11. Sources on this include: Reichel-Dolmatoff, G., 'Drug-induced optical sensation and their relationship to applied art among some Colombian Indians', *Art and Society*, Michael Greenhalgh and Vincent McGraw, Duckworth, London, 1978; Lewis-Williams, J.D., and Dowson, T.A., 'The signs of all times: Entoptic phenomena in upper Palaeolithic art', *Current Anthropology*, Vol. 29 (2), (April 1988), pp. 201–45; Lewis-Williams, J.D., and Dowson, T.A., *Images of Power*, Southern Book Publishers, Johannesburg, 1989; Dronfield, Jeremy, 'Migraine, Light and Hallucinogens: The neurocognitive basis of Irish megalithic art, *Oxford Journal of Archaeology*, Vol 14 (3), (1995), pp. 261–74

12. Two classic works on the subject are: Klüver, H., *Mescal: The 'Divine' Plant and Its Psychological Effects*, Kegan Paul, Trench, Trubner, London, 1928; Siegel, R.K., and West, L.J., (eds), *Hallucinations*, John Wiley, New York, 1975

13. Weahkee, 'Petroglyph area is sacred place' in *High Country News*, Vol. 29 (1), (1997), cited in Dennis Slifer, 1998, op.cit.

14. Davis, Tony, 'Horses and bikes push into petroglyph park', in *High Country News* Vol. 29 (1), (1997), cited in Dennis Slifer, 1998, op cit.

Chapter Two: **Patterns of Power**

1. Grim, J.A., *The Shaman – Patterns of Religious Healing Among the Ojibway Indians,* University of Oklahoma Press, Norman, 1983; Kroeber, A.L., 'Elements of Culture in Native California', *American Archaeology and Ethnology*, Vol.13 (8), (1922), p. 308

2. Cited in Grim, 1983, op.cit., p. 155

3. Roseau River Chapter, Three Fires Society, *Tie Creek Study,* Manitoba Department of Natural Resources, Winnipeg, 1990

4. Werlhof, J. von, *Spirits of the Earth*, Imperial College Museum Society, El Centro, 1987, pp. 24–31

5. ibid., p. 76

6. Hoskinson, T., 'Saguaro wine, ground figures, and power mountains: Investigations at Sears Point, Arizona', in R.A. Williamson and C.R. Farrer (eds), *Earth and Sky*, University of New Mexico Press, Albuquerque, 1992

7. As told to Constance Goddard Dubois by Old Mission Indians in 1905.

8. Hoskinson, 1992, op.cit., p. 159

9. Spier, L., *Yuman Tribes of the Gila River*, (1933), Dover edition, New York, 1978

10. Lepper, Bradley, 'Tracking Ohio's Great Hopewell Road', *Archaeology*, November/December, (1995)

11. Fagan, Brian, *Ancient North America*, Thames and Hudson, London, 1991, p. 393

12. See for examples: Devereux, Paul, *The Illustrated Encyclopedia of Ancient Earth Mysteries*, Cassell, London; Frazier, Kendrick, *People of Chaco*, W.W. Norton, New York, 1986; Gabriel, Kathryn, *Roads to Center Place*, Johnson Books, Boulder, 1991; Lister, R., and Lister, F., *Chaco Canyon*, University of New Mexico Press, Albuquerque, 1981

13. Kincaid, Chris (ed.), *Chaco Roads Project Phase 1*, Bureau of Land Management, Albuquerque, 1983

14. Furst, Peter, *Hallucinogens and Culture*, Chandler and Sharp, Novato, 1976

15. La Barre, *The Peyote Cult*, (1938), University of Oklahoma Press, 5th Edition, Norman, 1989, p. 257

16. Trombold, Charles, 'Causeways in the context of strategic planning in the La Quemada region, Zacatecas, Mexico', in *Ancient Road Networks and Settlement Hierarchies in the New World*, Charles Trombold (ed.), Cambridge University Press, Cambridge, 1991, p. 165

17. See, for instance: Folan, William, 'Sacbes of the northern Maya', in Trombold (ed.), 1991, ibid.

18. Urton, Gary, *At the Crossroads of the Earth and the Sky*, (1981), University of Texas Press, Austin, 1988

19. Aveni, Anthony, (ed.), *The Lines of Nazca*, The American Philosophical Society, Philadelphia, 1990

20. Hawkins, Gerald, *Beyond Stonehenge*, Hutchinson, London, 1973

21. Urton, Gary, 'Andean social organisation and the maintenance of the Nazca Lines', in Aveni, (ed.), 1990, op. cit.

22. Hyslop, John, 'Observations about research on prehistoric roads in South America', in Trombold (ed.), 1991, op.cit., pp. 29–30

23. Dobkin de Rios, Marlene, 'Plant hallucinogens, out-of-body experiences and New World monumental earthworks' in Brian Du Toit, (ed.), *Drugs, Rituals, and Altered States of Consciousness*, A.A.Balkema, Rotterdam, 1977, pp. 237–49

24. Dobkin de Rios, Marlene, *Hallucinogens: Cross-Cultural Perspectives*, (1984), Prism Press, Bridport, 1990

25. Cited in Spier, 1933/1978, op.cit., p. 247

26. Kalweit, Holger, *Dreamtime and Inner Space*, Shambhala, Boston, 1988

27. Ereira, Alan, *The Heart of the World*, Jonathan Cape, London, 1990, see also his BBC video, *From the Heart of the World*

28. Lekson, Stephen, *The Chaco Meridian*, Altamira Press, Walnut Creek, 1999

29. Freidel, David, Schele, Linda, and Parker, Joy, *Maya Cosmos*, William Morrow, New York, 1993
30. La Barre, Weston, *The Ghost Dance*, (1970), Dell, New York, 1972, p. 129

CHAPTER THREE: Death Roads and Funeral Paths

1. Magin, Ulrich, 'The old straight track on Dragon Mountain', *The Ley Hunter*, No.117, 1992
2. Campbell, Joseph, *The Way of the Animal Powers, Part Two: Mythologies of the Great Hunt*, Harper and Row, New York, 1988
3. Linton, Ralph, *The Tree of Culture*, Knopf, New York, 1969
4. La Barre, Weston, *The Ghost Dance*, (1970), Dell, New York, 1972, p. 126
5. Sheets, Payson, and Sever, Thomas L., 'Prehistoric footpaths in Costa Rica: transportation and communication in a tropical forest', in Charles Trombold (ed.), *Ancient Road Networks and Settlement Hierarchies in the New World*, Cambridge University Press, Cambridge, 1991, p. 62
6. Ibid., p. 64
7. Pennick, Nigel, and Devereux, Paul, *Lines on the Landscape*, Robert Hale, London, 1989, pp. 245–62
8. Sandén, Börje, *Rösaring Cult Site*, Upplands-Bro Research Institute for History of Culture, 1996
9. Palmer, John, 'The Deathroads of Holland', *The Ley Hunter*, No.109, 1989
10. Palmer, John: 'Walking a Dutch Corpse Road', *The Ley Hunter*, No.121, 1994; 'Lines on the Landscape', *The Ley Hunter*, No.126, 1997; 'Lykwei to Harich', *The Ley Hunter*, No.132, 1998
11. Palmer, John: 'Hellweg', 'A Rothenburg death road', and 'A Polish death road', The Ley Hunter, No.126, 1997; 'Willbroek death road', *The Ley Hunter*, No.127, 1997
12. Palmer, John, 'Crossing the border – The Meinweg Corpse Road', *The Ley Hunter*, No.131, 1998
13. Palmer, John, 'No Roman pedigree for Dutch death roads', *The Ley Hunter*, No.133, 1999
14. Palmer, John, 'Deathroads III', *The Ley Hunter*, No.114, 1991
15. Magin, Ulrich, 'The Mutterstadt Pilgrim's Way', *The Ley Hunter*, No. 117, 1992
16. *Handwörterbuch des Deutschen Aberglaubens*, Vol. 5, de Gruyter, Berlin, pp. 1121–2
17. Magin, Ulrich, 'German death roads not straight', *The Ley Hunter*, No. 126, 1997
18. To take just one well-researched example, country rambling author Laurence Main cites a Welsh corpse road in the Wrexham area that has been meticulously investigated by R.J.A. Dutton. It links the cemetery at

Gresford in the south to Harwarden monastery in the north. Detailed study of the course of this corpse way shows it to have fallen on 'a very straight line'. (Main, Laurence: 'A north Welsh corpse road', *The Ley Hunter*, No. 132, 1998, and his *The Spirit Paths of Wales*, Cicerone Press, Milnthorpe, 2000)

19. Quinn, Phil, 'Mapping the journey of the soul', *The Ley Hunter*, No. 128, 1997
20. Harte, Jeremy, 'Show me the way to go home', *3rd Stone* April–June, 1998
21. Hawkes, Gabrielle, and Henderson-Smith, Tom, 'Coffin Lines: And a Cornish spirit path?', *The Ley Hunter*, No. 117, 1992
22. Harte, April–June 1998, op.cit.; Friar, Stephen, *The Batsford Companion to Local History*, Batsford, London, 1991.
23. Ginzburg, Carlo, *Ecstasies: Deciphering the Witches' Sabbath*, (1989), Penguin Books, London, 1992, p. 5

CHAPTER FOUR: The Secret Life of Old Europe

1. Murray, Margaret, *The Witch-Cult in Western Europe*, (1921), Barnes and Noble Books, New York, 1996
2. Ginzburg, 1989/1992, op.cit., p. 10
3. Ibid., p. 14
4. Pocs, Eva, *Between the Living and the Dead*, (1997), Central European University Press, Budapest, 1999, p. 8
5. Ginzburg, 1989/1992, op.cit., p. 160
6. Purkiss, Diane, *The Witch in History*, Routledge, London, 1996, p. 93
7. Ginzburg, 1989/1992, op.cit., pp. 166–7. See also Carrington, Dorothy, *The Dream-Hunters of Corsica*, Weidenfeld and Nicolson, London, 1995
8. Pocs, 1997/1998, op.cit., p. 67
9. Ross, Anne, *The Pagan Celts*, (1970), Batsford, London, 1986
10. Duerr, Hans Peter, *Dreamtime: Concerning the boundary between wilderness and civilisation*, (1978), Blackwell, Oxford, 1985, p. 62
11. Pocs, 1997/1998, op.cit., p. 46
12. Ibid., p. 109
13. Ibid., p. 48
14. Ginzburg, 1989/1992, op.cit., p. 154
15. Pocs, 1997/1998, op.cit., p. 47
16. Ibid., p. 50
17. Ginzburg, 1989/1992, op.cit., p. 101
18. Pocs, 1997/1998, op.cit., p. 31
19. Ginzburg, 1989/1992, op.cit., p. 211
20. Ibid., p. 213

21. Davidson, Hilda Ellis, *The Lost Beliefs of Northern Europe*, Routledge, London, 1993, p. 28

22. Taylor, Tim, 'Gunderstrup Cauldron', in Fagan, Brian M., (ed.), *The Oxford Companion to Archaeology*, Oxford University Press., Oxford, 1996, p. 269

23. Pocs, 1997/1998, op.cit., p. 76

24. Devereux, Paul, *The Long Trip*, Penguin/Arkana, New York, 1997; Dobkin de Rios, Marlene, *Hallucinogens: Cross-Cultural Perspectives*, (1984), Prism Press, Bridport, 1990; Furst, Peter, (ed.) *Flesh of the Gods*, Praeger, New York, 1972; Harner, Michael, (ed.), *Hallucinogens and Shamanism*, Oxford U.P., New York, 1973; La Barre, Weston, *The Peyote Cult*, (1938), University of Oklahoma Press, Norman, 1989

25. Cited in Harner, Michael, 'Common themes in South American Indian Yage experiences', in Harner, Michael, (ed.), *Hallucinogens and Shamanism*, Oxford Univeristy Press, New York, 1973, pp. 155–6

26. Duerr, 1978/1985, op.cit., p. 202

27. Schenk, Gustav, *The Book of Poisons*, Rinehart, New York, 1955, p. 44–8

28. La Barre, Weston, 'Anthropological perspectives on hallucination and hallucinogens', Siegel, R.K., and West, L.J., (eds.), *Hallucinations*, John Wiley, New York, 1975, p. 25

29. Duerr, 1989/1985, op.cit., p. 155

30. Pocs, 1997/1998, op.cit., p. 77

31. Caciola, Nancy, 'Spirits seeking bodies: death, possession and communal memory in the Middle Ages', in Gordon, Bruce, and Marshall, Peter, (eds), *The Place of the Dead*, Cambridge University Press, Cambridge, 2000, p. 66

32. Ibid., p. 67

33. Gordon, Bruce, 'Malevolent ghosts and ministering angels: Apparitions and pastoral care in the Swiss Reformation', in Gordon and Marshall, 2000, ibid., p. 93

34. Cited by Palmer, John, 'Notes on church and corpse roads in Holland', *The Ley Hunter*, No. 127, 1997

35. *Handwörterbuch des Deutschen Aberglaubens*, Vol. 5., pp. 1121–2

36. Richardson, Ruth, 'Death's Door: Thresholds and Boundaries in British Funeral Customs', in Davidson, Hilda Ellis, (ed.), *Boundaries and Thresholds*, The Katherine Briggs Club, Thimble Press, Stroud, 1993

37. Ibid., citing Bertram Puckle (1926), p. 98

38. Menefee, Samuel Pyeatt, 'Dead Reckoning: the Church Porch Watch in British Society', in Davidson, Hilda Ellis, (ed.), *The Seer*, John Donald, Edinburgh, 1989

39. Atkinson, J.C., *Forty Years in a Moorland Parish*, Macmillan, London, 1891, p. 219

40. Palmer, John, 'The Folklore of Death: The Precursors', and 'The Precursors III', *The Ley Hunter*, No. 129, 1998

41. Simpson, Jacqueline, *Icelandic Folktales and Legends*, University of California Press, Berkeley, 1972, pp. 176–8

42. Palmer, John, 'A Dutch Spirit Route', *The Ley Hunter*, No. 126, 1997

43. Magin, Ulrich, 'An assortment of landscape lines in Germany – Real and Imagined', *The Ley Hunter*, No. 133, 1999, citing German archaeological sources

44. Pennick and Devereux, 1989, op.cit.; Devereux, Paul, *The Sacred Place*, Cassell, London, 2001

45. MacConnell, Sean, 'Discovery sheds new light on newgrange', *Irish Times*, 21 December, 2000

46. Keys, David, 'Godmanchester's temple of the Sun', *New Scientist*, 23 March, 1991

47. Burl, Aubrey, *From Carnac to Callanish*, Yale University Press, New Haven, 1993, p. 2

48. Coles, Bryony and John, *Sweet Track to Glastonbury*, Thames and Hudson, London, 1986, p. 43

49. Ibid., p. 64

Chapter Five: Last Voyage to Avalon

1. Ashe, Geoffrey, *King Arthur's Avalon*, (1957), BCA, London, 1974, p. 12

2. Green, Miranda, *Dictionary of Celtic Myth and Legend*, Thames & Hudson, London, 1992, p. 35

3. Evans Wentz, Y.W., *The Fairy-Faith in Celtic Countries*, (1911), Colin Smythe, Gerrards Cross, 1977, p. 218

4. Ashe, 1957/1974, op.cit., p. 21

5. Ginzburg, 1989/1992, op.cit., p. 107

6. Tabor, Richard, 'South Cadbury: Milsoms Corner', *Current Archaeology*, 163, Vol. XIV, No.7, 1999, p. 252 (The link between the boat burial and the mythic end of Arthur was not lost on Tabor, either.)

7. Brustle, H., (ed.), *Das Wilde Heer*, Robach, Freiburg, 1977, cited in Ulrich Magin, 'Ways of the Wild Hunt', *The Ley Hunter*, No. 118, 1993

8. The Peterborough Manuscript, *The Anglo-Saxon Chronicles*, Swanton, Michael, (trans. and ed.), (1966), Phoenix Press, London, 2000, p. 258

9. *Handwortbuch de deutschen Aberglaubens*, Vol. 3, de Gruyter, Berlin, 1933, p. 557 (Cited in Magin, Ulrich, 'The Medieval Christianisation of Pagan Landscapes', *The Ley Hunter*, No. 116, 1992)

10. Caciola, Nancy, 'Death, possession, and communal memory', in Gordon and Marshall, 2000, op.cit., p. 78

11. Hinze, Christe, and Diederich, Ulf, *Ostpreussiche Sagen*, Eugen Diederich, Munich, 1991. (Cited in Magin, Ulrich, 'The Flightpath of the Corpses', *The Ley Hunter*, No. 131, 1998.)

12. Courtney, M.A., *Folklore and Legend of Cornwall*, (1890), Cornwall Books, Exeter, 1989

13. Davies, Jonathan Caredig, *Folk-Lore of West and Mid-Wales*, (1911), Llanerch, Lampeter, 1992, pp. 149–50

CHAPTER SIX: Fairies, Witches and Werewolves

1 Mac Manus, Dermot, *The Middle Kingdom*, (1959), Colin Smythe, Gerrards Cross, 1973, p. 27

2. Pocs, 1997/1998, op.cit., p. 50

3. Evans Wentz, 1911/1977, op.cit., p. 33

4. Gregory, Lady, *Visions and Beliefs in the West of Ireland*, (1920), Colin Smythe, Gerrards Cross, 1979, p. 10

5. Kirk, Robert, *The Secret Commonwealth of Elves, Fauns, and Fairies*, (1691), Rare Text Library of Philosophical Research, Helios, Toddington, 1964, p. 5

6. Mac Manus, 1959/1973, op.cit., p. 22–3

7. Evans Wentz, 1911/1977, op.cit., p. 194

8. Ibid., p. 218

9. Mac Manus, 1959/1973, op.cit., p. 104

10. Gregory, 1920/1979, op.cit., pp. 180–4

11. Evans Wentz, 1911/1977, op.cit., p. 33 (This reference got into the popular 'earth mysteries' literature in the 1960s, and contributed to the spawning of the modern 'energy line' idea regarding 'leys'/'leylines')

12. Ryan, Meda, *Biddy Early: The Wise Woman of Clare*, (1978), Mercier Press, Dublin, 1991, pp. 79–80

13. Evans Wentz, 1911/1977, op.cit., p. 38

14. Ibid., pp. 230–1

15. Ibid., p. 33

16. Keightley, Thomas, *The Fairy Mythology*, (1892), Wildwood House, London, 1981, p. 520

17. Cited in Olding, Frank, 'Fairy Lore in 18th-Century Monmouthshire', *3rd Stone*, No 31, 1998, pp. 19–22

18. Dickinson, Bob, 'Lincolnshire Spirit Lines', *Markstone*, No. 8, 1993, p. 7

19. Ginzburg, 1989/1992, op.cit., p. 108

20. Davidson, Hilda Ellis, *The Lost Beliefs of Northern Europe*, Routledge, London, 1993, p. 122

21. *Landnámabók IV*, cited by Davidson, Hilda Ellis, *The Road to Hel*, Cambridge University Press, Cambridge, 1943, p. 117

22. Bottrell, W., *Traditions and Hearthside Stories of West Cornwall*, (1870–1880), Llanerch, Lampeter, 1989, p. 84

23. Harte, Jeremy, 'Hidden Laughter: The Dorset Fairy Tradition', *3rd Stone*, No. 29, 1998

24. Pocs, 1997/1998, op.cit., p. 80

25. County Folklore Vol. V, cited by Dickinson, Bob, 'Lincolnshire Spirit Lines', *Markstone*, No. 8, 1993, p. 6

26. Pocs, 1997/1998, op.cit., p. 77

27. Dickinson, 1993, op. cit., pp. 8–9

28. Quinn, Phil, 'The Spirit Flight of Molly N', *The Ley Hunter*, No. 126, 1997

29. Bottrell, W., 1870–1880/1989, op.cit., pp. 79–91; Hunt, Robert, *Popular Romances of the West of England*, (1881), Llanerch, Lampeter, 1990, pp. 109–13)

30. Atienza, Juan, 1981, cited by Ulrich Magin, 'Spanish Witch-Flight?', *The Ley Hunter*, No. 118, 1993

31. Desjarlais, Robert, 'Healing through images: The magical flight and healing geography of Nepali shamans', *Ethos*, Vol. 17, 1989, pp. 289–307

32. Allen, Nicholas, J., 'The ritual journey, a pattern underlying certain Nepalese rituals', in von Furer-Haimendorf, Christoph, (ed.), *Contributions to the Anthropology of Nepal*, Aris & Phillips, Warminster, 1974, p. 7

33. Humphrey, Caroline, 'Chiefly and Shamanist Landscapes in Mongolia', in Hirsch, Eric, and O'Hanlon, Michael, (eds.), *The Anthropology of Landscape*, Clarendon Press, Oxford, 1995, p. 153

34. The path or road image manifests in numerous ways in American Indian life – the straight earthen ridge leading to a sweat lodge entrance is a 'spirit road', as is the line of grain or meal laid out during a peyote ceremony. Also, the concept of the road as the lifeway of an individual is a key motif: in some American Indian societies there is a role known as a 'roadman'.

35. Humphrey, 1995, op.cit., p. 152

36. Vitebsky, Piers, *The Shaman*, Little, Brown, Boston, 1995, p. 156

37. Saward, Jeff, 'The labyrinth as spirit trap', *The Ley Hunter*, No. 133, 1998

38. Eliade, Mircea, *Shamanism: Archaic Techniques of Ecstasy*, (1951), Bollingen, Princeton UP, Princeton, 1972, p. 217; 111

39. Nebesky-Wojkowitz, Rene de, *Oracles and Demons of Tibet*, Mouton & Co., Holland, 1953, p. 369

40. Ibid.

Chapter Seven: The Mysterious Ways of the Gods

1. Magin, Ulrich, 'Church Lines', *The Ley Hunter*, No. 117, 1992

2. Magin, Ulrich, 'Central European Geomancy', *The Ley Hunter*, No. 119, 1993

3. Thiel, Eckard, *Niederlande*, Goldstadtverlag, Pforzheim, 1977, as one example among several others

4. Larkman, Brian, 'The York Ley', *The Ley Hunter*, No. 100, 1986
5. Heselton, Philip, 'Tunnel legends and landscape patterns of Holderness', *Markstone*, No. 9, 1993
6. Gurney, O.R., *The Hittites*, cited by Jim Kimmis, 'Making a Beeline?', *Essex Landscape Mysteries*, No.5, 1982
7. Hutt, Michael, *Nepal: A Guide to the Art and Architecture of the Kathmandu Valley*, Stirling: Kiscadale Publications, 1994, p. 33. See also Slusser, Mary Shepherd, *Nepal Mandala: A Cultural Study of the Kathmandu Valley*, Princeton UP, Princeton, 1982
8. Puhvel, Martin, *The Crossroads in Folklore and Myth*, American University Studies, Peter Lang, New York, 1989
9. Quinn, Phil, 'A Toast to the Recently Departed: Fairy Faith in the Bristol Region', *3rd Stone*, No. 26, 1997
10. Irish Folklore Commission Manuscripts, Vol. 744, p. 296. Cited by Puhvel, 1989, op.cit., p. 42
11. Puhvel, 1989, op.cit., p. 83
12. Ibid., p. 89

CHAPTER EIGHT: Road Hauntings

1. Harries, John, *The Ghost Hunter's Road Book* , Frederick Muller, London, 1968, pp. 104–5; O'Donnell, Elliot, *The Midnight Hearse*, (1965), Four Square, London, 1967, p. 94
2. O'Donnell, 1965/1967, op.cit., p. 94
3. Harries, 1968, op.cit., p. 55
4. O'Donnell, 1965/1967, op.cit., p. 94
5. Clarke, David, *Supernatural Peak District*, Robert Hale, London, 2000, p. 47
6. *Fortean Times*, No. 131, February, 2000, citing *Holme Valley Express*, 22 October, 1999.
7. Brown, Theo, *Devon Ghosts*, Jarrold, Norwich, 1982, p. 94–5
8. Harries, 1968, op.cit., p. 74
9. Jackson, Florence, and Ottewell, Gordon, *Walking in Haunted Gloucestershire*, Sigma, Wilmslow, 1994, pp. 107–8
10. Waring, Edward, *Ghosts and Legends of the Dorset Countryside*, Compton Press, Tisbury, 1977, p. 17
11. Jackson and Ottewell, 1994, op.cit., p. 107
12. O'Donnell, Elliot, *The Midnight Hearse*, 1965/1967, op.cit., p. 18
13. These A23 reports have been compiled from several sources, but notably from Rackham, John, *Brighton Ghosts, Hove Hauntings*, Latimer Publications, Brighton, 2001, and the research of Kevin Groves
14. *Fortean Times*, No. 137, 2000, citing *Kentish Express*, 13 January, 2000

15. Jackson and Ottewell, 1994, op.cit., pp. 116–17
16. Andrew Lucas, personal communication, October, 2000
17. Kevin Groves, personal communication, citing *West Sussex Observer*, 20 October, 1999
18. Cheryl Straffon, personal communication, November, 2000
19. Various sources, including: Grinsell, Leslie, *Folklore of Prehistoric Sites in Britain*, David and Charles, Newton Abbot, 1976, p. 107; Underwood, Peter, *Ghosts and How to See Them*, Index, London, 1993, pp. 10–12
20. *Fortean Times*, No. 137, 2000, citing *Kent Messenger*, 2 July, 1999
21. Goss, Michael, *The Evidence for Phantom Hitch-Hikers*, Aquarian Press, Wellingborough, 1984
22. Ibid., p. 46
23. Waring, 1977, op.cit., p. 27
24. Laurence Main, personal communication; Main, Laurence, and Perrott, Morag, *Welsh Walks: Dolgellau and the Cambrian Coast*, Sigma, Wilmslow, 1992, p. 45
25. Brought to my attention by Kevin Groves
26. Roberts, Andy, *Ghosts and Legends of Yorkshire*, Jarrold, Norwich, 1992, p. 30
27. Harte, Jeremy, 'Haunted Roads', *The Ley Hunter*, No. 121, 1994, citing Pike, Muriel, *The Piddle Valley Book of Country Life*, London, 1980
28. Alexander, Marc, *Phantom Britain*, Frederic Muller, London, 1975, p. 111
29. Quinn, Phil, 'Mapping the Journey of the Soul', *The Ley Hunter*, No. 128, 1997
30. Jackson and Ottewell, 1994, op.cit., p. 51
31. Ibid., pp. 52–3
32. Grimble, Arthur, *A Pattern of Islands*, John Murray, London, 1952, p. 47; pp. 148–53)
33. Sandra Maddox, personal communication, January, 2001
34. Harte, Jeremy, 'Cavaliers and Phantoms', *3rd Stone*, No. 26, 1997, pp. 7–8
35. Quinn, Phil, 'A Toast to the Recently Departed: the Fairy Faith in the Bristol Region', *3rd Stone*, No. 26, 1997
36. MacGregor, Alasdair, *The Ghost Book*, Robert Hale, London, 1955, pp. 163–4
37. Gelling, Margaret, *Place-Names of Oxfordshire*, Vols I & II, Cambridge University Press, Cambridge, 1953, 1954

CHAPTER NINE: Non-Human Shades of the Land

1. Williamson, Cecil, 'Close Encounter with a Demon Hound', *The Cauldron*, No. 78, 1995
2. Waring, 1977, op.cit., p. 5

3. Brown, 1982, op.cit., p. 113
4. Barbara Carbonell conducted her research in the 1920s, and her notes were published in James Wentworth Day's *Ghost Hunter's Game Book*, 1958, and in the archives of the Straight Track Club in Hereford Library. (These have recently been catalogued.)
5. Brown, 1982, op.cit., p. 115
6. Waring, 1977, op.cit., p. 3
7. MacGregor, 1955, op.cit., pp. 56–7
8. Puhvel, 1989, op.cit., 96–7
9. *The Ley Hunter*, No. 122, 1994 (Name withheld.)
10. Downes, Alison, 'The Horse–Man of Lincolnshire', *Animals and Men*, No. 9, 1996
11. Pocs, 1997/1999, op.cit., p. 79
12. Brian Bates, personal communication
13. Devereux, Paul: 'Portrait of a Fault Area', (with Andy York), *The News* (now *Fortean Times*), Nos 11 and 12, 1975; *Earth Lights*, (with Paul McCartney), Turnstone Press, Wellingborough, 1982; *Earth Lights Revelation*, (with Paul McCartney, David Clarke, and Andy Roberts), Blandford, London, 1989, 1990; 'Planet Earth's UFOs', in Devereux, Paul, and Brookesmith, Peter, *UFOs and Ufology*, Blandford, London, 1997, pp. 138–59
14. Just some: Lagarde, F., in *Flying Saucer Review*, Vol. 14 (4), 1968; Persinger, Michael, and Lafreniere, Gyslaine, *Space-Time Transients and Unusual Events*, Nelson Hall, Chicago, 1977; McClure, Kevin and Sue, *Stars and Rumours of Stars*, private, 1980; Long, Greg, 'Yakima Indian Reservation Sightings', *MUFON UFO Journal*, No. 166, 1981; Clarke, David, and Oldroyd, Granville, *Spooklights: A British Survey*, private, 1985; Derr, John S., 'Luminous Phenomena and their Relationship to Rock Fracture', *Nature*, 29 May 1986; Clarke, David, and Roberts, Andy, *Phantoms of the Sky*, Robert Hale, London 1990.
15. *Identified Flying Objects*, Equinox, Channel 4, November 1996. Later shown on Discovery Channel as *Earth Lights*, and on the National Geographic Channel.
16. Clarke and Roberts, 1990, op.cit.; Randles, Jenny, *Pennine UFO Mystery*, Granada, London, 1983; Devereux, 1989/1990, op.cit., pp. 87–115
17. Porter, Frank, 'Ridgeway Light', *The Ley Hunter*, No. 115, 1991
18. Harries, 1968, op.cit., p. 42
19. Dixon, Judy, 'West Witton Light', *The Ley Hunter*, No. 112, 1990
20. http://indy.hiof.no/~hessdalen/engelsk/ or http://www.hiof.no/crulp/proskekter/hessdalen/html/privat/privindex.html or simply put 'Project Hessdalen' into your Web browser search window to see if it can locate the site.
21. MacGregor, 1955, op.cit., p. 218

22. Pocs, 1997/1999, op.cit., p. 48
23. Gordon and Marshall, 2000, op.cit., p. 91
24. Blofeld, John, *The Wheel of Life*, (1959), Rider, London, 1972, p. 149–50
25. Walhouse, M.J., 'Ghostly Lights', *Folklore*, Vol. 5, 1894, p. 293
26. Tait, David, 'Konkomba Sorcery', in Middleton, John, (ed.), *Magic, Witchcraft and Curing*, The Natural History Press, New York, 1967, p. 156
27. Brown, 1982, op.cit., p. 125
28. Ibid., and *Journal of the Society for Psychical Research*, Vol. xxxiv, 1947, p. 74
29. Supplied by Kevin Groves, citing Green, Andrew, *Haunted Sussex Today*, S.B. Publications, 1997, p. 65
30. Rackham, 2001, op.cit., citing the *Evening Argus*, 26 February 1996

CHAPTER TEN: White Lady and Black Monk

1. Clarke, 2000, op.cit., 124
2. Trevelyan, Marie, *Folk-Lore and Folk-Stories of Wales*, (1909), EP Publishing, East Ardsley, 1973, pp. 197–8
3. Dewi Bowen, personal communication, January 2001
4. All cases from *Fortean Times*, No. 137, August 2000, citing the *Gloucester Echo*, 3 September 1998 and 19 April 2000. Guy Routh also in personal communication, April 2001
5. Claudia Copestake, personal communication, 21 March 2001
6. G.M. Stocker, personal communication, 19 October 2000
7. Supplied by Kevin Groves, citing Green, Andrew, 1997, op. cit., p. 20
8. Brown, 1982, op.cit., p. 123
9. Jackson and Ottewell, 1994, op.cit., pp. 13–14
10. Meredith, Bob, *The Haunted Cotswolds*, Reardon Publishing, Cheltenham, 1990, p. 33
11. Jackson and Ottewell, 1994, op.cit., p. 6
12. Paula Copestake, personal communication, 20 March 2001
13. Another family had an unnerving experience at Belas Knap one warm summer's afternoon: they laid out a picnic atop the mound, but during the course of the meal the tablecloth suddenly leapt into the air, scattering the items of food placed on it. Was it just a gust of wind or a poltergeist-like event? The family were convinced it was the latter, and packed up and left. Meredith, 1990, op.cit., p. 9
14. Green, Miranda, *Dictionary of Celtic Myth and Legend*, Thames & Hudson, London, 1992, p. 104
15. Davidson, Hilda Ellis, *The Lost Beliefs of Northern Europe*, Routledge, London, 1993, pp. 120–1
16. Davidson, Hilda Ellis, 'Hooded Men in Celtic and Germanic Tradition', in

Davies, Glenys, (ed.), *Polytheistic Systems*, Edinburgh UP, Edinburgh, 1989, pp. 105–24

Chapter Eleven: **Between a Rock and a Hard Place**

1. The dowser T.C. Lethbridge felt that the impressions we see as ghosts were mental images left in the ionised fields associated with waterfalls, pools, streams, woodland and underground water, but there is no actual evidence for such an idea. Probably the most lucid discussion of this approach was in his *Ghost and Divining Rod*, Routledge and Kegan Paul, London, 1963. A concise précis of his thoughts can also be found in Graves, Tom and Janet, (eds), *The Essential T.C. Lethbridge,* Routledge and Kegan Paul, London 1980, pp. 1–31
2. Green, Celia, and McCreery, Charles, *Apparitions*, (1975), Hamish Hamilton, London, 1989
3. Ibid., p. 2
4. Ibid., p. 4
5. Laughlin, Charles, McManus, John, and d'Aquili, Eugene, *Brain, Symbol and Experience*, Columbia U P, New York, 1992, p. 135
6. Siegel, Ronald, K., *Fire in the Brain*, (1992), Plume, Penguin, New York, 1993, pp. 83–90
7. Tandy, Vic, 'Something in the Cellar', *Journal* of the Society for Psychical Research, Vol.64 (3), No. 860, July 2000
8. Devereux, 1990/1999, op.cit., pp. 190–93
9. Harte, Jeremy, 'Haunted Roads', *The Ley Hunter*, No. 121, 1994
10. Clarke, 2000, op.cit.
11. Ibid., p. 33
12. Ibid., p. 36
13. Ibid., p. 40
14. Goss, 1984, op.cit.
15. Ibid., p. 67
16. Quinn, Phil, 'The devil's eye: Earth lights in landscape and folklore', *3rd Stone*, No. 28, 1997
17. Mark Spurlock, personal communication, October, 2000

Chapter Twelve: **The Magic Theatre**

1. I borrow this term from an important, pioneering paper by Laughlin, Charles D., 'Archetypes, Neurognosis, and the Quantum Sea', (1996), *Report No.* 95.6, International Consciousness Research Laboratories, Princeton. (3); and also *Journal of Scientific Exploration*, Vol. 10 (3), 1996

2. Jung, C.G., *On the Nature of the Psyche*, (1947/1954/1960), trans. R.F.C.Hull, Bollingen/ Princeton University Press, Princeton, 1969. (125) (From: *Collected Works 8: The Structure and Dynamics of the Psyche*)

3. Some investigators are looking at the possibility that the quantum phenomenon known as 'tunnelling' (when an electron passes through a barrier that in non-quantum, classical physics should be impenetrable) may take place at the synapses, the tiny gaps across which brain cells connect by means of electrochemical interaction. Others are exploring the possibility that brain cell structures can produce 'coherence' in weak electromagnetic fields surrounding the cells – coherence being a central concept in quantum physics referring to the interrelationships of an activity in one part of a quantum system with that in another, thus opening the possibility that neuronal processes could couple with the underlying vacuum energies. Yet other scientists are probing the possible quantum properties of water molecules in the lattices of cylindrical protein pathways within brain cells called 'cytoskeletal microtubules'. And these are only some of the investigations now taking place.

4. Graves, Robert, *The White Goddess*, (1948), Farrar, Straus, and Giroux, New York, 1966, p. 67

5. Green, Miranda, 1992, op. cit., p. 92

6. Ibid.

7. Jung, C.G., 1969, op.cit., p. 115

8. Stone, Alby, 'The road that makes things disappear: The path of the dead in Indo-European myth and religion', *Fortean Studies*, No. 5, 1998, pp. 122–35

9. Jung, C.G., 1969, op.cit., p. 126

10. This point is well made in Laughlin, C., 1996, op.cit.

11. Jaffé, Aniela, *Apparitions – An Archetypal Approach to Death Dreams and Ghosts*, (1957), Spring Publications, Irving, 1979. (pp. 205–6)

12. It has occurred to me that while archetypes might be phenomena of the mind produced at the interface between the micro quantum levels and the macro levels of matter and conscious mind, entoptic patterns (see Chapters One and Two) could be phenomena of the brain produced at that same interface. If archetypes and entoptic phenomena are thus related, complementary mind-brain phenomena, it could go a long way to explaining the stubborn motif of straightness appearing in so many archaeological features associated with spirit or funerary geographies.

13. This was more than some extravagantly romantic gesture, for at any sacred place when I am on my own I have a habit of appealing to the spirit of the place, forcing myself to suspend the disbelief in such a process that is borne out of my modern worldview. It is only a strange thing to do in our modern culture – a few generations ago it would have been quite normal, as it is still among the vestiges of traditional and tribal societies surviving in the

world today. While at such places I allow myself to believe in the invisible presences of counselling elders, though afterwards I always rationalise it in terms of giving my thought processes a change of mental scene, a stimulatingly different cognitive framework to clamber around within. It had worked enough times for me to know it to be a useful tool. Sometimes I have actually heard voices (I mean I had auditory hallucinations . . .), while on other occasions I have seen aspects of sites that my eyes had previously literally overlooked, or have had a sudden insight. In one way or another this approach has often resulted in my gaining useful information – some of it, even, of the kind that has made its way into peer-reviewed academic journals.

Index

Note: page numbers in *italics* refer to illustrations, page numbers in **bold** refer to tables.